NUEVA ESPARTA

EASTERN
COASTAL

L

AL

NDA

SUCRE

MONAGAS

TERRITORIO

EASTERN OIL

O

ANZOATEGUI

DELTA

AMACURO

G U A Y A N A

BOLIVAR

ORIO

MAZONAS

MAP 1

VENEZUELA:
TERRITORIAL DIVISION
AND GROUPS OF STATES

KMS 0   200   400

OCTOBER 1962   SCALE 1/4,000,000

Regional Development Policy

A Publication of the Joint Center for
Urban Studies of the Massachusetts Institute
of Technology and Harvard University

This book is one of a series published under the auspices of the Joint Center for Urban Studies, a cooperative venture of the Massachusetts Institute of Technology and Harvard University. The Joint Center was founded in 1959 to organize and encourage research on urban and regional problems. Participants have included scholars from the fields of anthropology, architecture, business, city planning, economics, education, engineering, history, law, philosophy, political science, and sociology.

The findings and conclusions of this book are, as with all Joint Center publications, solely the responsibility of the contributors.

Other books published in the Joint Center series include:

CHARLES ABRAMS, *Man's Struggle for Shelter in an Urbanizing World*. The M.I.T. Press, 1964.

WILLIAM ALONSO, *Location and Land Use*. Harvard University Press, 1964.

MARTIN ANDERSON, *The Federal Bulldozer*. The M.I.T. Press, 1964.

DONALD APPLEYARD, KEVIN LYNCH, and JOHN R. MYER, *The View from the Road*. The M.I.T. Press, 1964.

EDWARD C. BANFIELD and JAMES Q. WILSON, *City Politics*. Harvard University Press and the M.I.T. Press, 1963.

JOHN E. BURCHARD and OSCAR HANDLIN, editors, *The Historian and the City*. The M.I.T. Press, 1963.

RALPH W. CONANT, editor, *The Public Library and the City*. The M.I.T. Press. 1965.

BERNARD J. FRIEDEN, *The Future of Old Neighborhoods*. The M.I.T. Press, 1964.

JAMES Q. WILSON, editor, *Urban Renewal: The Record and the Controversy*. The M.I.T. Press. 1966.

NATHAN GLAZER and DANIEL MOYNIHAN, *Beyond the Melting Pot*. The M.I.T. Press, 1963.

CHARLES HAAR, *Law and Land: Anglo-American Planning Practice*. Harvard University Press, 1964.

KEVIN LYNCH, *The Image of the City*. The M.I.T. Press, 1960.

LLOYD RODWIN, *Housing and Economic Progress*. The M.I.T. Press, 1961.

STEPHAN THERNSTROM, *Poverty and Progress*. Harvard University Press, 1964.

SAM B. WARNER, JR., *Streetcar Suburbs*. Harvard University Press, 1962.

MORTON AND LUCIA WHITE, *The Intellectual Versus the City: From Thomas Jefferson to Frank Lloyd Wright*. Harvard University Press, 1962.

Regional Development Policy:
A Case Study of Venezuela

John Friedmann

The M.I.T. Press
Massachusetts Institute of Technology
Cambridge, Massachusetts, and London, England

For Manuela

PREFACE

This book is intended for students and practitioners in the field of economic development. It is an attempt to incorporate the dimension of space into a discussion of the strategy for national development in countries that have embarked upon a course of industrialization. Part I deals with general issues; the second part is a case study of regional development policy in Venezuela.

The idea for such a book first came to me a decade ago when I served as an advisor on regional planning in the Brazilian Northeast. It had become eminently clear to me then that regional development in a country the size and diversity of Brazil, and at approximately the same level of economic development, would have to become an integral part of national policy if major social conflict was to be avoided. But at that time, a rational basis for such a policy was still rather nebulous in my mind, and I postponed further thought on this subject. A second opportunity arose after I had returned to academic life in 1961. The Joint Center for Urban Studies of M.I.T. and Harvard had undertaken to advise the Venezuelan government on the planning of the new city of Santo Tomé de Guayana, which was to be the focal point for a dramatic effort at regional development. Through the good offices of the Joint Center, I was able to spend two summers doing field work in Venezuela. The present study is the result.

As I proceeded with it, the use of a special vocabulary became inescapable. May the reader forgive me if he should find the pages burdened with a jargon that is unfamiliar to him. At the same time, I expect that many of the new terms may find their way into regional analysis. In every case, I have tried to relate the concept to its referent in the real world and to make its meaning clear.

I must also apologize to those who would like to see more quantitative analysis in a study of this type. Unfortunately, many kinds of data were simply not available or were so unreliable that little would have been gained by using them. This was the case with regional income data, for example. On the other hand, even if precise benchmark data had been available, they would have been of little help in projecting the spatial pattern of Venezuela's economy for an entire generation. The margin of error could not have been calculated for so long a period, and the use of detailed statistics would have given the reader an impression of specious accuracy. Recourse was had to maps instead. These maps give rough impressions of spatial relationships, and the book is primarily an analysis of these relationships and their implications. Maps, of course, are also instruments for making quantitative statements, and indeed, some of the historical maps are quite precise. But when it comes to charting future spatial patterns, the maps provide only a visual synthesis without pretending to be accurate in every detail.

Special emphasis has been given in the study to the Guayana program, and it may be hoped that its conclusions will in some small way be helpful to those in the Corporación Venezolana de Guayana, who gave so generously of their time and energy during the preparatory stages. In particular, I wish to pay tribute to General Rafael Alfonzo Ravard, the brilliant and dynamic President of the Corporation, who not only gave unstinting support to the study but with his probing questions helped me to gain a more profound understanding of the regional issue in Venezuela's development.

Two young Venezuelan planners were closely associated with me during the months of field work. Many stimulating hours in conversation and sometimes heated debate were spent with José Alberto Rivas and Clemente Chirinos, both of whom contributed greatly to my thinking. In addition, Mr. Rivas is responsible for designing a number of the maps.

Great encouragement for the study came from Roberto Alamo Blanco, Chief Economist of the Corporation, Juan Andres Vegas, Chief of the Planning and Investigations Department, and Hector Font, Chief of the Human Development Division. I am deeply indebted to them for the many ways in which they facilitated my work in Venezuela.

Lloyd Rodwin, Chairman of the Faculty Committee of the Joint Center, not only helped in the original formulation of the study but also contributed useful critical comment at various stages during its completion. Alexander Ganz, the Joint Center's Chief Economist in Caracas, was unstinting in his generosity and I greatly value my association with him.

For reading portions of the manuscript in draft and helping me avoid the worst blunders, I wish to express my gratitude to Jorge Ahumada, Luis Lander, Eduardo Neira, Richard Meier, Britton Harris, Bernard Frieden, Edward Ackerman, Sam Warner, Jerome Milliman, William Alonso, and William Doebele. Peter Grenell carried out some income analysis which served as background to the study.

Last, but in no sense least, Harvey Perloff has my lasting gratitude and admiration. It is largely to him that this book owes whatever merit it may deserve.

JOHN FRIEDMANN

August 1965

CONTENTS

xii

GLOSSARY

ACTIVATION OF CORE REGIONS—the measures taken to realize the potential development prospects of a core region. Usually involves a heavy investment in urban infrastructure facilities.

CENTER-PERIPHERY MODEL—a conceptual model that divides the space economy into a dynamic, rapidly growing central region and its periphery. The growth of the center is viewed as being subsidized in part by the periphery.

CORE REGION—one of several types of development region. Similar to François Perroux's concept of *pôle de croissance* (growth pole). A metropolitan economy with a high potential for economic growth. In a hierarchy of core regions, at least four ranks may be distinguished: (1) national metropolis, (2) regional capital, (3) subregional center, and (4) local service center.

DEVELOPMENT CORRIDOR—a type of upward-transitional area connecting two or more core regions. The intensity of corridor development tends to be directly proportional to the product of the core region economies and inversely proportional to the distance separating them.

DEVELOPMENT REGION—an area delimited on the basis of common prospects and problems of development. Five types are identified: core region, upward-transitional area, resource frontier region, downward-transitional area, and special problem area.

DOWNWARD-TRANSITIONAL AREA—one of several types of development region. An area of old, established settlement whose essentially rural economy is stagnant or in decline and whose peculiar combination of resources suggest as optimal a less intensive development than in the past.

GROWTH POINT—a local service city, equivalent to a core region of the fourth rank or lower. Important in the reorganization of downward-transitional (depressed) areas.

GROWTH POLE—see core region.

INTEGRATION OF THE NATIONAL SPACE ECONOMY—achievement of a unified economy over the national territory, organized according to the principle of comparative advantage and having in view the maximization of interregional flows of mobile factors of production.

INTERMETROPOLITAN PERIPHERY—includes all areas intervening among metropolitan regions. The socioeconomic profile of the IMP is the reverse image of metropolitan virility.

LOCATIONAL FORCES—forces operating on the space economy and tending to alter its structural organization. Three types are distinguished: decentralization, focalization, and dispersion.

LOCATION INPUTS—conditions economically important to the location of a firm. Expressed as a requirement, they represent an effective demand on the part of firms seeking a new location.

LOCATION MATRIX—see location point.

LOCATION POINT—a subsystem of the national space economy with respect to which location decisions of firms and households are made. May be characterized by its supply of location inputs. (Also referred to as location matrix.)

PROGRAMMING REGION—an area delineated for the purpose of initiating a process of detailed programming for economic development. It need not coincide with development region.

REGIONAL DEVELOPMENT POLICY—a national policy for the economic development of regions and guided by objectives for the organization of the national space economy. One of the means for achieving the spatial coordination of sectoral plans and programs.

REGIONAL PROGRAMMING—the process of evolving detailed, operational programs for the economic development of specified regions. A series of linked investment projects are at the basis of a regional program statement.

RESOURCE FRONTIER REGION—one of several types of development region. A zone of new settlement in otherwise virgin territory. Contiguous (agricultural) and noncontiguous frontier regions are distinguished. The latter are usually associated with large-scale investments in a mineral or forest development scheme and involve substantial urbanization.

SPACE ECONOMY—the economy in its spatial dimension. Described in terms of either (1) point location and interacting flows of goods, capital, labor, and information or (2) regional constructs.

SPATIAL EQUILIBRIUM—a pattern in which no single firm or household is able to shift its location without reducing the output of the economic system as a whole.

SPATIAL ORGANIZATION—the structure of the space economy arranged according to certain social purposes, either implied or explicitly stated.

UPWARD-TRANSITIONAL AREA—one of several types of development region. An area whose natural endowments and location relative to core regions suggest the possibility of a greatly intensified use of resources. See also development corridor.

URBAN FIELD—the area over which a specified degree of urban influence is felt. Influence may be measured in terms of several indices, including trade, commuting, radio and television reception, newspaper readership, and telephone messages.

PART I

STRUCTURE AND PROCESS OF REGIONAL DEVELOPMENT

INTRODUCTION

My aim in this first part is to introduce the reader to the theory of regional development and planning. The reference to theory is perhaps pretentious. It might be more accurate to speak of propositions having broad generality. More specifically, I wish to demonstrate the place of regional development in national economic policy in a set of societies that have been called by various names but whÍch are conveniently classified as transitional to industrialism. As a result, I am concerned with national policies for regional development, a point of view that is not yet widely accepted but which is increasingly being adopted by national planners whom circumstances compel to think predominantly in geographic terms.

The traditional approach has been to view regional development planning (and associated planning for urbanization) as a concern with local issues primarily by local people and more especially by those who live in the economically distressed parts of a country. The concentration on national income accounts as a tool of development policy has blotted out the crucial significance of the regional element in national planning. The location of activities has been considered a matter of only secondary importance. Yet, national development is, in one sense, simply the composite of economic activities conducted in rather specific environmental settings. These activities combine in certain ways, more or less successfully, to yield an index figure for growth in the national accounts. In an economy in which resources are not fully employed, in which many important resources (and their potential applications) may not even be known, this disregard of the regional element can markedly diminish an economy's capacity for growth. Over and above the possibility of bringing additional resources into play, there is the question of the efficiency at which the economy operates, and this is to a large extent a question of the location of activities and the resulting pattern of interregional relations. The present study therefore regards the solution of specifically regional problems as an integral part of a general policy for the development of *all* regions that is pointed toward the attainment of national goals for the spatial organization of the economy.

In the five chapters that follow, the elements of a national policy for regional development are discussed. Chapter 1 traces the emergence of regional policy as a public issue and attempts to state the conditions under which it is likely to arise. Chapter 2 is essentially a series of interrelated propositions regarding the processes of regional economic growth. It serves as background to brief statements on the delineation of development regions (Chapter 3) and the national objectives for the pattern of activity location and the spatial allocation of investments (Chapter 4). The concluding chapter in Part I focuses on individual problem regions and states the major elements of an approach to their development.

These general principles are applied, in Part II, to a detailed investigation of the regional policy problem in Venezuela.

CHAPTER ONE

THE REGIONAL POLICY PROBLEM

Since the end of the Second World War, a number of questions have arisen to become central concerns of mankind. Among them is the triad of national independence, national economic development, and national planning. Regional policy appears to have been added as a fourth concern in recent years.

Regional policy deals with the locational aspects, the "where" of economic development. It reflects the need to deal with regional problems at the national level. It is by manipulating national policy variables that the most useful contributions to the future of regional economies can be made.

Regional policy is a direct outgrowth of the triad which has the nation as its basic mark of reference. Nations are not homogeneous; development does not affect all parts of a nation equally; and planners need a link relating isolated projects to national goals. If regional policy reflects the existence of geographic or spatial inequities, it also reflects an awareness of the importance of a regional approach to the implementation of national growth objectives. The significance of regional policy has been recognized for some time in centrally planned economies, such as Poland. But the necessity to think of regional problems in national terms has not been confined to them alone. It has also been discovered in the mixed economies of Common Market countries.[1] And the newly evolving nations of Africa, Latin America, and Asia are beginning to appreciate the fact that national investment strategies require a subaggregation along regional lines.

This sudden awakening to the spatial dimension of development occurred in Europe as a consequence of the rapidity with

5

which postwar changes transformed the economic life of the continent. An urban revolution—propelled by vast internal population transfers and the automobile—engulfed the remnants of Europe's nineteenth century cities. Old agricultural problem areas clamored for the attention of a population newly grown rich and demanded a rectification of ancient and patiently borne griefs. Technological progress often bypassed traditional centers of commerce and industry and left them to cope with obsolete facilities, high taxes, and an overaged but underemployed labor force. Finally, the spatial shifts in productive facilities which were predicted to follow from the realization in full of the objectives of a Common European Market raised serious problems of adjustment in the areas of rapid expansion—the "growth poles" of the New Europe—no less than in the areas of stagnation or decline.[2]

This explanation for the emergence of regional policy—rapid economic evolution and spatial dislocations—is valid also for transitional societies. But the specific occasion is, of course, different from that for central Europe. The central issue for the newly developing countries is, without question, the achievement of a high rate of economic growth in a national area that is often poorly articulated, poorly integrated, and whose resources are inefficiently and only partially used.

Phases of National Development

The sustaining thesis of this study is that regional policy appears as a function of the spatial transformations engendered by economic growth. Not only will the policy problems be different for each major period of national development, but the importance attached to regional policy will vary (Table 1.1).

Preindustrial societies need to pay little attention to problems of spatial organization. Most of their energies will be devoted to creating human and material bases for further industrial growth: fundamental improvements in education, health, agricultural organization, and transportation. At the opposite end of the scale are those national societies in which the output of manufactures as a proportion of total production has already reached

6

Table 1.1. Phases of National Development
and Regional Policy

Type of Economy	Preindustrial†	Transitional	Industrial	Postindustrial
Industry as Share of GNP, 1950–1955°	0–10%	10–25%	25–50%	declining
Importance of Regional Policy for National Economic Growth	inappropriate	critical	vestigial	shift to a new focus
Policy Emphasis	creating pre-conditions for economic development	creating a spatial organization capable of sustaining transition to industrialism	depressed area problems; area redevelopment; spatial adjustments to common market organization	urban renewal; spatial order and circulation within metropolitan regions; open space and amenities of landscape
Examples of Countries in each Category	Tanganyika Paraguay Bolivia Afghanistan Cambodia Burma	Venezuela Brazil Colombia Turkey India Pakistan Iraq Mexico	France Italy West Germany Japan Israel United Kingdom Canada Australia	U.S.A.‡

°Hollis B. Chenery, "Pattern of Industrial Growth," *American Economic Review*, Vol. I, No. 4 (September 1960), Table 1.

†Estimated. See Everett Hagen, "Some Facts about Income Levels and Economic Growth," *The Review of Economics and Statistics*, Vol. 42, No. 1 (February 1960), Table 1.

‡The turning point, it appears, was 1953, when manufacturing industry accounted for 32.1 per cent of the national income. The corresponding share of manufacturing for the average of the years 1960 to 1962 was only 28.6 per cent. Cf. U.S. Department of Commerce, Bureau of the Census, *Historical Statistics of the United States*, Series F 22–33; Washington, D. C.: U.S. Government Printing Office, 1960), and *Survey of Current Business*, July 1963, Table 7.

a peak and is beginning to decline, yielding to a service sector that has its own inner dynamics. Such societies—the United States is the outstanding example to date—are so completely integrated spatially that the regional focus is no longer an appropriate one as a basis for national development policy. Rather, spatial planning in postindustrial society involves chiefly urban

7

and metropolitan problems. Moreover, such a society is likely to be more troubled with the quality of the physical environment, the internal spatial adjustments occasioned by growth, and circulation than with generating growth through more intensive resource uses.

Transitional societies are clearly the most directly concerned with regional organization, partly because of the spatial shifts involved in moving from an agrarian to an industrial economy, partly because a large portion of their potential resources are still unutilized. A number of recent studies are beginning to shed light on the nature and extent of these problems.[3]

Vestiges of the regional problems of economic transition, especially long-standing problems of regional backwardness, continue into the period of mature industrialization. The affluence that comes with industrial maturity allows of noble gestures. And the favored treatment of heretofore neglected rural areas and the rebuilding of old cities are luxuries that need no longer be justified in every detail against the harsh criterion of the national growth rate.

Emergence of the Regional Policy Issue

Spatial aspects of development, it has been claimed, arise as a critical policy issue during a phase in the evolution of a national economy that has been loosely called transitional. This assertion may be more fully elaborated by sketching a simple model of how the economic space of a nation may be changed over several historical transitions, from early settlement to full industrialization. Venezuela, a society about to make a successful "breakthrough" to industrialism, will serve as a convenient prototype, but the model is intended to be more widely applicable.[4]

I shall begin by assuming that a previously uninhabited area is colonized from the sea, and that its initial settlements are founded along the coast where they serve as base camps for the subsequent exploration and occupation of interior regions. In due course, several of the early towns will grow into commercial centers of some consequence, each achieving dominance over a

8

loosely defined hinterland whose population is engaged in agriculture, cattle raising, and mining. One of these centers will be elevated to a loftier position over the rest as the administrative capital of the new province.

There follows a long period during which the colonial economy remains predominantly agricultural. With changes in export demand for primary products, different regions are, in succession, favored for intensive settlement, investment, and production. A number of new cities are established for administrative control as well as for the provision of essential services to the surrounding countryside. Their accessibility to the older centers on the coast will be decisive for the localization and subsequent expansion of these towns. But an interdependent system of cities will not yet come into existence. The several regional economies will frequently have closer commercial and even social ties with centers in the mother country than among themselves.

In course of further occupancy and settlement, spatial differentiation proceeds, as each regional economy acquires its own characteristic patterns in adaptation to external demand and to the local features of climate, topography, and natural resources. Social differentiation may parallel this tendency to ecological distinctness until a number of clearly defined regional complexes evolve. Toward the end of this period, the nation, now liberated from colonial rule, will appear to be composed of a congeries of relatively autonomous regional economies and sociocultural subsystems, each with its own administrative and commercial centers and traditional channels of export.

The next period is characterized by a cumulative process of industrialization and by dramatic shifts in the existing spatial patterns, reflecting the basic transformations taking place in the structure of the economy. Industrialization typically leads to a concentration of investments upon one or two areas, while much of the remaining national territory becomes locationally obsolete. A dualistic structure is thus imprinted upon the space economy, comprising a "center" of rapid, intensive development and a "periphery" whose economy, imperfectly related to this center, is either stagnant or declining.

9

The Center-Periphery Model

Since economic evolution continues beyond this stage, the preceding model remains incomplete and open to the future. It is appropriate, however, to break in at this juncture for, with the emergence of a center-periphery relationship, the regional problem is, for the first time, posed as an issue of national importance. Because of its critical contribution to the present analysis, a brief review of the literature pertaining to the center-periphery relationship is in order.

Meier and Baldwin, in an important text, have drawn attention to the existence of a center-periphery structure on a global scale. They claim to have discovered in this structure an important clue for understanding some of the key developmental processes during the nineteenth century.[5] The authors identify the center initially with England whence, spreading laterally to parts of western Europe and the eastern United States, it came to form what an American historian, writing for an earlier generation, had called the "world metropolis."[6] On this broad scale, the use of the concept may be regarded as chiefly metaphorical. Nevertheless, Raúl Prebisch of the United Nations Economic Commission for Latin America (ECLA) has used it as part of a fundamental explanation of Latin America's persisting economic backwardness compared with western Europe and North America. He lays particular stress on the long-run adverse terms of trade experienced by producers of primary products on the periphery in their commerce with nations of the world metropolis. Although controversy has raged about it, the Prebisch thesis has recently been gaining some support.[7]

Moving from a global to a continental scale, a study carried out by the United Nations Economic Commission for Europe finds that " . . . in all countries of Europe the levels of economic development tend to be lowest in the regions furthest removed from the relatively small areas which developed as the main European center of industrial activity, embracing England and the valley and outlet of the Rhine."[8] This pattern, according to the Commission, is presumably related to the structure of spatial relations: " . . . the smaller or larger distance has no doubt been in itself a powerful location factor contributing to mold the pattern of settlement inside most European Countries, making the regions nearer the center more, and those furthest removed from it less, attractive from the point of view of industrial location."[9]

At the next lower, or national, scale, Harvey S. Perloff and Lowdon Wingo, Jr., ascribe to the center-periphery structure a fundamental role in the development of the American economy.

The role of cumulative advantage is most clearly seen [they write] in the growth of the Middle Atlantic region and, later, of the Great Lakes region. Here are regions which have enjoyed access to national markets. Each was endowed with unusually good agricultural resources from the beginning, and the emergence of the minerals-dominant economy found each with excellent access to vast deposits of iron ore and coal. With these resources and market advantages, they developed into the most significant feature of regional economic growth on the American scene—the emergence of an industrial heartland coincident with the center of the national market.

The emergence of the industrial heartland set the basic conditions for regional growth throughout the nation—it was the lever for the successive development of the newer peripheral regions. As the input requirements of the heartland expanded, it reached out into the outlying areas for its resources, stimulating their growth differentially but in accordance with both its own resource demands and the endowments of the regions. The rapid growth of the U.S. economy was accompanied (and to some extent achieved) by this process of industrial nucleation.[10]

Finally, the center-periphery relationship has been intensively studied at the level of the city.

According to T. W. Schultz, economic development occurs in a specific locational matrix which is primarily urban and industrial in composition. It is at or near this matrix that economic organization, especially commodity and factor markets, work most efficiently.[11] A number of carefully elaborated empirical studies have given substance to this generalization.[12] Dissenting arguments have stressed the possible primacy in economic development of the agricultural sector, emerging independently of any urban focus.[13] But in order to achieve the sustained and

11

cumulative growth of a predominantly rural region, creation of an urban-industrial matrix appears, at least in an historical perspective, to be essential. And once it has come into being, the Schultzean hypothesis can be expected to hold in a general way: the further an area lies from an urban center, the less promising will be its outlook for development.[14]

World, continent, nation, and city—the center-periphery hypothesis appears on all the relevant scales of explanation simultaneously as cause and as effect of economic transformation. Although it has been heatedly debated, the balance of the evidence points strongly in its favor.

Recently, a number of attempts have been made to incorporate this thesis into a general theory of economic growth.[15] Each analysis proceeds from the empirical finding that industrial growth tends to be concentrated upon a few metropolitan regions or, to use François Perroux's vivid expression, the "growth poles" (*pôles de croissance*) of an economy. Gunnar Myrdal shows how the emerging center-periphery structure leads to cumulatively greater disparities through the operation of unrestrained market forces, while Albert Hirschman, chiefly concerned with development strategy, emphasizes the need to phase the investment process carefully over a sequence of regions, concentrating initially upon the points of rapid urban-industrial expansion, and moving outward into the periphery when the need for further public investment declines in relative importance at the center.[16] Hirschman views regional balances as a stimulus to national growth and urges a policy of "controlled disequilibrium" upon government planners.

This rapid and somewhat impressionistic survey of the literature which has grown up around the core-periphery concept during the last decade may be completed by drawing attention to some of the implicit structural relations that appear to govern the behavior of the two "regions."

First, the center-periphery relationship may be described as essentially a "colonial" one.[17] The emergence of a polarized structure will normally be accompanied by a series of displacements, from the periphery to the center, of the principal factors of production: labor, capital, entrepreneurship, foreign exchange, and raw materials in unprocessed form. Judging from this behavior, one would conclude, though without substantial evidence, that the marginal productivities at the center are vastly superior to those obtainable from investments on the periphery.

Second, insofar as the periphery remains a producer of primary, chiefly agricultural, materials, the secular trend in the interregional terms of trade will, on the whole, continue to be favorable to the center. In other words, manufactured goods produced at the center will grow progressively dearer than the traditional exports of outlying regions. Where this tendency exists, it may be aggravated by the maintenance of high protective tariffs for domestic industry at the same time that the prices of essential foods are artifically held low through direct government controls and subsidy schemes.

Third, growing regional inequalities will give rise to political pressures intended to reverse the traditional flow of resources to the center and to help raise per capita incomes on the periphery to a level of approximate equality with the rest of the nation. Since the periphery can often marshal imposing political strength at the national level, efforts in this direction are usually effective, at least with regard to the ability to mobilize additional resources. But this agitation in favor of the periphery—which is the real source of support for regional policy and planning—can have serious economic repercussions. An *unprincipled* redistribution of resources in favor of the periphery would significantly retard progress at the center and, consequently, for the country as a whole.

Spatial Equilibrium as an Alternative Model

Social scientists have argued that in an unfettered economy, under assumptions of perfect information and unhindered movements of labor and capital, the system of spatial relationships would, if disturbed, eventually return to a state of equilibrium. An optimal allocation of resources would consequently be achieved whenever the relevant factors of production are so distributed that further shifts among uses and locations are impossible without reducing the national product.[18] This model, of

13

course, also assumes given demand and supply conditions, and a given state of the arts. The equalization of returns to labor and capital may be stated as a logical corollary to this model. Or dynamically: capital will tend to flow from low- to high-productivity regions, and labor from low- to high-wage areas until, by a process of successive marginal adjustments in both regions, a spatial equilibrium is established. The equilibrium model, therefore, leads one to expect not a widening disparity in the rates of factor return and economic growth between center and periphery but a gradual convergence of these rates. Which model one adopts is decisive for the type of regional policy likely to be evolved. While the center-periphery model suggests the necessity for state intervention, the equilibrium model soothes policymakers by reassuring them that the unhindered operation of market forces will inevitably tend to establish a spatial equilibrium (and thus the highest degree of social well-being).

There is, however, a major difficulty with the equilibrium model: historical evidence does not support it. Disequilibrium is built into transitional societies from the start; the technological revolution is permanent; changes in demand and supply conditions are so rapid and their consequences of such magnitude, that they can scarcely be considered "marginal." The indisputable fact is that regional convergence will not automatically occur in the course of a nation's development history. Impressive evidence has been collected to show why the equilibrium mechanism that has been posited in theory will, in fact, break down. Even with a century and a half of sustained industrialization, the advanced economies of the United States and western Europe continue to be preoccupied with problems of depressed and backward regions inside their national territories.

The following may be cited as among the principal reasons for this failure of the world to correspond to theory:

1. *The failure of diminishing returns to set in at the center.*

The continued growth of even the largest metropolitan regions in the world contradicts the expectation of diminishing marginal returns to scale. Within a given metropolitan area, many

14

structural and locational changes may occur over time. But there is no evidence that metropolitan areas have ceased to grow anywhere as the result of presumed social diseconomies of scale in settlement. Profit incentives to seek out new and more productive opportunities on the national periphery may consequently be lacking.[19]

2. *The failure to perceive peripheral investment opportunities.*

As Hirschman has pointed out, private investors consistently overestimate the profitability of investments at the center relative to the periphery.[20] There are numerous reasons for this tendency, including a lack of objective knowledge about production opportunities on the periphery, the relative ease of making new investments at the center, the strong preference of enterprises for a metropolitan environment, and an absence of spontaneous interest in the periphery, except for relaxation from the rigors of a harried city life.

3. *Export demand for goods produced at the center.*

Growth at the center may be viewed as a function of the demand for regional exports. It is altogether possible, in fact, quite probable, that the central region's exports, chiefly of manufactured products, will grow more rapidly than agricultural exports from the periphery. In this event, and contrary to theory, a high-wage region, such as the center, may experience a greater growth of capital and a greater increase in money wages than surrounding low-wage areas. Existing inequalities between the two regions will consequently be intensified.

4. *Coincidence of center with the national market.*

Once a center emerges, the national market for goods produced in the modern sector will come to be concentrated upon it. This, in turn, will lead to further investment in market-oriented industries and services, and a cumulative growth cycle will be set in motion. In the industrial sector, the periphery is likely to acquire only those enterprises whose location

15

is determined by proximity to primary materials. As a country's development advances, the quantitative importance of such industries tends to be reduced to a small fraction of total production and employment.

5. *Location of quaternary services at the center.*

The center is almost always the high citadel of finance, education, research, planning, and control services of diverse kinds, including those of the national government. This array of service functions not only acts as a powerful attractive force on modern industry, but turns the center into the core of a permanent technological revolution. This tends to give a centrally located enterprises an initial advantage over possible rivals on the periphery and serves further to concentrate capital at or near central locations.

6. *Heterogeneity of populations.*

The center tends to have the largest proportion of foreign nationals, many of whom have come with the intention to pioneer new enterprise. Culture contact reaches a high peak of intensity at the center not only with foreign cultures but also with representatives of the several national subcultures who have migrated to the center. Cultural heterogeneity of this type is generally conducive to innovation and risk-taking.

7. *Inability of the periphery to make adjustments appropriate to constant socioeconomic change at the center.*

   a. High replacement rates on the periphery. Despite rapid outmigration from the periphery, the natural rate of increase is often so great as to prevent an absolute decline in peripheral populations. Thus what starts as a temporary condition of "overpopulation" on the periphery may become endemic.

   b. Disruptive effects of rapid outmigration. The selective nature of internal migrations tends to deprive the periphery of its youngest, most enterprising, and most educated population. Moreover, heavy outmigration from small communities may foreclose adjustments that might lead to a recovery and to subsequent growth on a sustained basis. Community leadership will tend to remain in the hands of traditionalists.[22]

c. *Lack of capital.* Just as the center tends to attract the best human elements from the periphery, so it will attract its "surplus" capital. Local capital for investment in modern enterprise is generally scarce. Moreover, peripheral poverty produces insufficient revenues for undertaking large-scale projects, and provincial governments are typically dependent on the good will of the national administration for contributions to their own miniscule capital improvement budgets.

d. *Inability and unwillingness to see the regional problem from a national perspective.* This perceptual difficulty often leads to improper investments and other development policies that by their very nature prevent an effective adjustment and do not lead to the desired multiplier effects.

It may be that, in the very long run, when the society has advanced into an era of prosperity and mass consumption, interregional inequalities can be made to dwindle into insignificance. There is evidence that, for at least one set of regions in the United States, income differentials have been steadily declining for almost a century.[23] But, as Easterlin points out, the process of income convergence has been an extremely slow one, and the "underlying factors which frequently worked against convergence were the dynamic ones: the development of new products and new techniques, resources depletion and discovery, changes in the structure and transfer costs, shifts in consumption patterns, and so on."[24] Thus, income convergence is not in any sense a necessary result of the development process.[25] Bela Balassa suggests that Myrdal's "spread effects" may become more powerful at a high stage of economic development when they may take the form of "increased demand for the underdeveloped region's products, rising proportion of mobile external economics, transmission of technological knowledge, and relocation of plants in response to wage differentials."[26] However, this is empty counsel for newly developing areas if it is suggested that spread-effects such as these will automatically take care of the

17

periphery in the good course of historical time. Although the government can make use of technological possibilities and changing demand structures in order to promote the development of peripheral economies, this is clearly a matter of deliberate planning. On the whole, the unrestrained forces of a dynamic market economy appear to be working against a convergence of the center and periphery.

Projects, Programs, Plans

If further proof were needed of the bankruptcy of the equilibrium model as a basis for policy prescription, one might cite the persistent search for more adequate guidelines. However, regional policy extends beyond the formulation of principles of spatial resource allocation. It points to a process for generating investment projects and aggregating them over spatial subsystems of the economy.

Although regional programs are intended to meet the requirements of local development, they should also dovetail into the pattern of objectives for national economic growth. The sum of regional programs should therefore spell out the investment component of a national strategy for development; the sum of regional projects for any one year must be identical with the national capital budget. These are the relations in principle. In practice, of course, the parts may badly fit to one another.

By extending a bridge from global national plans to programs and projects, regional policy creates conditions favorable to an increased participation of local people in the planning process. It reduces distance to the government by involving people in considerations that have immediate consequences for them. Creating this additional channel for expressing their wants and grievances may render national planning more difficult, since persuasion and compromise are basic tools for building that minimum of consensus which is necessary to democratic action. But it may also aid planning by a more thorough airing of possibly immature ideas conceived by national planners, by injecting local realism into schemes that are perhaps inappropriate in their existing form, and by making certain that new undertakings

18

are understood and supported by local populations. This essentially *political* dimension of regional policy is tremendously important; but I shall not be dealing with it here. It belongs to another realm of discourse.

CHAPTER TWO

THE PROCESS OF REGIONAL DEVELOPMENT

Planners who would interfere in regional development must understand the process by which it is generated. Unfortunately, little is known about the way the aggregate of local activities produces growth in national income or how economic growth in one area of the nation is transmitted to other parts. Little, indeed, is known about the substructures of the spatial system, and the influence that the spatial pattern of activities has upon national growth. The presence of such an influence—acting through external economies and diseconomies, the propensity to innovate and to invest, and the variable costs of moving both people and products—is undeniable. At issue here is the magnitude of the influence and the character of the process by which it is exerted.

The outlines of such a process are nevertheless beginning to emerge from current writings, though our newly acquired knowledge has not yet hardened into doctrine.[1] An adequate regional theory has to meet two requirements. First, it must clarify the reordering of spatial relations that occurs under conditions of growth. It must be able to account for changes in the boundaries of regional subsystems. Second, it must explain the changing influence of spatial patterns on system-wide growth. Regional theory is, therefore, not a theory about regions with fixed boundaries but about the spatial incidence of economic growth.

In the following, I intend to present a way of thinking about the process of regional development in this sense. Although I shall make no effort to state in rigorous form the quantitative relations among the variables that account for the facts of subnational economic growth, I hope to lead the reader to consider a set of interrelated propositions concerning the process under study.

Propositions Concerning the Spatial Incidence of Economic Growth

Regional economies are open to the outside world and subject to external influence. In an interdependent economy, there are no "closed" regions, hermetically sealed against all impulses beating against imaginary walls. Whether interdependency takes the form of trade relations or the exchange of information, there is no part of the space economy that is not bound into a series of overlapping networks of this sort. The degree to which any given area is "open" to the outside world will, of course, vary from place to place; so will the composition of the flows terminating and originating in one locality. Mountainous areas predominantly devoted to subsistence farming will have fewer external relations than sprawling urban regions in the plains. Similarly, the spatial subsystems of a backward economy will be less interdependent than the subsystems of a postindustrial society, such as the United States. And, other things remaining the same, the smaller the spatial subsystem, the greater will be its dependence on a network or external supporting relations. Whole countries tend to have more closure than subnational areas; large multistate regions will be more autonomous than single cities. Topography, type of economy, stage of development, and size of region are the main variables to be considered.

What is the meaning of the degree of closure (or openness) of regional economies? Quite simply it is this: their economic behavior will be variously subject to external influence; the degree to which local decisions are able to shape the future of regional economies will partly depend on the degree of closure. Closure suggests autonomy of choice; openness implies a measure of dependency. Nations tend to be more autonomous than regions, and large nations more so than small ones; but even national areas, which tend to have maximum closure, cannot escape the sweep of historic forces, of peace and war, world-wide depressions or periods of great buoyancy and confidence. Subnational areas are subject to all these as well as to more exclusively national trends in tastes and fashion, the geographic spread of market areas, and the rate and pattern of investment. They are constrained to respond to the behavior of the system as a whole. They are essentially reactive economies.

Regional economic growth is externally induced. The initial impulse for the economic growth of a given subarea comes usually from the outside. For this to happen, the particular resource combinations of the local area must give it a comparative advantage in supplying external demand efficiently. Its leading economic sectors will consequently be oriented to exports. This may be a specialized crop, such as tropical fruit or Imperial Valley lettuce; it may be oil or iron ore; it may also be an aircraft or petrochemical industry, or a national defense establishment.

Comparative advantage is not given in nature; it is always created by human effort. Resource surveys may discover primary materials in demand on world markets; a new routing of railroads or highways or a new structure of transport rates will alter the relative attractiveness of all parts of the space economy for supplying national markets or receiving strategic imports; technological innovations, such as a new smelting process, may suggest new opportunities for those subnational economies that are able to combine efficiently the relevant factors of production.

The initiative to exploit the opportunities created in this fashion will usually come from outside the region, especially during the first stages of growth. Entrepreneurship and capital will tend to be heavily concentrated in the more highly developed regions and will be attracted into new areas to the extent that profitable opportunities are perceived. Since individual and social calculations of returns on investment may diverge, some of the burden of development may be shifted to the public sector. External economies must be created through judicious investment in those facilities that will induce the flow of private capital into the region. Public investments may include the buildup of highways, energy supplies, irrigation works, housing, schools and hospitals, sewage systems, and similar facilities that, if they are not borne by the public sector, will have to be supplied, usually on a less than optimal scale, by the private investor himself. The resulting costs to the individual firm may effectively preclude investment in any form whatever.

Successful translation of export sector growth into growth of the residentiary sector depends on the sociopolitical structure of the region and the local distribution of income and pattern of expenditures. In the preceding section, a distinction was implied between the export sector of an economy and its residentiary activities. The latter are wholly oriented to serve market demand internal to a given region. This classification is arbitrary since, by enlarging regional boundaries, it is possible to reclassify export industries into residentiary, the reverse effect being accomplished by contracting boundaries.[2] Nevertheless, for a set of *fixed* regional boundaries, the distinction is a valid and useful construct. If initial investment in the export sector of a regional economy is to result in further expansion, this first impulse must be translated into an active buildup of the regional market and the productive facilities needed to serve it. This is not an automatic process, however, and many regions soon reach a plateau of relative stagnation because of their inability to accomplish the essential measures of "translation." Political jargon refers to this situation—in which an export sector under external control fails to set off a spiral of internal development—as colonial domination.[3]

The size of the multiplier effect will depend, therefore, on a number of variables that are difficult to isolate but of supreme importance in determining the response of the region to the initial impulses received. Will local entrepreneurs be encouraged to invest in the region? Will the government provide the infrastructure necessary to render private investment in the residentiary sector economic? What is the wage structure of the export sector? Will it permit a rapid expansion of consumer demand? What percentage of the profits generated in the region will be reinvested in new productive facilities within it? How much of the new demand is for items of luxury consumption that must be imported?

In the extreme case, local entrepreneurship will be suppressed; no infrastructure investment will be undertaken beyond what is essential to support the export sector; wages paid to export workers will be held to a subsistence minimum; profits concentrated in the hands of "foreign" entrepreneurs will be taken out of the region; and the high salaries of managers and other "foreign" personnel stationed in the region will be spent chiefly on luxury imports. Under such conditions, no significant regional multiplier will result from the original investment.[4]

Local leadership is decisive for successful adaptation to external change. Yet the quality of leadership depends on the region's development experience. Opportunities have to be perceived and seized by someone. Foresight and the willingness to assume calculated risks are hallmarks of imaginative leadership. To the extent that a region's economic growth hinges on successful adaptation to external changes, local leadership must display these qualities to a high degree. Regional economic growth is, above all, a competitive game. From the standpoint of comparative advantage, wholly unique resource endowments, though they may exist, are rare. It is rather with respect to the quality of a region's infrastructure and the more generalized regional *image* that productive investment decisions are generally made. The efficiency of local administration; the ability to maintain law and order; the reputation of an area's schools, universities, and hospitals; the volume and quality of its housing stock; the quality of its recreational facilities—all these may have decisive influence on what is popularly known about a region. Under conditions of rapid growth, the problem is to provide enough of these facilities and the services they hold to sustain further growth and ease the process of transition to economic maturity.[5]

Slow-growing or stagnant regions face a more difficult situation. Their future is beclouded; the risks are greater. At the same time, the financial means available to them are few. Investment here will generally have to *precede* an upturn in the economic life of the region. A shrewd assessment of the economic currents sweeping the nation will have to be made and specific investments pinpointed that will reintegrate the region into the national economy.

What are the capabilities of local leadership in this respect? Can it effectively organize commitments to respond to these challenges? Does it have an accurate judgment of the situation? Can it act with resolution? The quality of local leadership will depend, in part, on its general value orientation (modern or traditional), on the pattern of its expectations (optimistic or pessimistic), on its orientation to the external world (cosmopolitan or local), on its sense of responsibility (collective or individualistic), on its risk-taking propensities (forward-looking or conservative), and on its abilities to inspire the actions of others.

In many countries, the public sector economy is so thoroughly centralized that little scope remains for the exercise of local leadership. In this event, all decisions affecting local areas will be made by central government bureaucrats whose interest in local areas is, at best, marginal and usually not sustained. The capabilities for adaptive planning at the regional level are therefore greatly reduced.

The leadership capacities of a region will vary in accordance with its past development experience. In cases of economic backwardness, for instance, the pseudo leadership supplied by the national bureaucracy may, in fact, fill a void created by a history of large-scale outmigration. Migrants tend to be selected for age, sex, education, financial means, and possibly the degree of future-orientation. Those who remain may lack the charisma to organize their communities to cope successfully with the flux and flow of external events. They will tend to be ill-informed, indecisive, tradition-bound, pessimistic, largely unaware of the changes in the world outside their local domain, familistic and factionalistic in their politics, and conservative in the willingness to assume risks.

Much the reverse situation is likely to hold for areas of heavy inmigration where an altogether different group of men is likely to step into the available leadership roles. The structure of the space economy thus exerts a subtle but pervasive influence on the ability of regions to deal with their own problems. And because the system is self-reinforcing, leadership capabilities between the center and periphery will tend to spread further apart.

Regional economic growth may be regarded in part as a problem in the location of firms. Abstracting from regions, in a disaggregated approach to the problem of the spatial incidence of economic growth, we may obtain valuable insights from location theory. To demonstrate this, two new terms will be introduced: location inputs and location points. *Location inputs* refer to the conditions that are economically important to the location of a firm. Expressed as a requirement, they represent an effective demand on the part of firms seeking a new location. According to a recent formulation by Ruttan and Wallace,

The forces which determine the location of a particular firm, the level of production of a particular product, and the total level of economic activity in a particular region can be classified under five broad categories: (1) transportation rates on inputs and final products; (2) the geographic location of inputs and product markets; (3) supply schedules of production factors or inputs; (4) production functions or input-output ratios (technology); (5) demand functions for products. This is a more precise classification system than the "orientation" approach which attempts to analyze the factors affecting location in terms of whether the firm or industry is primary materials, market, or labor oriented.[6]

The supply of location inputs can be determined for any spatial subsystem, such as a city or urban region, with respect to which location decisions are usually made. Such subsystems I shall call *location points*.

In principle, it is possible to sum the individual location inputs for all firms in the economy which at a given time are seeking a new location and arrive at a total demand function for such inputs. Similarly, location inputs can be aggregated into a supply function for all location points extending as a frequency distribution over the location surface. If demand and supply functions are now superimposed, and assuming that the supply functions are spatially fixed in the short run, those points whose supply of location inputs most closely approximates the modal value of the demand function will obviously be favored, on the average, in all location decisions. They will receive the largest amounts of new investment.

This pattern is immediately translated into performance. For regional progress is attributable, first, to the shares that each location point obtains of the nation's fast and slow-growing industries and, second, to the actual growth in the output of the particular industry mix found at each location. The total growth pattern, then, may be regarded as the outcome of matching specialized regional advantages (supply of location inputs) with specialized industrial location requirements (demand of location inputs).[7] Incidentally, this formulation also explains why a pattern of spatial distribution may diverge from what is considered optimal from a national standpoint. Faulty matching can lead to gross inefficiencies in the performance of the whole economy.

We may think of each successive time period as a new round of investments. By altering the spatial distribution of markets and sources of raw material supplies, each round will lead to small changes on the supply side of location inputs. But the demand side, too, will be subtly affected. Historically, it is possible to observe an orderly progression in the modal requirements for elements of location from those that are relatively fixed in space, such as primary material and energy sources, to those that are more mobile, such as educational and research facilities. At the same time, a strong drift towards metropolitan markets may be observed.

As long as regional resources remain unevenly developed, with some regions showing large unexploited potentials for a given pattern of demand and technology, very real economic differences will exist in the relative attractiveness of individual location points, especially during the early phases of economic growth when spatial immobilities fall within the modal range of location input demand. But as increasingly all points of the space economy are brought close to their full potential contribution in the short run, as transportation and communications are extended nationally, and as the marginal costs of movement across space are reduced, the choices among location points tend to become, over large segments of the location surface, relatively indifferent from a purely economic standpoint.

It is, of course, true that some firms require rapid access to centers of style, fashion, research, and world-wide communications. But these centers are becoming, if not ubiquitous as yet, more widely spread. In the United States, for instance, centers of high fashion have sprung up in Miami, Dallas, Los Angeles, and Chicago, all having approximately equal access by jet plane, to the intimate salons of Paris and Rome that continue to pace the world's *haute couture*. New York has lost its monopoly position because of more rapid and less costly connections among world cities and the spread of cosmopolitan values throughout the country. The total increase in the size of the market and the regional distribution of population are, of course, important contributing factors. But the result is clear: the women's fashion industry no longer needs to crowd upon New York and is free to choose among a half dozen cities whose number will, no doubt, increase with time.

This growing indifference among location points is counterbalanced by a weighing of extraeconomic elements which furnish a criterion for more refined distinctions among communities. I refer to the quality of life, especially the quality of the educational system, climate, and cultural and recreational opportunities. Except for climate, which is supremely place bound, these other elements are the result of community action and a will to attain high standards in the design of urban culture.

Although the supply structure of location inputs will be gradually transformed under the impact of economic development, it is at any given time severely constrained. First, it is patterned into a system of cities of different sizes, carrying out a variety of functions and spaced in a more or less regular way. It is likewise molded into commodity and labor market areas whose reach across space is fairly stable. Second, it is given form by the existing structure of transport rates which, in effect, assigns a set of weights to location points according to their relative accessibility from each other. And finally, it is constrained by national legislation for minimum wages, tariffs, interest rates, and subsidies, which tend to have pronounced, spatially differentiated repercussions. National policies must, therefore, be regarded as parameters that are critical to the performance of regional economies.

Economic growth tends to occur in the matrix of urban regions. It is through this matrix that the evolving space economy is organized.[8] The location decisions of most firms, including those in agriculture, are made with reference to cities or urban

28

regions which, in the previous section, I have called location points.[9] This is for essentially two reasons. First, cities represent identifiable points in the space economy; from a location standpoint, the internal areas of cities tend to be regarded as relatively homogeneous; site selection may be treated as a problem distinct from the choice of a location. And it is with respect to cities—as identifiable economic subsystems—that measurements regarding the supply schedules of labor, material inputs, energy, and transportation may be taken. The second reason is by far the more significant, however. It has to do with a category of external economies which Walter Isard has called "urbanization economies."[10] They result from the spatial juxtaposition of firms, but unlike scale economies, they are independent of the firms' output. As urbanization economies accrue, the cost curves of production will fall, although the output of each firm remains the same.[11]

It has proved impossible to measure urbanization economies. They are nonetheless of outstanding significance in determining the incidence of economic growth. From the vantage point of the investor, a metropolitan location—and in developed countries this may include an area of from ten to fifty miles from a central city—may offer many nontrivial advantages. A metropolitan location will allow the investor to dip into a large, diversified labor pool, appropriating to himself the investment in human skills whose cost was borne by others. It will provide him with ready access to a specialized, well-organized capital market. It will put him within easy reach of buyers and sellers who are themselves located within the metropolitan region or may wish to contact a number of potential suppliers and customers during a single visit. It will offer him a wide range of specialized services each of which may realize economies of scale by meeting the demand of many customers concentrated upon a single market area. It will reduce his costs by allowing him to share with other firms and with the urban population at large in furnishing and maintaining an adequate urban infrastructure. And it will enable him to exploit technical linkages by drawing inputs from nearby firms or selling to others, and thus to realize additional savings.

29

These multiple advantages lead to metropolitan concentrations which, in turn, arrange themselves into a complex spatial system of interdependencies. This much is known. It is perhaps less widely understood that agricultural activity is structured much in the same way. Some of the most productive counties are located within the metropolitan belt of the urbanized north-eastern seaboard in the United States. According to Jean Gott-mann, "In average value of farm products sold per acre, New Jersey, Rhode Island, and Connecticut lead all other states in the Union. Eight counties in Megalopolis are among the first hundred in the United States in the value of all farm products sold."[12]

On the basis of intensive research on the location of agricultural production, William Nicholls arrives at the critical explanation.[13] In brief, it is that agricultural production is, on the whole, more efficient in the vicinity of cities, so that farming incomes tend to be higher there. He ascribes this to the operation of labor, capital, and product markets that function under heavy spatial constraints. Land rents tend to fall off with distance from the urban core, so that land is intensively used near the city to produce high-value products such as vegetables, mushrooms, nursery stock, poultry, eggs, and dairy products. A competitive labor market attracts nearby farm labor into the city and forces farmers to change to more capital intensive methods of production. And since the city depends for part of its food supply on the surrounding countryside, financing farm investment often presents less of a problem there than in remote and, for the city dweller, somewhat obscure regions. Where transport facilities are poor, this pattern is probably even more pronounced.

Summarizing, we may regard economic activities ordered in space through (a) a system of cities, arranged in a partial hier-archy, according to the functions performed by each city and (b) the corresponding areas of influence, or urban fields, that surround each of the urban centers in the system. Since function tends to be correlated with city size, the latter may be used as a convenient though imperfect index of a city's relative position in the hierarchy.[14] This system of spatial organization undergoes change with economic growth at any point within it. As a basis for measuring these effects, four hypotheses will be proposed. Assuming total population to remain constant, a perfectly even distribution of population, resource, and income over a perfectly even plain, and constant technology, the following propositions may be advanced.

a. *The population of an urban field will be proportional to the population of the central city;* thus, large cities will control larger dependent populations, distributed over larger areas, than smaller cities.

b. *The spatial incidence of economic growth is a function of distance from a central city;* thus, economic growth will be more intense in the proximity of cities than at distances further away; troughs of economic backwardness will tend to occur along the intermetropolitan periphery.

c. *The growth potential of an area situated along an axis between two cities is a function of the density of interaction between them;* thus, economic activities will tend to be drawn into an axis roughly in proportion to the product of the populations of each city, divided by some function of the distance separating them.

d. *Impulses of economic change are transmitted in order from higher to lower centers in the urban hierarchy;* thus, large cities play a key role in extending growth across the entire system of the space economy.

Flows of labor tend to exert an equilibrating force on the welfare effects of economic growth. But contradictory results may also be obtained.[15] For the past two centuries, the world has witnessed one of the most dramatic population movements in history in the steady stream of migrants from rural areas to cities. This movement reflects not only the almost universal preference for urban culture but also man's continuing search for a more dignified way of life.

In societies whose resources are fully used, labor tends to flow from low-wage to high-wage areas; but where there is a significant amount of unemployment, the flow is also from areas of low to those of greater opportunity for remunerative work. Although unemployment is more visible in cities than on farms, the rural migrant will tend to regard his period of joblessness in the city as only a temporary condition from which he may soon escape. In fact, within a rough margin, he may calculate the period during which he must expect to live without paid work. Against this, he has to weigh his almost certain inability to improve his income in his home community. This "balance" explains the curious phenomenon of continued migration to cities in face of unemployment rates that run as high as 10 or 15 per cent. Beyond a certain level of urban unemployment, migration will, of course, decline. The critical level appears to depend on the extent of rural misery and is reached, in many underdeveloped economies, at about 15 per cent. Urban unemployment thus acts as an automatic stabilizer upon the rate of cityward migration.

Whether motivations are for higher wages or more work, it is primarily an increase in income that is sought. Other frequently cited reasons for migration, such as the dreariness of rural life compared with the presumed gaiety of a whirl among the dance halls, taverns, and movie palaces of the big city, or the greater educational opportunities and better housing thought to exist there, must be considered, if at all, as ancillary to the main drive for individual material betterment and social esteem.

The basic hypothesis relating migration to regional development is the equalization of the marginal returns to comparable labor across the space economy. The outflow of labor is supposed to raise wages, while an inflow of labor will depress them. Over the long run, a convergence of wage rates in all regions is supposed to occur. A weaker formulation of this idea is expressed in terms of the effects of migration on real family (or per capita) income. Here, the movement of labor is supposed to bring about a convergence of economic welfare among regions. Both propositions are well established in economic literature.

There are serious difficulties in testing them that arise from differences in the cost of living between rural and urban areas, the noncomparability of standards of living, and the vexing problem of comparing city jobs with farm work to achieve rough comparability for labor. The most precise statistical analyses so far have been carried out for the United States, where the following empirical regularities, among others, have been noted:[16]

    a. There has been a convergence of per capita personal incomes among states since 1880. The differences among states is narrowing over time.

    b. A group of states has persistently experienced slower-than-average growth of earnings per worker in nonagricultural occupations.

Although income differences appear to have narrowed among states over the seventy years of the study, complete equalization has not been achieved. In 1950, the Middle Atlantic states had a per capita income 19 per cent above the national average; but income in four East South Central states was 42 per cent *below* the average for the country as a whole. After several generations of economic growth, large parts of the United States continue to suffer severe economic depression. Moreover, much rural poverty has simply been transferred into city slums where it reappears as a social rather than as a regional problem. One fifth of the American people, or 32 million in the prosperous year 1957, live below the poverty line. An estimated three fourths of them reside in cities.[17]

With respect to wages, classical theory maintains that the rate of return to labor should rise in areas of outmigration and decline in the regions of ingathering. This appears to be contrary to fact, however. Wage rates have, in fact, shown a tendency to rise more rapidly in the high-wage target areas of migration, that is to say, in urban regions that also received the bulk of new investment. Continued high rates of capital growth appear thus to have more influence on the structure of wage rates than do labor transfers.[18] Where investment opportunities tend to be consistently overvalued for urban regions, as in developing countries, this tendency of wage rates to respond to capital flows contributes to a gradual divergence in the average returns to labor between the center of national development and its periphery.

Would the convergence theory for family (or *per capita*) income fare better in transitional societies? The facts do not support one's faith in the *automatic* working of the theory. At best, the convergence takes place on a time scale of centuries. This is scarcely enough to satisfy the high aspirations of the people who have only a single lifetime to look forward to. A wide variety of government programs may therefore be needed to overcome the normal tendency for economic growth to occur primarily in a few urbanized regions.

First, the volume of migration must be increased by various forms of direct and indirect subsidy, or the rate of natural increase in outmigrant areas must be reduced. For the failure of incomes to converge more rapidly can be ascribed, in part, to a failure to reduce sufficiently the pressure of population upon resources.

Second, the ability of the remaining rural population to carry out adjustments in the organization of farming made possible by outmigration must be strengthened. Adjustments may include consolidation of fragmented lands into units of economic size, reform in the pattern of land ownership, conversion of farming from subsistence to commercial types, and development of marketing organizations, among others. This may require new legislation (land reform), expanded agricultural research, improved information services, and large-scale technical assistance programs.

Third, the flow of capital into low-wage regions must be increased. This may involve conducting resource surveys to uncover new investment opportunities, the establishment of agricultural or regional development banks with extensive participation of public capital, changing the image potential investors have of low-wage regions as yielding only low returns on capital, and large investments in urban infrastructure at selected locations.

Fourth, heavy outlays for education and training programs are indicated to qualify urban migrants for skilled work in the cities, thus forestalling the accumulation of urban poverty, as well as to prepare peasants for the commercial, scientific management of their farms.

The extent to which any of these measures should be undertaken is, of course, a matter for public policy decision. This question will receive close attention in Chapter 4.

Where economic growth is sustained over long periods, its incidence works toward a progressive integration of the space economy. It was noted earlier that in the course of successful economic growth spatial subsystems change their boundaries and are rearranged. This process tends to follow in an orderly progression, culminating in the full integration of the national space economy. How this typical sequence may be visualized is shown in Figure 2.1.

The initial pattern, characteristic of a preindustrial order, is also a relatively stable one. It is exaggerated here, since completely closed economies probably do not exist. But the volume of interregional relations in preindustrial societies is generally small, and the diagram serves to bring out a salient feature: the existence, in relative isolation from each other, of a number of largely self-sufficient economies.

In contrast to the first, the second pattern must be regarded as inherently unstable. It is the result of a disruption, usually externally induced, of the spatial equilibrium maintained by a preindustrial order.

The spatial pattern suggested for this stage is that of *primacy,* the domination of the space economy by a single urban region. Historically, this pattern has been associated with both development and underdevelopment in the indices of economic performance.[19] But in a dynamic view, primacy may well be harmful to the aspirations of new political elites. For primate cities tend to feed upon the rest of the nation. Instead of generating a new socioeconomic order and new wealth, they feast on what may be extracted by the sweat of poor, provincial labor.[20] The reason for this essentially colonial relationship is that any center unopposed on the periphery by countervailing powers will yield excessive influence in making basic political decisions. The periphery, therefore, is drained, and national progress will fail to occur, except as it accrues to a small elite of urban consumers at the center. The problem of primacy is not, as is frequently assumed, the absolute size of the central urban region—

1. *Independent local centers, no hierarchy.* Typical preindustrial structure; each city lies at the center of a small regional enclave; growth possibilities are soon exhausted; the economy tends to stagnate.

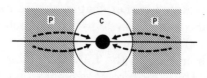

2. *A single strong center.* Structure is typical for the period of incipient industrialization; a periphery (P) emerges; local economies are undermined in consequence of a mass movement of would-be entrepreneurs, intellectuals, and labor to the center (C); the national economy is virtually reduced to a single metropolitan region, with only limited growth possibilities; continued stagnation of the periphery may lead to social and political unrest.

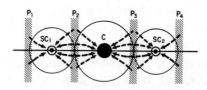

3. *A single national center, strong peripheral subcenters.* The first stage toward a solution during the period of industrial maturation; strategic subcenters (SC_n) are developed, thereby reducing the periphery on a national scale to smaller, more manageable intermetropolitan peripheries (P_n); hypertrophy of national center is avoided while important resources from the periphery are brought into the productive cycle of the national economy; growth potential for the nation is enhanced, but problems of poverty and cultural backwardness persist in intermetropolitan peripheries.

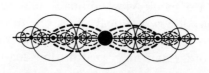

4. *A functionally interdependent system of cities.* Organized complexity is the final solution to be aimed for during the period of industrial maturation, but it will subsequently give place to other configurations; major goals of spatial organization are fulfilled: national integration, efficiency in location, maximum growth potential, minimum essential interregional balances.

FIGURE 2.1. *A sequence of stages in spatial organization.*

36

it may, indeed, grow to any size whatever—but of the *distribution* of sizes over the whole spectrum of cities. Interregional balance and an hierarchical system of cities are essential conditions for national development.

The third pattern is transitional to the fourth. The simple center-periphery structure is gradually transformed into a multinuclear structure as investments are focused upon a number of strategically placed subcenters. The national periphery is replaced by *intermetropolitan* peripheries that represent less of a threat to the stability of the system, for they will be weak politically, and consequently will be easier to manage. Nevertheless, if the momentum for economic development is maintained, further changes will be imposed upon the spatial system. The intermetropolitan periphery will be gradually absorbed into nearby metropolitan economies, and in the final stage of "organized complexity" major goals of spatial organization are fulfilled: national integration, efficiency in the location of individual firms, maximum potential for further growth, and minimum essential interregional balances. Whether further patterns lie beyond this stage must, in the absence of historical experience, remain an open question.

Summary

Our propositions may now be brought into a synoptic view. Together, they demonstrate that more than a knowledge of purely economic relations is required to understand the processes of regional economic growth. The propositions represent an attempt to bring together in the study of a major social phenomenon a variety of different subject fields. Some aspects of this phenomenon are, indeed, best studied by economics, but the investigation of others will need to draw on expertise in sociology (propositions 3, 4, 7), political science (3, 4), and geography (6, 8). A general theory of the spatial incidence of economic growth, if it is to have value as a guide for public policy, will have to receive contributions from all the major social sciences. It may therefore be hoped that sustained work on regional theory will soften some of the more artificial barriers that currently divide the academic world and point the way toward a truly unified science of human behavior.

The eight propositions are restated:

1. Regional economies are open to the outside world and subject to external influence.

2. Regional economic growth is externally induced.

3. Successful translation of export sector growth into growth of the residentiary sector depends on the sociopolitical structure of the region and the local distribution of income and patterns of expenditure.

4. Local leadership is decisive for successful adaptation to external change. Yet the quality of leadership depends on the region's past development experience.

5. Regional economic growth may be regarded, in part, as a problem in the location of firms.

6. Economic growth tends to occur in the matrix of urban regions. It is through this matrix that the evolving space economy is organized.

7. Flows of labor tend to exert an equilibrating force on the welfare effects of economic growth. But contradictory results may be obtained.

8. Where economic growth is sustained over long periods, its incidence works toward a progressive integration of the space economy.

CHAPTER THREE

THE PROBLEM OF REGIONAL BOUNDARIES

What are the proper regions for planning? It is frequently asserted that the most important task facing the planner is regionalization, that nothing of substance can be accomplished until the "right" set of regions has been identified. This problem is heavily encrusted with muddled thinking. Should planning regions encompass and exhaust the whole of the national territory? Should they serve administrative as well as analytical and planning uses? What criteria should be used to draw their boundaries?

No striking consensus has emerged from the discussion. There is a sense of significance about it, yet also frustration over the failure to discover a workable set of true, all-purpose planning regions. Many countries have attempted an areal division of their national territories for planning, but with each new criterion, another regional configuration appears. In view of the failure to reach agreement on what appears to be so basic a matter, other regional policy questions are frequently shunted aside.

The formal literature on the subject of regionalization is extensive; a recent review lists no less than 291 titles.[1] Yet for all the intellectual passion this subject has engendered, it is, in a dispassioned view, of only secondary interest. Two aspects of the problem, often confounded, must be separated. First, it is indeed essential for regional planners to acquire understanding of the structural form of spatial relationships in an economy. Economic activities and households are always arranged in certain density patterns over the landscape. Connected by an intricate web of functional linkages, they fall into complex but recognizable spatial patterns—local subsystems of the space economy. Geographers have evolved elaborate techniques for mapping labor and commuting sheds, market areas, regional patterns of communications and financial transactions, and the hierarchy of urban settlements.[2] They have advanced beyond this to mapping subtle areal differentiations in economic health and experimenting with simulation models of spatial patterns.[3]

All this represents factual knowledge and poses no problems beyond those inherent in the statistical and cartographic methods used. The controversy I referred to pertains to the second, or normative, aspect of regionalization, that of finding a set of *optimal* planning regions. One is not surprised that the ball has been fumbled. One approach is to proceed in a wholly arbitrary way, looking upon regionalization as simply a problem in the spatial aggregation of data. This solution may be satisfactory in the interest of administrative convenience. Since the question of an optimality criterion does not arise, however, nothing further need be said about it. Alternatively, one may wish to identify one or more patterns according to a stated purpose. It is the purpose that will furnish the decision rule. But no single purpose is capable of standing for *all* purposes, and if the search is for the latter, the enterprise is headed for failure from the start. The notion of a region for "things in general"—or of multipurpose regions as they are called—fails to provide enlightenment. One may as well proceed by a random drawing of boundary lines.

It is worth recalling that quite different criteria may be derived with equal logic from the same purpose, as in finding that set of regions which has optimum closure for stated problems of development. There has to be no symmetry in the design of regions. Regions may vary in character, extend over only sections of the country, be noncontiguous and of varying size, and even overlap to a degree. Regional boundaries, moreover, are changed as a result of economic development. During periods of rapid social and economic transition, boundary lines will frequently have to be redrawn. What is required, therefore, is a nonsymmetrical set of planning regions stated in dynamic terms.

Geographers distinguish between two major types of regions.[4] The first is bounded according to the occurrence of one or more features with respect to which the area is *homogeneous*. The second incorporates areas that stand in an active relation to each other, whose futures are linked by the flows of people, information, goods, or financial investments among them. These are regions of *interdependency*. They need not be, strictly speaking, nodal regions—a pattern that turns out to be only a special case of the more general type.[5]

For planning purposes, both types of regions are relevant. Best results may be achieved when a pattern of interdependent regions is superimposed for analysis upon regions that are identified by the common problems they pose for economic development. Five so-called development regions may accordingly be distinguished:

1. *Core regions* are characterized by their high promise for economic growth. Structurally, they will consist of one or more clustered cities, together with an encompassing area that may be conveniently delimited by the extent of daily commuting or, alternatively, by the distribution of agricultural activities that furnish sustenance to central urban populations. Their problems will be manifold: how to sustain growth, how to absorb newcomers into the local labor force and provide for their needs, how to organize a livable physical environment that is also efficient, and how to manage the increasingly complex affairs of a metropolitan society, voracious in its hunger for space.

2. *Upward-transitional areas* include all settled regions whose natural endowments and location relative to core regions suggest the possibility of a greatly intensified use of resources. They, too, are areas of net inmigration. Instead of being focused upon a single, dominant center, however, they may encompass several cities. The economic development of upward-transitional areas will generally occur as a response to rising commercial demand at the core. Their problems are consequently associated with rapid economic growth: agricultural adjustment to more capital-

41

intensive farming, improvement in agricultural marketing organization, improvements in farm to market and intercity transportation, urbanization, and industrial development. Since their economies will show a strong admixture of forestry, agricultural, and cattle-raising activities, these areas are typically less concentrated and less urbanized than core regions. *Development corridors* connecting two or more core regions represent a special type of upward-transitional areas.

3. *Resource frontier regions* are zones of new settlement in which virgin territory is occupied and made productive. Contiguous and noncontiguous frontiers may be distinguished. In the former, a movement of population into new areas occurs, usually along a broad front adjacent to already settled regions. Supply lines will be relatively short, and the new areas will be readily incorporated into the existing structure of the national economy. New colonization will be predominantly agricultural. Problems encountered in the settlement of a contiguous agricultural frontier may include the building of transport and communication lines, the founding of agricultural communities and marketing centers, the construction of irrigation works, the subdivision of farming land, and the extension of basic administrative and social services to the new communities. The *noncontiguous* resource frontier, on the other hand, is usually associated with large-scale investments in a mineral or forest development scheme and involves substantial urbanization. Such regions tend to occur as isolated pockets of development at a considerable distance from metropolitan cores, but may eventually become core regions themselves. They are inevitably based upon a city as the agent for transforming the wilderness into an environment suitable for long-term habitation. Major problems arise from (1) the need to create a new locational matrix on the settlement frontier that is competitive with already established centers in attracting and holding a suitable labor force and (2) the need to integrate the new regional complex into the national space economy.

4. *Downward-transitional areas* are old, established settlement regions whose essentially rural economies are stagnant or in decline, and whose peculiar resource combinations suggest as

optimal a less intensive development than in the past. They furnish the bulk of migrant workers to points of concentrated development. Occasionally, a downward-transitional area may also be a city whose economy is declining because of its aging industrial structure or the loss of its primary resources base (mining regions). The problems of such cities are typically associated with general obsolescence and with overpopulation relative to existing possibilities for development. They also include problems of adaptation to new external conditions and of transition to an economic order in which they can become reintegrated into the national space economy.

5. *Special problem regions* belong to a category of area that, because of the peculiarity of their resources or location, demands a specialized development approach. They will often include regions along national borders, water resource development regions, regions suited to the intensive development of tourism and fisheries, and military zones.

One may visualize these development regions as forming an abstract pattern in which a core area occupies the center of a spatial system. This core would be surrounded by a band of contiguous areas whose economies are generally upward-transitional, and these, in turn, would be enclosed by an extensive zone in a state of downward-transition. At certain points along the rim of this zone would be the new settlement or resource frontier regions. Special problem areas would be interspersed at random throughout the system.[6]

The main driving force determining the behavior of this interdependent system of regions is, of course, the economic dynamism of the core region itself. It is the center that will stimulate investment in adjacent areas, encourage a centripetal drift of population from downward-transitional to more promising areas, and create the distant, noncontiguous frontier regions in response to its own pressing needs.

Although it represents a gross simplification, this description suggests the systemic relations that underlie all regional policy. The special problems arising from regional growth (or decline) cannot be attacked in isolation. For instance, a partial solution to structural poverty in downward-transitional areas may lie in undertaking intensified investment programs for adjacent core regions. But the fate of core regions, in turn, will rest on the ability of the nation to maintain minimum acceptable living levels in areas of decline. Problems of urbanization, land use, public utilities, housing, and transportation will predominate in the metropolis, while the policy emphasis in upward-transitional areas will be on problems of organization in agriculture, settlement, interregional transportation, and industrial development. In the downward-transitional areas, population resettlement, community development, and rural land-use adjustments will call for priority attention. The interrelatedness of these problem complexes underscores the need for a national approach to regional development. Interregional competition alone cannot be relied upon to achieve the optimum spatial arrangement of population, industrial and agricultural production, basic services, and transport-communication systems.

The identification of development regions and their interrelated problem complexes tells us nothing regarding the regional administration of development programs or the wisdom of spatially coordinating these programs. Development regions simply have maximum closure with respect to a given problem set. They are fully compatible with a number of alternative administrative regions, such as municipalities, states, or specially designated areas for coordinating development programs. Development regions are not programming regions. Their chief function is to assist in the analysis of socioeconomic and environmental problems and in the formulation of development strategies at the national level. The question of programming regions is a pragmatic one for which no general answer can be given. In the final chapter of Part II, several possibilities are discussed for Venezuela. The issue of administration, however, is even there left open. It touches on complex questions of local-national relationships that must be resolved in the unique political context of each nation.

CHAPTER FOUR

GOALS FOR SPATIAL ORGANIZATION

A national policy of regional development must be designed to deal with the diverse problems of development regions as a comprehensive system of interdependencies. The need for such an approach has been stressed in the last chapter; it is easily demonstrated by pointing to the impact that migration flows, stimulated by regional policy, will have on both the target areas and home regions of migrants. The direction and magnitude of these flows, and their consequences for regional development, enter the determination of regional policy in a significant way. To focus policy exclusively on target areas or, alternatively, on the home regions of migrants is to lose much effective leverage for inducing economic change.

But if the policy problem is viewed from the standpoint of the system as a whole, as I propose to do, what objectives should the planners have before them? What should be the national goals for regional development? To ask this question is to locate its answer within the context of a policy for national economic growth.

Goals for regional development must be adapted to the current phase in the evolution of an economic system. The outline of a policy for transitional economies must reflect their historical condition and will differ from an equivalent outline for industrial or postindustrial economies. In the case of the former, regional policy will appear as part of a process of nation building; in the latter, it will deal chiefly with residual problems of spatial organization. The difference is between *structural* changes in which the parameters themselves are rearranged and *incre-*

mental changes within a relatively stable system of organizational constraints.

This is the first requirement. The second is that regional policy goals must be consistent with dominant national aspirations. The regional problem is subordinate to the more general purposes of a nation, including its desire to achieve greatness; its striving for economic strength and political influence; its drive for modernization; and its concern for the well-being of its citizens. National purposes are not obtained simply by adding local or regional preferences, although regional interests must always be respected. They constitute virile symbols that are accepted by the population as valid and legitimate.

National economic planners have a job to do. They must nudge the economy to a higher average level of performance and, at the same time, maintain a set of critical variables, such as money supply, external payments, investment, consumption, and employment, in a reasonable balance. The location of investment and the spatial incidence of economic growth are variables that belong to this set and are consequently subject to explicit policy determination.

Goals or Criteria

The literature on economic development has shown a good deal of interest in the question of investment criteria.[1] This reflects, no doubt, the preference of the academic mind for logical decision rules of the following kind: choose that course of action which will maximize net social product. Criteria of this type fail to discriminate among historically specific situations. Maximizing criteria, for example, can be applied with equal logic in Timbuctoo and Vladivostok. Political leaders and planners, on the other hand, immersed in the details of unique situations, painfully cognizant of the multiple changes that press upon them, and aware of the symbolic function that basic policy pronouncements tend to have in the exercise of national leadership, are inclined to refer to goals and objectives rather than criteria. Goals appear to them as desirable "end states."

46

They differ from general purposes insofar as they are placed within a definite time limitation. Whereas the guiding purpose may be "equality of opportunity" to be achieved at an indefinite future time, the relevant goal may be expressed as the attainment of a certain level of employment by year x, or a certain annual rate of change in the growth of the national product. As distinguished from criteria, goals may be said to represent historical statements of aspiration.

Which, then, goal or criterion, is the more appropriate concept for use in policy? The great advantage of a criterion is its logical precision, its derivation from general propositions about economic relationships and social welfare. A goal has the advantage of historical relevancy.

Happily, it is possible to combine the two modes of expressing policy guidelines. For goals may also be used to distinguish among action alternatives and may consequently serve as historically relevant criteria. Suppose that the goal is a 20 per cent reduction in family income differences among a given set of regions by a certain year. Every alternate course of action can then be tested for its probable contribution toward this goal. In fact, through simulation procedures, it may be possible to test entire programs for their consequences against a set of interdependent objectives.[2] If testing is impractical because appropriate models do not exist or the data themselves are unavailable, it may still be possible, in a weaker formulation, to check the probable consistency of a proposal with the goal. To return to the earlier example, will a given investment advance the objective of reducing family income differences? If it does not, the project should be abandoned. There may, of course, be countervailing and more trenchant reasons for undertaking it, regardless of the consequences for income equalization. But, where the will is present, the objective can be used as an effective constraint on policy choice. It will tend to eliminate from further consideration those projects that fail to make a significant net contribution to its achievement. It will set the logical boundaries for an evaluation of the costs and benefits of individual projects.

The Allocation of Investments in Space

Writings on the spatial allocation of investment funds have been less numerous than the outpouring of ideas on the problem of sectoral allocation.[3] Nevertheless, enough has been said to polarize the controversy around a series of alternate choices. The debate has raged chiefly around the following paired sets of regional strategies:

- growth versus welfare
- imbalance versus balance
- concentration versus dispersion

In each paired alternative, the "hard line" has usually been taken by academics while the "soft line" has found its champions among practitioners and politicians. Although in many respects similar, the three pairs are sufficiently differentiated to justify their separate appraisal.

Growth versus welfare. The choice implicit in the first pair is between achieving a maximum rate in the growth of the national product and a redistribution of income in favor of the poorer regions of a country. The national planners in Venezuela are fully aware of the dilemma imposed on them by this dichotomy. They write:

There exist two equally valid criteria, each of which, however, leads to diverging and even opposite results.

The first is related to the needs for accelerated development believed to exist in certain regions due to the present depressed state of their economies. This criterion asserts that the task of the central government is, in the first instance, to use its resources to stimulate development in the more backward areas of the country, so that these areas might, within a reasonable period, attain to levels of living that are more compatible with those in the rest of the nation.

The other criterion is oriented towards a better utilization of resources. Accordingly, resources should be invested wherever the rates of return to the national product and to foreign exchange are highest. The application of this criterion is defended on the grounds that thus the maximum benefits will accrue to the nation as a whole and that backward regions will eventually participate in them.[4]

48

As the quotation intimates, the "hard line" is equivalent to economic common sense. It assumes that poorer regions will ultimately benefit from the working of an automatic "trickle down" effect that will come about partly through an equalization of incomes from migration and partly through an increased producer demand in the growing regions for raw materials and an expansion of their markets. It assumes further that higher returns of investment can be obtained by continued investment in high-income regions. Beyond these assumptions, economists argue that a redistribution of existing income will accomplish only a sharing of poverty, not its eradication, and that, before substantial welfare claims can be made, the total volume of resources must be increased. They argue, further, that the propensity to save (and to invest) tends to be greater in rich than in poor regions, that considerations of efficiency due to lower transportation costs and external economies point toward continued emphasis on investment programs for regions that have already demonstrated a capacity for sustained economic growth, and that the pursuit of such a policy will facilitate essential structural transformations in social values and aspirations. This is a persuasive case that is not easily brushed aside.

Political thought, on the other hand, favors a redistribution of income in the short run. Politicians are prone to capitalize on any unrest that may be generated by entrenched misery; some of them may even stir emotions where unrest fails to appear of its own accord. As proof of the failure of the automatic working of the "spread effects" of economic growth, they will point to the presumed widening in the welfare gap between the growing and the backward areas.

Posed in this manner, the issue is genuine enough, and the resulting dilemma an awkward one. But the dichotomy that seems to compel commitment to either one or the other position is false on at least three counts. First, the ultimate justification for economic growth is the welfare of the community and of its families. Second, the equalization of regional incomes in transitional societies, as I have tried to show in Chapter 2, is not an automatic process but may, indeed, require positive public action if, within a reasonable period, it is to be achieved.

49

Third, and most important, the problem of policy is not so much a choice between growth and welfare or determining the just proportion of each, but how effectively to meet the challenges of economic transformation in *all* development regions simultaneously. No part of the effectively settled national area can be neglected; different policies and programs must be devised for each. A system-wide approach to regional policy will transcend the issue of growth or welfare in a synthesis that sees the problems of development in different regions as mutually contingent on each other.

Imbalance versus balance. The choice in the second pair of concepts is between concentrated development in areas of high social returns (core regions) and essentially equal development efforts in all parts of the space economy. This dichotomy has been crystalized by Albert Hirschman who has become identified with a development strategy of "controlled imbalance."[5] Hirschman's model declares disequilibrium to be high virtue; its avowed purpose is to devise a policy for sustaining a process of economic transformation. Over time, Hirschman asserts, imbalances will tend to be self-correcting through a variety of market and nonmarket mechanisms. Although this process may be more costly than "balanced" growth in the utilization of resources, various sectoral and regional imbalances will ultimately call forth more resources and investment than would otherwise have been available. According to Hirschman, the "analysis of a prospective investment project should, above all, try to evaluate its effects on further development decisions instead of conventionally concentrating on its own prospective output and productivity."[6] Equilibrium is simply a parameter for policies whose main intention is the achievement of a high rate of growth.

Hirschman is fully aware that the economic system must not stray too far from the main path; where the gap in economic development between center and periphery is gaining, he favors a policy that will reverse the trend to regional divergence by establishing, within the periphery, new core regions and consequently a new set of spatial imbalances. Implied is the progressive extension of a system of cities into the periphery as the optimum path of national development.

This is a valuable insight, but a major difficulty remains: How is the policymaker to know when he is perched on the narrow edge of optimal imbalance or has exceeded it? When does "optimal imbalance" become just plain inefficiency? As a criterion, therefore, Hirschman's is at best an ambiguous one, incapable of being directly applied to problems requiring decision. Its value obtains chiefly from its emphasis on an investment planning process in which the historical future is explicity considered for its relevance to the present.

In contrast to Hirschman, proponents of the "soft" approach to regional development support a simplistic criterion of "balance."[7] Whatever magic this word may have, it is insufficiently potent to overcome the vagueness of its meaning. The concept of optimal or controlled imbalance may be unclear; that of balance only compounds confusion. First, the regions: Which set is to be balanced? The problem of maintaining economic balance—any kind of balance—becomes more difficult the smaller the unit area considered. Counties are more difficult to balance than states and these more difficult than major subdivisions, such as North and South. But a set of regions must be stated if the degree of balance is to be measured. It is untrue that all kinds of balances can be achieved in all possible regions at the same time. States or provinces are frequently cited as the relevant areas for comparison; they have a political rationale. But what makes sense politically may not be logical or desirable from an economic standpoint.

Second, what should be balanced? Is it total investment in the aggregate or in each sector? Is it investment divided by population, families, or unit area? Is a balance to be achieved by having all regions grow at equal rates? Or should poor regions grow at a faster rate to allow them to catch up with regions that are better off? Is balance expressed in average income per family so that eventually all regions will be approximately equal in this respect?

Clearly, one cannot remain indifferent among these choices; each alternative has different policy implications and different consequences for economic growth. Balance according to any of these meanings might be a sensible criterion if the productivity of capital were everywhere the same. But it is not; hence a difficult choice is posed.

Despite the confusion engendered by the criterion of balance, it does point to the importance of tracing alternate development politicies for their effects on the economic welfare of different areas. For the political element in development policy is not to be discounted. When the imbalance in real family income becomes unbearable, dissatisfaction may turn violent. This, in turn, will undermine the social and political stability of the nation and jeopardize the very growth process itself. Many strongly regionalized economies—Turkey, India, Venezuela, Canada, Algeria, Indonesia, Nigeria, Pakistan, Belgium, Czechoslovakia, Yugoslavia—have at various points in their histories had to confront internal conflict engendered by regional inequities. Some nations, such as Brazil, have been led to the threshold of bankruptcy by their inability to handle these conflicts successfully.

Concentration versus dispersal. The choice here is quite similar to that between imbalance and balance, except that the dichotomy is expressed in purely spatial terms. The first term refers explicitly to the core region concept. It is the only one of the three sets of criteria that specifies a desirable form for spatial organization.

As serious students have recognized, however, the dichotomy, as in the previous cases, is a false one. Lloyd Rodwin has therefore suggested a strategy of "concentrated decentralization."[8] This synthesis recognizes the need to bring areas other than the principal national center into the development process and to locate new core regions in the periphery. The strategy is consistent with the long-term regional development process described in Chapter 2. The gradual attrition of the periphery was there explained as part of a normal sequence of evolution. In Rodwin's concept, it appears as a policy criterion for regional development. He remains mindful of the failure of dynamic economies to generate self-equilibrating forces of sufficient strength, of the possible diseconomies of large urban concentrations, and of the genuine economic opportunities that may be created on the periphery.[9]

52

At the same time, Rodwin's criterion makes use of the notion of imbalance by arguing in favor of a certain concentration of resources in the activation of core regions. This would make it possible to exploit potential complementarities in investment, creating the urbanization economies that serve as an inducement to private investment, and capitalizing on the symbolic value of a dramatic development effort having internal dynamics of its own. Concentrated decentralization implies a commitment in selected locations to what Paul Rosenstein-Rodan has called the "Big Push" theory of economic growth.[10]

Rodwin's formulation appears to incorporate a variety of criteria that, outside a spatial frame of reference, are antagonistic to each other. Insofar as he advocates concentration, he favors imbalance in the space economy; but he also supports greater interregional balance in development by invoking the principle of decentralization. And he sides with the theorists of balance by favoring the idea of development programming for new core regions through the simultaneous creation, as a matter of public policy, of the technical and economic linkages that are essential to the process of growth.

For all of its virtues, however, Rodwin's criterion fails to discriminate sufficiently among development regions and their problems. Activation of new core regions is not enough nor, indeed, always appropriate. An effective regional policy must deal as a system with the separate developments of core regions, upward- and downward-transitional areas, resource frontiers, and special problem areas. And for this purpose, a comprehensive set of objectives is needed. It is to this question that I now turn.

Spatial Organization as an Objective

In an earlier chapter, I showed that economic growth inevitably alters the spatial arrangement of activities. But at any given moment, this pattern may be less than optimal, either in its short-run welfare effects or in its consequences for the longer-run prospects of growth in the economy. The mathematical proof of optimality is all but impossible in a dynamic, complex system organized to meet a multiplicity of purposes. It is much

53

easier to decide when a pattern is nonoptimal (because recognizable problems exist), just as it is easier to decide on the direction an improvement should take without commitment to an optimal end-state.

Whether or not problems of spatial organization exist and, consequently, whether public action is in any sense appropriate will depend on the social purposes around which the system is organized. For a problem, by definition, appears whenever an incongruity exists between an ideal future and the imperfect present. Similarly, measures of corrective action must be, at least, not inconsistent with declared social purposes, though the relationship, in principle, should be a stronger one. A statement of social purposes is clearly an essential condition for properly orienting a public policy for regional development.

In the transitional societies with which I am concerned, the dominant ideology advances the general goal of achieving and maintaining a high rate of national economic growth with all this implies for structural change and modernization. Since regional policy must fit into this normative framework, I shall posit as its major goal *the achievement of that spatial structure of the economy which, at any point in time, is judged to be satisfactory for promoting and sustaining an efficient process of economic growth.* Spatial organization is thus regarded as a means for approaching the ultimate economic purposes of a society. The first test of a given spatial pattern of activities will be found in answer to the question: Does it effectively support national economic development?

Transitional societies are characterized by the center-periphery structure of their economies. Subsidiary objectives are consequently two in number:

1. The gradual elimination of the periphery on a national scale by substituting for it a single, interdependent system of urban regions.

2. The progressive integration of the space economy by the extension, on a national scale, of a system of efficient commodity and factor markets.[11]

Each of these subsidiary goals, though closely related to the other, points to a different variable in spatial organization. The first calls attention to the integrative role that cities perform in the economy. It suggests an approach to regional policy and planning based on a hierarchy of urban centers. The second places emphasis on the operation of product and factor markets (labor and capital) and directs attention to the institutional structure of trades and services, the flows of information, and the geographic mobility of labor. Both goals imply the desirability of growing regional interdependence and areal specialization of production within a national system.

Further specification of these goals is possible. They may be expressed separately for the performance of the total system of spatial interaction, the selection of core regions as a device for stimulating economic growth, the location of individual projects, and the achievement of interregional balances in the critical variables bearing on welfare.

Some overlap among these more specific objectives should not detract from their immediate usefulness for policy. Since policy planners may address themselves variously to systems, core regions, projects, and the welfare effects of economic growth, they may welcome an effort to state objectives separately for each of these key terms.

Full integration of the national space economy. An adequate structure of the space economy, viewed as a pattern of systemic relations, must be regarded as an overriding consideration in spatial planning. Although individual investment projects may each be located in an optimal way from the standpoint of their separate profitabilities, the whole system of spatial relations may yet fail to function effectively. As long as the economy is focalized upon a single, dominant center, the economic calculus for investments will repeatedly suggest central locations. This failure to tie peripheral regions into a national system may eventually retard the rate of progress of which the country as a whole is capable. The goal of integration, therefore, is essential for a nation initiating its drive to industrial maturity. It has in view the breakdown of a pattern of regionalized economies partly closed to commerce with one another and holding on a steady course toward an interdependent national system, based on the principle of comparative advantage.

The means proposed for reaching this objective involve the creation of an urban hierarchy which will span the effectively settled national territory and of a national system of market areas for capital, labor, and commodities. The first of these suggests an emphasis on the location and functional role of cities. The second points to the creation of an adequate institutional structure that will facilitate the shift from local and regional to a nationwide system of market areas.

Opportunities for the further expansion of the economic system. Many of the important ends of a transitional society can be subsumed under the general purpose of a sustained increase in the volume of national production. The strategy of moving from a highly unbalanced and centralized spatial order to an interdependent system of cities and market areas on a national scale will have to further and support this dominant concern. But the basic processes of modern economic development unfold chiefly in an urban setting from which, through a series of complex linkages and multiplier effects, they eventually spread to encompass the whole nation. The problem is to choose that minimum number of core regions in which concentrated investment on a large scale is likely to trigger the rapid expansion and full articulation of the space economy.

This strategy will foster imbalance in the spatial allocation of resources. But as soon as one rejects the untenable notion of regarding all areas as, in some sense, equally endowed and consequently deserving equal treatment, one has no choice but to fall back on a strategy of "concentrated decentralization." This goal, then, instructs the planner that, ignoring for the moment other facets of the problem, a basic criterion for the selection of core regions should be the enhancement of conditions for the further expansion of the space economy.

Efficiency in the location of new investment projects. This goal cannot avoid some ambiguity. What is a project? How should efficiency be measured? To get across the first hurdle, I shall define a project as any coordinated investment undertaking. Thus, a factory, an industrial complex, or an irrigation scheme may each be regarded as a separate project for our purpose. The second hurdle is more difficult to surmount.

Efficiency is usually defined as a measure relating input to output, with the costs of overcoming distance included among the input elements.[12] An efficient location is therefore one in which the surplus value generated (for example, profits or net benefits) is equal to or greater than at any alternate location. The actual calculation, based on a comparative analysis of costs, may be rather difficult, however, and the reader is referred to the extensive literature that has accumulated on this question.[13]

It remains to be emphasized—and it is a principle too frequently neglected—that investment projects should accomplish their purpose without extended subsidy or income transfers unless a clear-cut public function will be served. For the private sponsor, a project has to yield a satisfactory rate of return, where profit opportunities elsewhere in the economy will serve him as a standard of judgment. The location of the project must so balance accessibilities to materials, labor, and markets as to satisfy the sponsor's aim in this regard. Diversion of public funds for his continued maintenance in an unprofitable location is unlikely to be thought of as an action consistent with the public weal. The same argument can be advanced with respect to government investments, where the criterion of efficiency requires an accounting that will fully reflect the real costs of capital and operation.[14] "In the context of a planned economy," writes Louis Lefeber, "conscious policies to maintain efficient resource allocation are crucial. They must be based on pricing policies that properly reflect changes in the demand and supply conditions prevailing in diverse markets; and investment policies must be responsive to the signaling of the price system."[15]

Minimum essential balances in major components of the level of living. Among the shortcomings of the strategy of concentrated decentralization is its failure to identify the point where the consciously fostered imbalances begin to undermine and threaten the stability of the social system. The other face of "optimal imbalance" is "minimum balance"; the term "essential" is inserted into this phrase to draw attention to the fact that some measure of balance in the levels of living among major regional units is a condition for successful economic growth.

This formulation invites a series of related questions: What is the *essential* minimum? To what set of regions should the criterion apply? How does one know whether a proper balance has been achieved? These questions are pertinent, but they cannot be answered with rigor. "Minimum essential balance" is as elusive a concept as public interest, region, development stage, or periphery—all of which refer to phenomena that tend to dissolve under logical scrutiny. And yet, one cannot quite do without them.

The basic meaning of "minimum essential balance" is a pragmatic one—politicians will signal the oncoming crisis when the essential minimum has not been met.[16] Unfortunately for planners, politicians are unable and usually unwilling to define the precise moment when the minimum has been *exceeded*. Nevertheless, the consequences of regional imbalance are largely political. Enough of a balance in living levels should be maintained to prevent social dissatisfactions (which are always present) from upsetting the political equilibrium that provides the basic institutional framework for sustained national economic growth. Some of the benefits of economic development must be spread to those areas that would normally be left behind the general push of progress. Ultimately, the goal of rapid growth in production may not be wholly separable from that of distribution and welfare, and the problem of linking the two in a logical manner remains a major challenge to theories of social change.

The Uses of Goals

As abstract principles, these goals have only small value. They tell us that the periphery should be more closely integrated into the national economy; that development efforts should be concentrated; that projects should be efficiently located; and that all of the goals ought to be made subject to the political constraints of maintaining sufficient balance in the

58

regional welfare effects of economic growth to prevent social unrest from upsetting the basic political equilibrium of the nation. They are national goals that tell us nothing about the objects of development efforts in a specific area.[17] They are equally silent on questions of general economic policy—prices, taxes, money supply, tariffs—which form the background to regional policy and must be evaluated for their consequences for regional growth.

Their principal use will be to orient national planners and serve as a constraint on allocative decisions. The goals must be stepped down, ultimately to touch base with specific projects for investment. It is here that they are made concrete and realistic. Supplementing broad value considerations, a programming process must be initiated that renders meaningful what would otherwise remain abstract and tantalizing in its vagueness.

Programming focuses on projects and their interrelations. As a process, it works upward through the hierarchy of government decision making until it meets the goals descending. On point of contact, crucial choices must be made, resulting in the actual commitment of public resources. Each project and each program must be carefully evaluated for consistency with the goals for spatial organization. The fit can never be a perfect one because the consequences of action cannot be stated with certainty and are known only in part. An element of risk will always attach to choice. The measure of consistency, moreover, will be an expert judgment that is prone to error. Nevertheless, it is better for programming decisions to be made in the context of specific value criteria than in total ignorance about the desired direction of development.

CHAPTER FIVE

APPROACHES TO THE DEVELOPMENT OF REGIONS

The goals reviewed in the preceding chapter may serve as a guide to the present discussion of strategies for the development of different types of regions. As a start, I shall briefly state what I believe to be some of the major preconditions for a successful development of regions in a national context. The emphasis will be on policy considerations that apply transregionally. I shall then turn to the specific planning problems, respectively, of core regions, resource frontiers, and downward-transitional areas. In Chapter 3, these regions were defined in accordance with a criterion of maximum closure for a cluster of common development problems. Within each region, these problems are so closely related that only a comprehensive approach can make them yield.

When strategy is carried over into action, planners confront difficult organizational issues. Sectoral programs must be integrated spatially. Regional programs must be linked to both projects and national policy. And local initiative must be constrained by central direction in order that a measure of the common good may be obtained. These problems are intricate and not well understood as yet. I shall return to consider them in the final chapter of this book.

Preconditions for Regional Development

The "open" character of regional economies suggests that a good part of their growth is shaped by outside forces. Regions are inserted into a network of functional relationships, and how the larger design is arranged will strongly influence the character and possibilities of regional economic performance. Regional growth must be regarded as primarily the result of an adaptive process. It is by changing the parameters which restrict their choices, that regions may uncover new opportunities for action.

The following conditions favorable to regional growth are set down despite the fact that they are also symptomatic of national development. They were drawn from among all the variables that might have been considered, with a bias for those processes that are normally undervalued because they are intangible: the acquisition of new knowledge, geographic mobility, the increased circulation of ideas, and local leadership.

A *sustained high rate of national economic growth* is an objective to which most other values must give place. Where the economy is relatively static, where living levels consequently decline, political crises are produced that leave no energies to deal imaginatively with regional problems. In this sense, regional development must be thought of as a certain luxury, a project that is carried forward when the national future is regarded with some confidence. Not only do national crises interfere with a rational consideration of the locational aspects of development but the shortage of resources and the low volume of new investment nationally diminishes the chances of any region to improve its relative economic status.

Regional development is the result of an investment process. It is consequently easier to achieve in a rapidly expanding economic framework than in a contracting one. This is especially true for ameliorating the gross inequities inherent in a center-periphery structure. The periphery is unlikely to be integrated into the national economy when few changes of any kind occur. Growth is, indeed, as much a psychological as an economic phenomenon. It creates an expansive mood that leads people to assume greater risks and to regard the future optimistically. It leads them, among other things, to entertain the possibilities of increased investment on the periphery and sets into motion a political process—a crisis of another sort—that fixes national attention on the problems of the periphery.

Regional economic growth is also dependent on the *volume*

61

of scientific and technical research. There is a common-sense thesis that argues that transitional societies need not engage in significant research since technology can always be imported. This view is held in error: a country so inclined may find itself forever in the backwaters of progress. Undertaking its push toward modernity in a scientific age, it may trail continuously behind the industrialized nations unless it ceases to rely exclusively on borrowed technology and concentrates on building up its own research instead.

Basing development on technology imports has three unfavorable consequences: it leaves the exploitation of monopolies based on invention in the hands of foreign enterprises; it forgoes the possible gains from novel factor combinations more suited to the national environment than the technology imported; and it fails to make the most productive use of natural resources.

The solution is to concentrate in a few areas of comparative scientific strength and to devote large funds to furthering the knowledge industries. Failure to do so means that unique production possibilities will go unused, particularly where discovery and invention are main vehicles for transposing national growth into regional product. Since modern industry is founded on research, the existence of research facilities has itself become a powerful condition of location. The loss of research functions to other countries will reduce the volume of investment that might otherwise have occurred.

Increased geographic mobility is a third condition of regional development. The functions of internal migration are those of economic adjustment. Kuznets and Thomas have stated the essential relations.[1]

1. Given a country's fixed area, the mere increase in population will, in the absence of technological change, modify the population-land ratio and affect unequally the economy in various parts of the country. The population will then tend to migrate in adjustment to such unequal economic impact.

2. More population in thinly settled areas, resulting from population growth but still assuming no technological change, is likely to uncover natural resources (other than land) valuable to the settled areas. This should stimulate further migration.

3. By far the greatest and most pervasive effect of economic growth on internal migration is through the differential effect of technological progress on economic opportunities associated with different locations.

4. Population redistribution in response to the differential impact of economic growth on economic opportunities in different parts of the country could presumably be carried through either by differing rates of natural increase or by internal migration . . . . it is internal migration that provides the main mechanism of adjustment; and it is internal migration that accounts for most of the population redistribution indispensable as an accompaniment to economic growth.

To summarize: without mobility, the economic structure of a country and, consequently, its spatial structure freezes and becomes extremely vulnerable. Expressed as the search for economic opportunities in geographic space, mobility is a condition of continued economic expansion and technical progress. Despite the magnitude of the process, the volume of internal migration relative to the needs for adjustment is not nearly great enough. Needed is not only greater movement from the farms to cities, but also increased intraurban and intrarural migration.

The failure of the economy to grow at a sufficient pace may hold migration to below-optimal levels. But the sources for this condition must also be sought in the migration process itself: the lack of adequate information about job opportunities, the costs of movement that are borne by migrant families, the difficulties of personal adjustment to an unaccustomed mode of life. Some guidance by the state is needed in improving information systems, granting subsidies to migrant workers, adding to investments in urban housing, training for job mobility, and undertaking programs of resettlement.

Migration is closely related to *upward social mobility*. A development society is a fluid society whose members have ready opportunity and the skills adequate to advance their incomes and social position. A society thus geared to change places heavy demands on individual capabilities. But where poverty and ignorance are critical thresholds, the responses will be weak. Poor peasant lads move to the cities to become there part of a faceless, shapeless proletariat, constrained by inabilities and want of knowledge to perform throughout their lifetime the most menial jobs. Nor are children favored to rise above the station of their fathers. Rural poverty pours into the cities and there perpetuates itself.

To acquire communication skills is fundamental to achieving upward mobility. Unable to receive the signals emanating with growing frequency from his environment, the illiterate person lives in a world he only half comprehends and to which he can ill adapt himself. Hence his frustration. But illiteracy is not the only obstacle. More important still is the constant upgrading of technical competences that modern civilization imposes as a condition of personal success. And the key to this is education. Harbison and Myers express this point of view persuasively.

In all countries people think of education as a main avenue to jobs and careers. In the underdeveloped countries, schooling may be looked upon as an "escape route" from the bush to a white-collar job in the government. Students in the advanced countries go to universities in order to qualify for positions of high status and pay. Learning for the sake of learning is a noble objective of a few scholars, but learning in order to prepare for jobs and careers is the goal of the vast majority of the people. Thus, the social and political pressures for education are powered by economic motivations. And for this reason, an educational system which fails to prepare persons for available jobs is clearly out of balance and is by any definition inefficient.[2]

A further characteristic of regional poverty is isolation, especially from new ideas. Successful regional development requires the *increased circulation of ideas*. Geographic and vertical mobility are part of this process that extends, however, far beyond them. Economic growth can be analyzed by the impact that new knowledge and new values have on observed behavior. Regional economic integration that appears as a prime national objective is indeed measured by the increased flow of information among all points of the location surface.

As generators and consumers of new information, cities occupy a key role in this process. It is by moving to the city that rural migrants learn to participate in the new society, that they acquire more refined arts, that their aspirations are raised to a high peak. Far from eviscerating cultures, cities revitalize them. Increasing the cities' capacity to absorb a migrant population,

64

economically into jobs and socially into the many urban realms of life, is one of the ways to assure an adequate circulation of ideas. A massive shift of resources to develop radio and television stations, to build up a large publishing industry, and to underwrite the creative talent necessary for a sustained high level of output is yet another path. Every effort should be made to reach the subliterate strata of the population and to saturate them with the symbols of modernity. The result will be a kind of permanent unquiet, a movement and uneasiness of conscience, a breakdown of familiar meanings and their reassembly around new forms of life that provide the seedbed for cultural and economic transformation on a grand scale.

Community leadership is a vital element in this process. Social change comes to a head in the districts, cities, rural towns, and villages of a country. The search is frantic for those who are able to channel this change and render it meaningful. The state cannot be everywhere. It is hidden, remote, inaccessible. It acts with imperfect knowledge of local detail and in a manner largely disinterested in the fate of the individual person. The state is a merchant in statistical averages, in large and powerful social abstractions. It cannot truly heed the uniqueness of a local situation. Social and economic transformation is rather a communal process, a groping for opportunities in the interstices of central government action. The choice is to adapt to outside changes, to adapt successfully, or fail. And in making this choice, the role of local leadership is vital.

A transfer of responsibility must occur, and with this, a transfer of the material means to do the job. This argues for a devolution of governmental functions, for increased reliance on local action to get things done, for greater popular involvement at the points where development becomes specific and concrete. It argues, too, for the establishment in local communities of schools, banks, health clinics, newspapers, and telephone exchanges that, drawing on the local citizenry, relate the isolated single area to the vast turbulence of change outside. It argues for the creation of local planning units, citizen councils, and civic groups as a means for harnessing latent energies to constructive jobs. Mistakes will be made, surely, and power must be circumscribed.

65

But in the growing complexity of modern life, the errors will be less and power is less likely to be abused where a positive communal response to external change can be obtained.

Development Approaches: Introduction

The regional approach to development differs radically from sectoral planning. Its purpose is to achieve an integration of individual sector programs for the solution of problem complexes on a regional scale.

Integration is the key word here. But, it should be noted, this need not imply coordination. It is sufficient to know, in principle, what an integrated approach should be. Some disaggregation of programs is always necessary during implementation, partly because there are practical difficulties in bringing several agencies together in a common undertaking, partly because regional subdivisions for administrative ends do not coincide with development and programming regions, partly also because any development effort must be based on projects and simple project chains that are often conveniently organized along sectoral lines. What is important, however, is for every project to have its assigned place in a comprehensive regional scheme, to perform a definite role within a total strategy. Because of the vast amount of energy required to make it work, coordination should be reserved to those few programs whose successful conclusion depends on a network of supporting actions. A rural resettlement program may require the joint participation of half a dozen or more agencies. A forest conservation program, on the other hand, may be carried out independently of school construction. This is the essential meaning of the separation of integrated programming from coordinated action.

In the following description of strategies, I am running the risk of occasional glibness. I will be encroaching on areas that have been staked out by many disciplines for years. I do not pretend to be more knowledgeable about schools than schoolmen, about farming than farmers, about roads than road builders. My aim is simply to show how schools, farms, and roads must be brought into a regional synthesis so that the encompassing ends of development are served.

The *scale* of the effort in each region must, of course, be left to central policy determination. Here the problem is not so much a decision on priorities in space but on the character of the development tasks in each of the regions. The immediate aim is to show, for instance, how rural resettlement, demographic concentration around smaller growth points, and resources appraisal in downward-transitional areas may ultimately benefit core regions by reducing the volume of potential migrants and thus facilitating the absorption of a smaller number of migrants into metropolitan environments. To demonstrate this adequately would represent a forward step in our understanding of the processes of regional economic growth.

Core Regions

National economic development is, to a large extent, identical with the development of core regions. From one fourth to one third of national investment may be spent there, and for good reason. For core regions perform a critical role in the process of industrialization and are major centers for trade, finance, and government activities.

The economic growth processes of core regions are often said to stay in motion automatically. But this is an inaccurate description. Economic growth is the result of many choices and commitments. There is, to be sure, considerable feedback into core region growth; success thrives on success, and core regions conjure up hopeful images of future life. The pressures to adapt to growth are relentless. From a purely private standpoint, core regions offer economies of scale at any size. Whatever diseconomies appear are the result of an inadequate spatial structure and poor physical planning.

The growth of a core region may slacken, however, when leading export markets shift or the structure of location inputs changes, leaving the region in a less favorable supply condition. These phenomena lie beyond the control of core region elites.

67

And, as with some of the older industrial centers in Europe and the United States, they will decline.

There are two further reasons why growth in core region economies may fail to occur or occur more slowly than it should. First, for lack of foresight or sufficient resolution, the elites may fail to adapt effectively to changing external events. Core regions, indeed, are almost continuously engulfed in crises. Those who have visited them report that a third of the population may be living in shack towns, that water and electricity supplies may be severely rationed, that peak hour traffic creates a monumental convulsion of traffic. Once these problems have become endemic, the capacity for growth will be reduced and the region will fall below its potential level of production. It is true that a continuing crisis situation also generates pressures for solving many of the urgent problems of urbanization; in this sense, Hirschman's strategy of imbalance may work. On the other hand, it is difficult to grasp why the method of hurling resources at one strangulation point after another in desperate attempts to survive should be called "optimal."[3] What is a typical situation under rapid growth is not necessarily the best condition for sustaining growth. Factory shutdowns because of power shortages are not optimal. Nor are breakdowns of internal circulation. In addition, there is the physical and psychological harm inflicted on the population by persistent shortages of decent housing, the nagging nonavailability of water, erratic food supplies, poor sanitation systems, overcrowded substandard schools, interminable travel times to work, and insufficient recreation areas.

The second reason for the possible failure of core regions to grow is that they are still lingering in a provincial pregrowth atmosphere, waiting to be roused. How to bring such areas to the point where growth can be sustained will be discussed in the following section. In the activation of new core regions, the essential problem is to get a certain rhythm of growth under way. But in already existing core regions, it is to maintain that rhythm. Some means for doing so will now be discussed.

The basic thesis may be stated thus: core regions in transitional societies are prone to suffering adverse economic and social consequences from the appearance of major *points of strangulation* within the fabric of their development. These may include:

1. Shortages and poor performance records in water supply, waste disposal, electric power supply, and telephone communications.

2. Inefficient location of work places relative to worker residences and the internal circulation network.

3. Inefficient internal circulation as reflected in high transport costs, unusually long journeys to work, congestion, and totally inadequate means of public conveyance.

4. Inefficient spatial organization of the core region economy as reflected in (3) and in the excessively high costs of providing public services.

5. Inefficient absorption of migrants into the core region economy as reflected in high rates of unemployment and marginal employment, low upward mobility, a high incidence of crime, and substandard residential areas.

6. Inadequate provision especially of middle income housing, giving rise to social dissatisfactions and extremist political behavior on the part of the older resident groups.[4]

7. Undesirable internal organization of the core region from the standpoint of personal orientation within it, and of the availability of public amenities, especially recreation areas.

These "strangulation points" do not equally affect the performance of the core region economy. But each brings some influence to bear and, where these influences overlap, their combined impact will definitely harm achievement of a satisfying growth experience.

Three conditions help to determine a strategy directed at eliminating many of these strangulation points. First, the rate of the expected economic growth in core regions is high. Second, given a statement of national growth parameters, future core region growth is highly predictable. And third, the participation of the public sector in total core region investment is very high. With these conditions in mind, the main elements of a strategy for core region development may be proposed.

The need to plan ahead. Where economic growth can be

expected to occur, there is no special virtue in "imbalance." On the contrary, persistent shortages, inadequacies, and malfunctioning of essential urban services will lower the average production of the region and reduce its capacity for further growth. It is not a question of some growth or none at all but of its rate. And this will be lower where a failure adequately to provide for growth leaves core regions in a state of perpetual disorder.

The principal failures are shortsightedness and an unwillingness to act on reasonable expectations. What is needed is the adoption of a *regional capital budget* that will relate programs of public investment to the expected growth rate in population and employment.[5] The budget will arrive at an integrated statement of all programs in utilities, transportation, communication, housing, industrial estates, education, health, and amenities required to sustain the projected levels of demographic and economic growth and furnish preliminary estimates of total costs, together with expected sources of financing.

Where a national capital budget has been prepared along sectoral lines, the regional budget will need to be integrated with it. Alternatively, it will appear merely as a summing up of the functional items in the national budget across one or more core regions. An adequate time horizon also is important. Because of the lead time required for major construction projects, the regional capital budget should be prepared for a period of from four to six years.

Experience with capital budgets has not always been as satisfactory as theory would have it.[6] Frequent revisions are usually necessary, and the current annual budget almost never reflects the program as originally drawn up. However, the purpose of a regional capital budget is not its precise execution according to a preconceived design. Together with the background of analytical studies, it may rather be viewed as a model of the regional economy that has to be adjusted frequently. Its principal advantage lies in the joint consideration of all investments in a medium-term perspective. Adjustment of any one part of the budget would automatically lead to comparable changes in all other parts. Officially, only a single year of the budget needs to be acted upon by the legislature. The remainder of the capital budget and any supporting documents will serve primarily as information necessary for a just consideration of the items included for the budget year.

Need for an adequate regional form. This part of the strategy for core region development will be taken up under three topics: the nature of the programming region, the construction of a development map, and the optimal size of region.

a. The programming region. In Chapter 3, criteria were presented for the delineation of a set of development regions. The subject of programming regions was left undetermined since decisions concerning them will depend mainly on local conditions. In the case of core regions, however, it is possible to go one step beyond this. For core regions are areas where development criteria for regional boundaries coincide with those for programming. In capital budgeting, therefore, the entire core region should be treated as a single subsystem of the economy. Its parts are too closely interdependent to allow for their consideration in separation from each other. Their relation to the central city and to each other is what, in fact, renders core regions the special type of development regions they are. And this implies that transportation, housing, education, water supply, and all the rest should be extended as a network serving the entire area. Local political circumstances, such as the existence of multiple governmental authorities in the region, may render this approach impractical. Nevertheless, national decisions on the allocation of resources to different regions require a broader frame of reference than is given by the range of municipal authority alone. Plans and programs for national support of core region developments must be formulated for the entire problem area. Additional gains will be made if insistence on this criterion should happen to encourage closer coordination of the governments and agencies that are active in core region development. But coordination itself is not a condition of effective regional programming in a context of national planning.

b. Regional development maps. The location of new public facilities must be considered jointly and related to existing spatial patterns of settlement, work places, and circulation routes. In this way, mutually supporting activities can be identified.

Industrial site selection, for instance, may be evaluated together with a geographically determinate network of public utilities, housing projects, and the location of interregional transportation. This appears to be no more than ordinary common sense, but joint consideration of investments is not the rule where planning is fragmented and where different time horizons and different investment strategies are used. Frequently, the locations of several related facilities fail to reinforce each other. Housing projects may be built without connection to main water lines or health clinics may be remote from residential concentrations. This is a common happening in the core regions of transitional societies, especially where construction is in the hands of national agencies accustomed to operate in partial secrecy.

There is consequently need for a device that will enable the planners to evaluate the spatial consistency of projects that are included in the regional capital budget. This device is the *regional development map*. It may be visualized as a series of detailed map overlays in which are recorded, first, various essential features of the region's dynamic landscape—the direction of its expected population growth, its economic and residential areas, its pattern of traffic flows, its major problem areas—and, second, the spatial pattern of any investment projects proposed, not only public where information is available but also private. The map would include projected information on the following:

—roads and highways (capacity, condition, expected traffic volume)

—railways, ports, airports, and other means of public transportation (capacity, condition, traffic volume)

—facilities for power supply (main distribution grid, generating and transformer stations)

—facilities for water supply (capacity, water quality)

—waste disposal systems (capacity, type, units not served, pollution)

—communication facilities (location of central stations, areas not served, quality of radio and TV reception)

—housing (quantity and quality of the existing stock)

—public services (health, education, recreation)

—industrial and commercial facilities

72

This information should be projected for the same length of time as the capital budget, but only the first budget year needs to be determined with any finality, representing, as it does, a preliminary commitment. The map will show the spatial constraints that must be respected and furnish a means for testing what I have called the spatial consistency of projects. Its possible use as a control device will be discussed further on.

It is clear that careful and conscientious use of the map will also be reflected in the composition of the capital budget. The former is not merely an automatic plotting of the data collected in the latter. The development map will be elaborated on the basis of longer-range studies. It will take into account urban design criteria and will evolve out of a succession of detailed measurements whose aim is to establish the performance characteristics of alternative regional forms for their over-all efficiency with respect to internal movement, supply, and the cost of public services, as well as their visual quality, that is to say, the ease of individual orientation within it, its visual differentiation, and the sense of place and space it tends to create.[7]

c. The optimal size of region. This subject is a source of endless speculation on the part of planners.[8] But it may be safely regarded as a pseudo question to which an answer cannot be given, *even in principle.* If size—however measured—is to be the dependent variable, its optimality must presumably be determined on the basis of an efficiency measure relating inputs to outputs. Thus, it should be possible to assert that the greatest efficiency is reached in core regions within the range of x and y size of population.

Now, it is possible to obtain fairly reliable estimates of the costs of urban investment and services and even of the social costs of urbanization (for example, traffic congestion, noise, frequency of face to face relations, and so forth). The inputs can therefore be determined with some accuracy. But what is the output of a city? The concept defies measurement. Cities certainly contribute something to the social economy of a nation, but it is impossible to be very specific about it. That is the first and also the major difficulty.

The second difficulty has to do with the concept of regional size. Size of population is always an arbitrary measure in the case of regions. The region is not clearly demarcated, it is a portion of a larger continuous space characterized by differences in density configuration. If suburbs are included, why not ex-urbia; and why not also satellite cities and subcenters, and beyond them, related rural areas and still more distant urban concentrations within the wholesale trading area of the core region, and beyond *them*, all the other places with which some functional relations are maintained? If size is indeterminate, the concept of optimality cannot be applied to it.

What does appear feasible, however, is a measure of the total cost of servicing an area whose size is given but whose internal spatial structure is variable. The question of the optimal size of region should thus be reinterpreted as a question regarding the efficiency of internal spatial organization. Here, the measurements may be difficult to perform, but they are potentially operational. An adequate regional form is an efficient form. Unfortunately, no comparative data exist anywhere for formulating even tentative hypotheses. The study of this subject remains a major challenge to city planning theory.

Need to link physical and developmental planning. What has been said in the preceding section suggests the need for close integration of physical and economic (developmental) planning and programming in core regions. If regional capital budgets and development maps are planning instruments that state the same investment program in financial and in spatial terms, they must be jointly elaborated and subjected to simultaneous revision when required. This suggests the need for creating a planning-programming staff in each core region that will include urban designers, city planners, and development economists.

The difficulties inherent in a joint operation are indeed formidable. Mutual forbearance is indicated; a common vocabulary must be adopted; a common set of purposes will have to inform the activities of each profession. Economists and urbanists are not accustomed to work in harmony. Their ideologies, theories, concepts, and techniques are the result of altogether different traditions. It is nevertheless possible to create an environment in which each profession can be true to its own heritage and

74

yet learn enough of the other to be respectful of its unique potential contribution to a specific task. Economists will have major responsibility for constructing the regional capital budget, urbanists for the development map. Both instruments are different expressions of the same phenomenon: the desired direction of future growth. Professionals in both traditions will use efficiency concepts; economists, in addition, will study questions of financial feasibility, while urbanists will operate with design criteria derived from image studies and professional judgment. The outcome is a product more complex in concept and structure than either would have been able to achieve alone.

Need for more adequate controls. To implement the planning algorithm, controls are needed. Both capital budget and development map can be used for this purpose. For the current year, it is possible and indeed essential to require adherence to both the budget and the map: the construction and location of individual projects must be authorized in both these documents.

It is a fairly simple matter to insist on this requirement for public investments. Private investments are more difficult to channel in the appropriate direction. Since no capital budget exists for private investment, the only recourse left is the development map. One feature of this map might be a broadly conceived *zonal plan* that could be used to authorize private construction. The development map would thus exert a double influence. First, it would convey to private investors a sense of public intention with respect to the location of key investments in urban infrastructure (up to 80 per cent of total investment in core regions). This constitutes valuable information on which private decisions can be based. Second, the map would include indications of desired directions of growth by major activity groups and identify land reserved for residential, commercial, industrial, and various public uses. These determinations should be kept quite general and adaptable to change.[9] Overly precise specifications would be harmful on two grounds: an adequate rationale for detailed land-use planning, backed by precise quantitative measures, is usually lacking; the relevant decisions are therefore arbitrary and not especially persuasive. At the same time, too much design detail renders forms inflexible and poorly suited to the requirements of rapid expansion. With annual growth rates of 10 to 15 per cent, precise control procedures are in any case unthinkable. But growth may be channeled to achieve a generally desirable physical form for the region. Functional efficiency, orientation, social, and aesthetic considerations would be the main criteria applied in laying out the broad land-control zones for private use.

The main elements of a strategy for core region development may now be restated.

First, formulate a medium-term regional capital budget.

Second, formulate a medium-term regional development map that expresses and modifies the budget.

Third, for planning and programming purposes, treat the region as a single economic subsystem.

Fourth, consider the location of all proposed public facilities jointly.

Fifth, consider the efficiency of alternative regional forms.

Sixth, to implement (1) through (5), create a planning-programming staff for each core region in which economic development and urban design functions will be linked.

Seventh, use the capital budget and development map as a control device for public investment in infrastructure.

Eighth, use the development map as a control device for private investment by adopting a rough-grained zonal plan for major categories of land use.

If this strategy in carried out, specific strangulation points may be eliminated, and an optimal for core region development may be pursued.

Resource Frontiers

Resource frontiers have been important in the economic histories of many nations, including the United States, Canada, the Soviet Union, Australia, China, and Brazil.[10] The problems they define are, for the most part, common ones arising from the special circumstances that provide the initial impulse for their development and from the physical characteristics of their location.

In the following pages, I shall present a model of resource frontier development. It is based on extensive reading about the role of the frontier in national progress, including recent accounts for Alaska and Canada, personal observation in northern Brazil, and a detailed analysis of the available materials for the Guayana region in southeastern Venezuela. The model is consequently a composite picture and a perfect rendering of no actual situation. It will be possible, however, to derive from it the elements for a general strategy that may be adapted for resource frontier development in any part of the world.

Resource frontiers come into existence with the discovery of a major natural resource or resource complex and a commitment on the part of private firms or the government to exploit the commercial opportunities that it presents. Generally, the resources in question will be minerals, such as iron ore, uranium, gold, diamonds, bauxite, manganese, copper, or petroleum, although extensive forest and fishery resources may also occasion significant investments. In view of the large distances over which electricity can be economically transported, hydroelectric potential will normally constitute only a secondary attraction for regional development. However, its presence in an area otherwise richly endowed with basic resources may be a major influence in determining the strategy for the development of the region. As defined here, resource frontiers do not include those regions that are formed primarily by the expansion of agriculture into new areas. The agricultural frontier has its own characteristic behavior and is excluded from the present discussion.[11]

The presence of large-scale and economically attractive natural resources is a basic condition of frontier development. In the case of private enterprise, this will always be the chief motivating force and a satisfactory rate of return on investment the compelling interest in the undertaking. But the concerns of government may go beyond the relatively straightforward problem of resource extraction. Governments may be preoccupied,

77

for instance, with the permanent settlement of the region, with building a base for the further exploration and development of heretofore uninhabited areas, with the creation of interregional multipliers, or with drawing the resource frontier more closely into the orbit of the national economy. Although a single motivation may prevail, the purpose of a government in resource frontier development is likely to be a far more complex set of intentions than the maximization of profits.

A major characteristic of resource frontiers and, indeed, the chief reason for many of the planning problems they present, is their relative *remoteness* from existing centers of population. Resource frontiers are noncontiguous areas, separated from the main centers of population by long stretches of largely uninhabited wilderness. Their very remoteness suggests that, in the past, these areas were not considered prime land for settlement and cultivation; indeed, resource frontiers are almost always located in distant regions inhospitable to man: tropical forests and savannas, tundra, mountains, and deserts. Such areas will be uninviting by comparison with an already humanized landscape. To render them permanently habitable will be a costly undertaking. Their very remoteness renders the provision of access routes difficult and, in any event, expensive relative to the amount of traffic likely to be carried. The logistics of the new area becomes a major problem that will contribute to the high cost of living and production in the area.

The remoteness of frontier regions suggests that their development must be *focused on a city:* resource frontiers are urban frontiers. The city is the main civilizing agent that transforms the wilderness into an environment suitable for long-term habitation. "The towns were the spearheads of the frontier," writes Richard C. Wade in his scholarly analysis of early urbanization in the American West. "Planted far in advance of the line of settlement, they held the West for the approaching population. Indeed, in 1763, when the British threw up the Proclamation Line along the Appalachians to stop the flow of settlers, a French merchant company prepared to survey the streets of St. Louis, a thousand miles through the wilderness. Whether as part of the activity of the French and Spanish from New

Orleans or of the English and Americans from the Atlantic sea-board, the establishment of towns preceded the breaking of soil in the transmontane West."[12] What was true of the agricultural frontier of the midwestern prairie is to an even greater extent true of resource frontiers as defined in this study. The "city" may be a small town, perhaps originally only a fort. But it is the artificial physical environment and urban institutions that must be created before the major enterprise of resource explora-tion can seriously get under way.

Because of their relative isolation, cities on the resource fron-tier perform only *limited central-place functions*. Relative to their size, their trade and service sectors are generally atrophied. Hence, these cities do not form part of the national system of central places which is based on a hierarchy of service func-tions. They are instead highly specialized cities whose chief purpose is to support and maintain the primary resource activ-ities in the area. Some processing and manufacturing may ulti-mately be added to the economic base of the city, but this will be chiefly in those branches of industry which O. D. Duncan and his co-workers have classified as "first and second stage resource users" producing for a nonfinal market.[13] The hinter-land or service areas of resource frontier cities will, as a rule, be small, with city growth chiefly dependent on the behavior of the demand function for the products exported from the region. There may be ways of overcoming this limitation by considering frontier cities in a more comprehensive regional setting and, especially, by relating their development to progress in the more densely populated parts of the country—in short, by closely linking frontier resource development to the national economy. But the remoteness of frontier regions often works against such a solution.

Exports are the principal reason for the existence of resource frontiers. Unless there is a strong and continuing external de- mand for the potential products of the region, resource fron-tiers will not come into being, nor will they be able to maintain themselves. This fact establishes a clear-cut scale of priorities. The region will produce very little of what it consumes itself—hence, its import quotient will be high—and it will export, both to national and international markets, nearly everything it produces. Resource frontiers are "open" regions to an unusual extent. As highly specialized and export-oriented communities, they will be especially sensitive to fluctuations in the relevant export markets. The heavy initial investment required for the creation of resource frontiers is, therefore, a calculated gamble that the markets will hold. Private investors will be prone to base their calculations on a quick recovery of their initial investment. There is something inherently ephemeral about resource frontiers, a trait that will be reflected in the entire way of life of the new communities. How to transform the resource frontier into a permanent base of settlement constitutes a major challenge to public policy.[14]

Frequently, the important export markets will be foreign, and principally it will be *foreign interests* that are committed to the development of resource frontiers.[15] As a result, the frontier may operate quite independently of the national economy and, indeed, be subject to policies that have only a tenuous relation to national interests. This raises the questions of integration once more, but in a new context. To maintain control of the frontier is one of the principal reasons why national governments have, of late, shown a growing concern for their development, and more generally, for national resources policies. Foreign "enclaves" in this highly sensitive field are widely regarded as undesirable.

The *typical growth curve* of the population of resource frontiers is closely related to the conditions described. After an initial boom, which normally lasts for only a short period, there will be a tendency for population growth to level off: the maximum size of the community will generally be reached within a few years after its founding. Because of its close relation to the export base of the frontier economy, total population, together with the wages and salaries paid to them, may never reach the *minimum critical size* that would allow any but the most rudimentary forms of residentiary activities to locate in the area. The local market will generally be too small to attract local service industries to the region. Consequently, a cumulative growth process will not be set into motion. But where continuous growth is, from a national standpoint, desirable, it may be necessary to provide initial large-scale subsidies to push the local economy beyond the threshold of a minimum critical size. By the same reasoning, it may be necessary to bring the whole community into existence during a relatively short period through a coordinated and intensive development effort that will create the essential external economies. Unless self-sustaining growth can be achieved, population may fluctuate about a maximum level for a time—possibly even for decades—but will ultimately decline as production becomes more mechanized, the original resource supply is exhausted, or further exploitation is rendered uneconomic because of changes in the structure of demand. Sustained growth and, consequently, permanence can only be assured by a *diversification of the region's economic base.*[16]

The development of resource frontiers is usually carried out as an *integrated investment program* under a single executive authority. The development organization will also have to bear a substantial portion of the total development costs, including overhead investments in housing, community facilities, utilities, health, education, and transportation. Although some of these costs may eventually be recovered, this situation poses a serious problem for accounting and, ultimately, for the competitive position of the region. If the principal investments are private, depreciation charges for social overhead must enter into the total cost of production. This would put firms in the region at a disadvantage relative to those that need not bear this particular expense. If the investments are largely in the public sector, however, a major portion of the overhead can be written off on national accounts and need not directly influence the costs of production. Nevertheless, investment in community overhead must be included in a total assessment of the economic consequences of the project. As a result, initial investment per unit of output will be high.

Factors adding significantly to over-all expenses are the *high transportation costs* for supplies, especially during the initial phases of construction and operation, and the continuing *high costs of labor.* Labor costs may actually reach prohibitive levels, if one bears in mind the high turnover rates for workers and the cost-of-living and special "hardship" bonuses that may need to be paid to attract technicians and skilled workers of high quality.[17] Relatively high labor costs may continue well beyond the initial construction phase and make it imperative to use only the most advanced types of mechanized equipment in construction, mining, and industrial operations. While this will tend to reduce total labor requirements, it also has the adverse effect of keeping both the city and the local market small, and consequently renders the attainment of cumulative growth more difficult. In many situations, this practice will call a dualistic social structure into existence: an elite of professionals, technicians, and managers together with a relatively small but highly paid skilled work force will face a proletariat of unemployed, underemployed, and service workers who will barely succeed in surviving on the fringes of the local economy.[18] A broad middle stratum will generally be missing.

The entire *social structure* of resource frontiers tends, in fact, to be a rather peculiar one, at least during the early stages of development. Generalizations are difficult, since reliable information on a comparative basis is scarce. In general, single working men will predominate in the population. The community will also be composed largely of transients. There will be many new arrivals, but few will come with the intention to settle for a lifetime. The management and technician groups, in particular, will tend to be quickly rotating, working under contract for periods of only limited duration and considering their stay within the area as but a passing phase in their professional careers. For these reasons, it will be difficult to establish a class of professionals who will opt for a permanent home in the city.

The common work force may be even more shiftless.[19] Nevertheless, a core of more permanent settlers may in time appear, leading to tensions between an ingroup with distinctly local interests and a more cosmopolitan outgroup which, though it has no permanent roots in the community, will have control over its destiny by reason of its social and economic position.[20] In any event, the problem of achieving a sense of self-identification with the local area may be a rather difficult one—especially where such identification does not play as important a role, culturally, as it does in Europe, the United States, or Canada. Consequently, even the simplest kinds of community facilities may have to be provided by the development authority.[21] Few details are known about social structure and behavior in modern resource frontiers, but what small evidence there is, points to a highly stratified society with little internal cohesion.[22] This is contrary to the widely held notion that frontier life is inherently egalitarian.

Time and again in the foregoing description of resource frontier development, the problems of permanence and integration have had to be raised as among the most compelling issues. What is at stake here is a question of social objectives, whether productive efficiency or permanent settlement is to be the primary goal of regional development. The two cannot be held completely separate, of course, since permanent settlement would require an appropriate economic base and this, in turn, impose the criterion of productive efficiency on the entire operation: the region's output for export must remain competitive in national, but especially in international, markets. Continuing insolvency—implying an endless stream of public income transfers to the region—would be a serious "drag" on the total national development effort and could be justified only with extreme difficulty in view of all other requirements.

Principles of resource frontier development. The preceding discussion may now be summarized. There are three national objectives that can be regarded as typical for resource frontiers: permanence of settlement, integration with the national economy, and sustained economic growth. These objectives cannot always be achieved. Where the resources base is not diversified, or where remoteness to national markets is excessive, resource frontier development is likely to remain a transitory phenomenon, loosely related to national objectives and highly vulnerable to fluctuations in world markets. But where the conditions are reasonably fulfilled, the following elements of strategy may be considered.

a. Establish a regional authority for development. It is imperative that the development of resource frontiers should be subordinate to national purposes, especially during its initial stages. So long as the region is controlled by a few large private concerns—whether they be foreign or national—whose primary interest is in a quick return on their investment, no substantial progress can be made toward the objectives outlined earlier. The important questions are whose interests ought to prevail in forging the strategy for regional development and whether private profit or social gain should be chief criterion for determining the direction of investment. Where social gain is the preferred option, the first task will be to bring resource frontier development under a single regional authority capable of acting in the national interest. Such an authority would be responsible not only for general planning and project programming but also for implementing major phases of the program.

b. *Create a new location matrix.* The regional development authority should lay the basis for mobilizing additional private resources on a large scale. For this it is necessary to create an environment competitive with other location matrices in the national economy.

Every resource frontier needs an urban focus that will provide the external economies of scale and the amenities associated with urban life that are likely to attract private business. Public resources will be inadequate to furnish not only the basic overhead for regional development but also the main stock of productive facilities. Major reliance will have to be placed on private enterprise for supplying the productive plant of the region. Since location decisions are usually made on the basis of a comparison among alternative "matrices" in a national economy, the advantages of the resource frontier must be dramatically persuasive to overcome the reluctance of entrepreneurs to venture into territory that it unknown to them.

c. *Achieve a minimum critical size as quickly as possible.* Every economic activity has a threshold determined by the minimum economic size of the enterprise. This threshold will vary with the size of the market and the costs which enterprise itself has to absorb. To the extent that these costs can be shifted to the public sector or to other firms, the threshold size will be reduced. It is therefore necessary to create agglomerations of a

84

size that will provide both a fair-sized internal market and sufficient external economies to push regional growth to the point where it is capable of sustaining without harm to itself a gradual reduction of public inputs.

This requirement imposes a heavy initial burden on the public treasury and compels the development authority to assume risks whose benefits will be diffused and whose ultimate payout may be slow in arriving. No private firm can be expected to assume this role: its profits must be high and quickly made. It would be totally unrealistic to demand that any single firm absorb a major share of regional development costs during the initial period. To insist on this would render its activities unprofitable and bring it quickly to the edge of bankruptcy.

d. Reduce physical isolation. One of the greatest obstacles to resource frontier development is the isolation of the region from other parts of the national and world economy. This condition must be overcome if the total strategy is to succeed. It is therefore necessary to plan for multiple transport and communication linkages that will provide alternative access to the rest of the world. Air, sea, and land routes need to be constructed to provide a flexible system of transportation. Local telephone, telegraph, radio, and television networks should be connected with national and international systems from the start. And the costs of transport and communication should be reduced through subsidies, if necessary, in order to bring the region nearer to the main centers of metropolitan activity.

e. Reduce the cost of living. High living costs are typical for resource frontier regions and are immediately reflected in the wage and salary scales for skilled workers and management. This, in turn, will raise production costs and render the competitive position of regional firms more difficult to sustain.

High living costs are usually the result of an insufficient local supply of basic commodities and services, especially food, internal transport, housing, and specialized consumer services. These basic causes have to be attacked. Encouragement should be given to develop sources of local food supply, to provide adequate, low-cost public transportation throughout the region, to furnish sufficient housing for various population groups, with special emphasis on middle-income groups, and to create a market for locating consumer services in the region, leaving a margin for effective competition.

f. Diversify the economic base of the region. This element of the strategy is implied in all that has gone before, but it needs to be especially emphasized, for it is too narrow an economic base that lies at the root of many of the difficulties that resource frontiers experience. The bases here are natural resources and the intermediate products produced by the initial industries. In the effort to diversify, a detailed program must be worked out, with industrial promotion closely geared to the actual possibilities of the region and the expected pattern of development. Timing is a critical element here, for planned complementarities can be brought into existence only simultaneously or in a predetermined sequence. Some of the uncertainty can be reduced by the participation of public capital in private ventures. In all instances, however, the direction of effort should be the creation of the largest number of functional linkages in the region. Only in this way can a cumulative growth process be set in motion.

g. Create a basis in community. This, in a sense, is the most difficult of challenges. The government must encourage the development of a viable regional community that overcomes the dualism between the educated and the noneducated, the elite and the masses, the cosmopolitans and the locals. Potential leadership groups must be attracted to the region as permanent residents. To accomplish this, the region must be made halfway agreeable to them. Education for their children should be of a high quality, cultural amenities should be brought in or created locally, and the recreational opportunities of the region should be developed.

A leadership group, however, must be able to lead. It must have tasks to perform and the means to carry them out. This implies a transfer of authority from national public organizations to local communities and a legal structure that will enable local leaders to exercise this authority legitimately. It is especially important that local communities have the financial means to carry out programs of local improvement and the technical know-how to apply resources efficiently. Neither is likely to occur immediately, but both should become a long-range aim of public policy.

Downward-Transitional Areas

In transitional socities, the problems of distressed, downward-transitional areas are those of structural poverty in an environment that offers but limited scope for more intensive resource use. Their poverty is "structural" in two senses. First, because it is a direct outgrowth of the relative position of the region within the interregional system of the space economy. The economic performance of downward-transitional areas is the exact opposite of core regions whose inner dynamism—largely associated with external economies of scale—pushes them to always more capital-intensive methods of production and consequently to higher levels of productivity.

So long as ameliorative efforts are confined to a pattern of fixed regional boundaries, structural poverty is not easily reversed. And because the situation is persistent, it tends to fall into a self-reinforcing pattern that renders development efforts extremely difficult. Structural poverty appears as the most intractable of socioeconomic problems precisely because it evolves into a way of life that is spatially contained. This is the second sense in which poverty may be regarded as "structural." A profile of the characteristic subculture of poverty is attempted in the adjoining Table 5.1.

The problem is doubly and triply compounded where poverty coincides with a clearly defined ethnic or religious group whose social standing is viewed as inferior to that of the dominant elite. The Peruvian Indian and the American Negro are in this hapless position. Prevented by malice and prejudice from rising in society, the victims, crowded together in rural and urban slums, constitute a classical example of the disinherited proletariat whose only effective recourse is a social revolution that will destroy the artifice by which it is held down. But even thoroughgoing revolutions cannot alter the precariousness of life in downward-transitional areas, which is ingrained into the social and spatial structure of a country.

87

Table 5.1. Characteristics of Structural Poverty in Downward-Transitional Areas

1. *Economics:*
   Family subsistence farming and/or commercial cultivation of export crops under absentee owners with tenant, share-cropping, or wage arrangement; low productivity per unit of labor and land; low rate of capitalization; fragmentation of agricultural holdings; alternatively, old mining regions.

2. *Resource Use:*
   Land-use practices ill adapted to the physical environment, including terrain; lack of response to shifts in market demand; small potential resources base (soils, forests, minerals) and its gradual deterioration and attrition; backward technology and low skill levels.

3. *Demography:*
   High fertility and mortality rate: potential population "explosion," high rate of selective outward migration of surplus labor, leading to long-term deterioration of the region's human capital stock; high dependency ratios.

4. *Sociocultural Patterns:*
   Tradition-bound localism; increasing awareness of the outside world joined to a recognition of incapacity for constructive action and self-improvement; security-oriented because of slim margin of survival; widespread apathy and fatalism; high illiteracy rate; ethics of "amoral familism."

5. *Spatial Structure:*
   Peripheral locations, frequently in mountainous areas with relative isolation of communities from each other and from the larger world outside; predominantly village pattern of settlement or shifting cultivation with high degree of dispersal of individual farm units; few central places and inadequate provision of central services.

6. *Standard of Living:*
   General impoverishment of the population: nutrition and health deficiencies; high rate of infant mortality; low life-expectancy; high level of indebtedness; lack of means for major change in life position; substandard housing; involuntary idleness; rising absolute—often relative—income gap in comparison to major core regions and upward-transitional areas.

7. *Development Potential:*
   Low, relative to existing population: inability to support present numbers at adequate levels of living.

The purpose of these remarks is to underscore the difficulties obstructing improvement in downward-transitional areas. Yet, even if quick solutions cannot be expected, the situation is not entirely hopeless. Two approaches will be discussed as elements of a comprehensive strategy for attacking structural poverty in its typical geographic domain. First in order are those measures that must be taken primarily outside the region; in second place are measures that focus primarily on structural changes within it. Both approaches assume that a major regrouping of population is both necessary and possible. In Chapter 2, I showed that the volume of migration from downward-transitional areas is often inadequate to restore an interregional equilibrium to the economy. To allow for significant readjustments of agricultural and land-use practices, rural densities must be reduced, and this implies increased migration over customary levels. Yet for all of its importance, a regrouping of population is not a sufficient condition of regional progress.

Approaches outside the region. Downward-transitional areas are surrounded on their perimeter by actual or potential growth regions, including metropolitan economies (core regions), resource frontiers, and upward-transitional areas. These regions stand in a double relation to areas in downward-transition. As major poles of internal migration, they are the preferred target regions for the rural proletariat. But as *centers of growth,* they also reach outward into declining areas for their share of markets and supplies. The stores, banks, industries, and communications media of downward-transitional areas are, to a large extent, the creatures of core region interests and are directly controlled by them. The fate of core regions is consequently of immediate relevance to a solution of the problems in distressed areas.

This relationship may be viewed in yet another perspective. Core regions (and, to some extent, other growth regions as well) are the principal beneficiaries of poverty in downward-transitional areas in the sense that they withdraw more from these areas than they return (Figure 5.1a). Four major transfers may be effected. Downward-transitional areas usually have a net export balance to core regions; they supply core regions with a continuing stream of cheap labor that embodies in itself a high

89

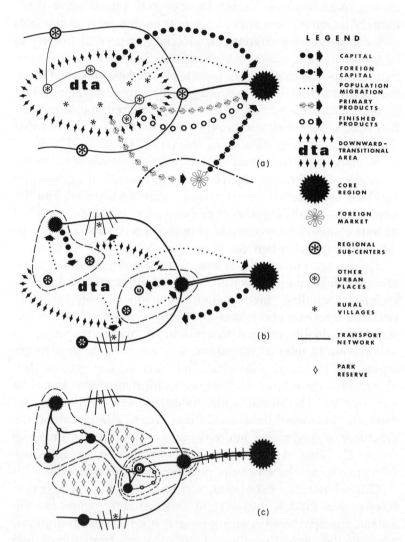

LEGEND

●●▶ CAPITAL

●◐●▶ FOREIGN CAPITAL

••••▶ POPULATION MIGRATION

⇜⇜▶ PRIMARY PRODUCTS

○○▶ FINISHED PRODUCTS

✦✦✦✦ dta ✦✦✦✦ DOWNWARD-TRANSITIONAL AREA

✹ CORE REGION

✿ FOREIGN MARKET

⊛ REGIONAL SUB-CENTERS

✳ OTHER URBAN PLACES

✳ RURAL VILLAGES

— TRANSPORT NETWORK

◊ PARK RESERVE

FIGURE 5.1. *Stages in the development of downward-transitional areas.*

order of personal capability and a not inconsequential stock of education; they export staple food crops to core regions at lower prices than the commodities they import: their internal terms of trade are typically unfavorable; and where they also earn foreign exchange from the sale of their primary products on world markets, their earnings are applied to investments primarily in core regions. These one-sided and decidedly unfavorable relationships explain, in part, the reluctance of core region elites to deal resourcefully with the problem of structural poverty. The poverty of surrounding regions turns out to be one of their chief assets.

But apparent advantage may, in a longer-term perspective, turn around and become a major obstacle to further progress. In technical language, the dependency relation of downward-transitional areas may have dysfunctional consequences for core regions. The populations of downward-transitional areas may be unwilling to contribute indefinitely to the sybaritic well-being of core regions without some show of reciprocity.[23] Political instability is the price that must be paid. Long before this, however, migration to core regions will have led to the appearance of strangulation points that reduce the capacity of core regions for further growth.

A paradoxical situation may thus ensue: on the one hand, core region development will feed on downward-transitional areas; on the other hand, failure to reciprocate by ameliorating the conditions of structural poverty in these areas may undercut the very growth processes on which the continued upward trend of core regions depends. The paradox can be carried still further; for a high growth rate of core region economies can also be a major force in hastening economic improvements in downward-transitional areas. By draining downward-transitional areas of their excess labor, internal adjustments in their economies are favored. What appears as a dysfunctional consequence at first can, *if appropriate supporting actions are taken,* be turned into a major drive to reduce the basic imbalance of interregional flows. The paradox may be resolved by introducing the principle of reciprocity.

These considerations suggest a number of distinct approaches to the development of downward-transitional areas. First, regions of influence must be defined which, while extending deep into the heart of downward-transitional areas, are centered on existing or potential core regions along their margins. The boundary of these influence areas may be determined by measuring the wholesale trade areas, the regions of origin for migrants, and the major raw material and food supply areas for the core region.[24] These regions may be useful not only for programming purposes; they may also in time contribute to bring to consciousness an identity of regional interests. Such an achievement would be of some consequence when it is borne in mind that downward-transitional areas need a very substantial inflow of enterprise capital. The main locus of this capital is in the core regions and proximity coupled with a felt identity of interests may lead to a structure of investment incentives that is more favorable to downward-transitional areas than in the past.

The second approach would be to activate potential core regions on the edge of downward-transitional areas and thus to raise substantially their capacity for absorbing rural migrants. Location is an important element in this strategy. If the purpose is to draw excess labor in larger numbers than before from the distressed region, migration patterns must be considered. Now, migration tends to be related both to distance and to "intervening opportunities."[25] The closer the jobs are to potential labor sources, the larger will be the expected response of migrants. Conversely, the farther away investment occurs from the home region, the less will be the impact on migration. Proximity of core regions to downward-transitional areas is therefore a significant policy variable.

If proximate core regions are selected, however, the over-all effect may be rather too much migration, up to the level of the equilibrium unemployment rate. Assuming that the cost of absorbing workers in an urban environment may be from five to ten times the equivalent cost in rural communities, this would impose a heavy burden on the community. A third approach, therefore, would aim at diverting some of the potential migration stream to rural resettlement areas in the vicinity of the distressed region.

Resettlement projects could be planned in rather rudimentary fashion in the beginning, using contributed labor as much as possible, little irrigation, and a rather low level of investment in overhead facilities. Despite the austerity of resettlement projects, migrants might still be drawn to them in preference to cities, so long as a livelihood is assured them in a relatively familiar environment. The chances for viability would be very much increased if resettlement projects also provided a variety of social services and a rather intensive level of technical assistance. Communal savings might be reinvested and eventually step up the over-all productivity of the projects. Since the labor force thus withdrawn from downward-transitional areas will have had a marginal productivity close to zero, maximizing resettlement on fertile agricultrual land outside the region may well result in a net gain for the economy. At the same time, it would reduce the costs of urbanization from levels that might have been incurred.

In summary, then, four measures external to the region are proposed (see also Figure 5.1b):

   a. Identify function or influence regions both for programming and for creating an identity of interests between core regions and downward-transitional areas.

   b. Encourage the return flow of capital from core regions to downward-transitional areas.

   c. Enlarge the absorptive capacity of potential core regions along the perimeter of downward-transitional areas through carefully staged programs of investment.

   d. Undertake large-scale rural resettlement schemes by extending the agricultural frontier along the edges of downward-transitional areas.

All of these measures will have to be supported by generally improving the accessibility of downward-transitional areas to the outside world.

Approaches inside the region. None of the measures proposed will be successful, however, unless appropriate actions are taken that will take advantage of the internal opportunities created by migration to points outside the region. A key role here may

93

be assumed by those intermediate-sized urban regions that appear to have a relatively high capacity for growth. Once identified, these urban regions may be activated as "growth points" for their respective areas of influence. Growth points may thus be defined as fourth- and fifth-order centers, lower on the scale than core regions but performing equivalent roles for greatly reduced areas. Their functions will be to provide essential central services to the areas surrounding them as well as additional employment in light processing and labor-intensive manufacturing plants, to focus upon themselves a network of local, regional, and interregional roads, to serve as major market and distributing centers with adequate storage and warehousing facilities, and to draw population from surrounding rural areas as a secondary target of migration.

A systematic study of central service location for growth points would lead to a setting of approximate standards based on population-service ratios for a number of critical central services, including (1) regional development banks, (2) agricultural production loan banks, (3) savings institutions, (4) regional secondary schools, (5) vocational training schools, (6) communications media (telephone, telegraph, radio, television, newspapers, libraries), (7) regional hospitals and clinics, (8) consumer and producer cooperatives, (9) storage and warehousing facilities, and (10) regional cultural facilities (cinemas, auditoriums). The adequacy of existing services would be measured against potential service areas—assuming a given network of local and regional roads—and deficiencies as well as surpluses would be noted. On this basis, programs could be worked out to make up any deficiencies through direct government investment, subsidy programs, and more indirect incentive systems. The purpose would be to supply standard services to the population of growth points as well as to outlying communities at a level that permits each enterprise and service to operate efficiently and economically. All the services mentioned will, in one way or another, assist in promoting regional growth: the banks in capital formation, the schools in education for change and upward mobility, the communications media in linking the region with the outside world, the regional hospitals in raising levels of pub-

94

lic and private health, the cooperatives in lowering the costs of both production and consumption, the warehousing in effecting the efficient transfer of commodities from the region to other parts of the national economy, and cultural facilities in cementing central city–hinterland relations and in assisting in the transmission of modern values to tradition-bound regions.

Each growth point would also center upon itself a network of highways. Some of these would be simple farm to market roads, others would provide internal connections for the system of growth points, and still others will carry interregional traffic. A pattern of bus routes should be carefully worked out (and the necessary equipment provided) that will link all essential points in the regional economy and provide ready access for the impoverished rural population to growth points. Incidentally, the road network would also encourage migration, helping to relocate population around each growth point and thus contributing to a lowering of rural densities that is considered to be a precondition for the far-reaching agricultural adjustments that are needed.

A major creative role in the development of downward-transitional areas is assigned in this scheme to a regional university that would be located in one of the growth points selected for activation. It would perform a variety of functions that are of critical importance. First among these is research on all aspects of regional development. An enormous amount of technical research must be accomplished before detailed programs can be carried out. It would be unreasonable to expect any planning agency to recruit a research staff sufficiently large and diversified to survey regional resources, carry out agronomic investigations, engage in research on social change and community development, study central-place functions, investigate the characteristics of optimal transport networks for the region, and accomplish all the other research necessary in support of planned development. It would be even more unreasonable to expect the country's national university to give sustained support to research in these areas. The research function is therefore essential, and in assembling a university teaching staff, arrangements should be made from the start to allow the faculty sufficient time to do research.

A second major function of a university is teaching, but a regional university cannot for obvious reasons compete in quality and breadth of effort with the main national centers of higher education. It must restrict its teaching to a few technical fields where it can perform with distinction and at the same time contribute directly to the development of the region. Teacher training, civil and mining engineering, agriculture and forestry, social sciences and planning might in the beginning constitute the core faculties.

In addition to research and teaching, the regional university would undertake adult education programs on a large scale, ranging from ordinary extension work to special programs in leadership training. The latter might take the form of intensive short courses for potential community leaders whose curriculum would include a series of seminars and workshops on aspects of development in the region, problems and methods of community organization, specific problem-solving methods (industry, housing, water systems, afforestation, and so on), dynamics of small group behavior, and national, regional, and community planning. If three such courses were held during a year, with twenty participants in each, a tremendous revitalization of community spirit and community effort could be brought about in a comparatively short period of time. No less than three hundred local community leaders could be trained within five years!

I have emphasized the development of growth points in this discussion because the concept is new and has yet to be applied experimentally. But if growth points are once established, more traditional approaches to agricultural adjustment may be considered. This could involve a changeover from subsistence to commercial farming and a better adaptation of agricultural practices to the natural conditions of the land. Usually, it will also require the introduction of new types of production (for example, dairying or horticulture), heavy capitalization, consolidation of fields, changes in land ownership, improved marketing organizations, and expanded information systems. The subject is vast and highly specialized. I can only hint here at its importance in regional development.

Some parts of downward-transitional areas will not be able to

96

support a rural population at a socially acceptable level of living. They are unsuited for agricultural production and should be evacuated. Usually mountainous and picturesque, these areas may be prepared as national park land for the delectation of metropolitan populations. They should be regarded as high-priority areas for the planned resettlement of entire villages on more productive land.[26]

This account of development in downward-transitional areas has purposely avoided the role of river basin development that is usually made the focus of any discussion on regional development.[27] I believe that the importance of water resources in regional development has been excessively valued. Although expensive, complex undertakings, their contribution to economic development is questionable. This judgment rests primarily on what is known about the process of regional development. The origin of regional development is typically the export of primary materials to external markets. But to sustain growth, multiplier effects must be captured and harnessed to urbanization. The role of core regions and growth points has been stressed for precisely this reason. The development of water resources may contribute to regional exports; but unless it does so on a major scale, it is not likely to improve the structural imbalance among regions. Even under the most favorable conditions, it will represent only a start toward higher performance. Water and power are essential ingredients in production. But to invest in them is only one of many measures that will further the process of regional growth. Others, not linked directly to natural resources, may lead to equally significant and even superior results.

The strategy for the internal development of downward-transitional areas may now be recapitulated (Figure 5.1c).

1. Identify as major growth points those urban regions of intermediate size that have a high capacity for future growth.

2. Measure the adequacy of central services at the growth points selected.

3. Bring central services at growth points to performance levels judged to be adequate on the basis of estimated population-service ratios.

97

4. Expand and improve the internal road network of the region, focused on growth points.

5. Plan the network of bus routes to provide for the maximum access of rural population to growth points as well as to points outside the region.

6. Develop a network of storage and warehouse facilities based on growth points.

7. Explore the possibilities of developing light processing and labor-intensive manufacturing industries at growth points.

8. Establish a major regional university that will concentrate its efforts on regional research, technical education, and adult education, including agricultural extension and leadership training.

9. Undertake all measures necessary for a changeover in agriculture from subsistence to commercial farming.

10. Transform areas of excessively low agricultural productivity into national park reserves.

No priorities have been indicated, and the preceding list is mainly a catalogue of things that might be done. The actual sequence of a program for distressed areas will depend on the importance of these regions in national development policy, on the character of the region, on the kaleidoscopic pattern of opportunities for action, on the nature of the various planning agencies responsible for regional programming, and on the orientation and persuasiveness of regional leadership. A major instrumentality for action, however, will be the university. For not only must knowledge precede action (even though knowledge is never complete for action) but action is also channelled best through local institutions. The university can become a major innovating and catalytic agent in the region. The choice of an outstanding and dedicated man for rector of the university is therefore essential.

SUMMARY

1. Regional policy typically arises as a problem in national economies that are in transition to industrialism.

2. The spatial structure of these economies is best described by a center-periphery (spatial disequilibrium) model. A powerful central region reduces the rest of the space economy to the role of a tributary area that is drained of its resources, manpower, and capital.

3. This disequilibrium is a structural one. As a result, the automatic working of the market does not re-establish a spatial equilibrium but reinforces the initial structural imbalance. Even where equilibrating tendencies persist, a balanced interregional system may require several generations to come into existence.

4. A lasting center-periphery relation is harmful to a country. It leads to extreme inequities in welfare among regions; it encourages the underutilization of natural resources; it is conducive to the inefficient location of new industries; it has a politically destabilizing effect; it contributes to the problems of rapid, concentrated urbanization at a single center; and it tends to restrict development of a consumer market on a national scale.

5. The center-periphery model suggests that the space economy—whatever its configuration—must be viewed as an interacting system of relationships. Regional development must therefore be approached in full cognizance of the interdependencies that extend across the whole of the national territory.

6. Because of the character of the space economy as a system and because normal equilibrating forces are too weak to rectify the center-periphery imbalance within a reasonable period, regional policy planning must be introduced in transitional economies at the national level.

7. The chief concern of regional policy planning is with the spatial incidence of economic growth. Its intention is to set broad sectoral investment programs with a specific geographic context and thus to contribute to their efficient implementation.

8. To achieve its objectives, regional policy planning seeks to influence both economic activity and household location decisions, chiefly by guiding public investments in overhead capital.

9. The location of new investments and the corresponding settlement pattern may, among other social values, affect the capacity for growth of the economy, the efficiency of production activities, the distribution of income, and the level of spatial integration of the economy. A mathematically precise spatial ordering of activities that will optimize these values cannot be obtained. But each of the criteria may be used, in succession, to test the desirability of a proposed investment allocation.

10. The tasks of regional policy planning may include

a. delineating development and programming regions;
b. formulating objectives for the spatial organization of the economy in the context of national planning;
c. engaging in regional economic, sociological, and geographic investigations;
d. establishing an interregional data system;
e. drawing up a general system of priorites for regional investments;
f. formulating development strategies for each of the major development regions identified that may serve as a reference guide for the specification and evaluation of more detailed regional programs;
g. initiating and providing continuing support of a comprehensive programming process in a number of key areas;
h. evaluating proposed investment projects for their locational efficiency, their consistency with other planned investments on the ground, and their implications for regional development.

11. In evolving an appropriate development strategy, each region will require a different approach, depending on whether it is a core region, an upward-transitional or downward-transi-

100

tional area, or a resource frontier. At the same time, the set of strategies must be coordinated in order to achieve the best over-all effects in terms of national objectives. Development of the economy of one area is interdependent with the development of all the other regional economies and cannot, therefore, be approached as if it were an isolated phenomenon. The precise degree of interdependency, however, needs to be empirically established.

12. The development of regional resources for export to other areas may be important to initiate a process of economic growth. But this process is not likely to be sustained unless it is accompanied by extensive urbanization and expansion of regional markets. Regional policy planning is therefore closely linked to general policies for urban development, including housing and internal transportation, and to the physical planning of particular cities.

13. Core regions together with development corridors and resource frontiers perform a critical role in generating impulses of economic development and transmitting them to other parts of the space economy.

14. The normal sequence of development is from higher-ranking to lower-ranking core regions in a hierarchy of such regions.

15. The structural disequilibrium of a space economy in transition may be attenuated by the activation of new core regions on the periphery.

PART II

A CASE STUDY OF VENEZUELA

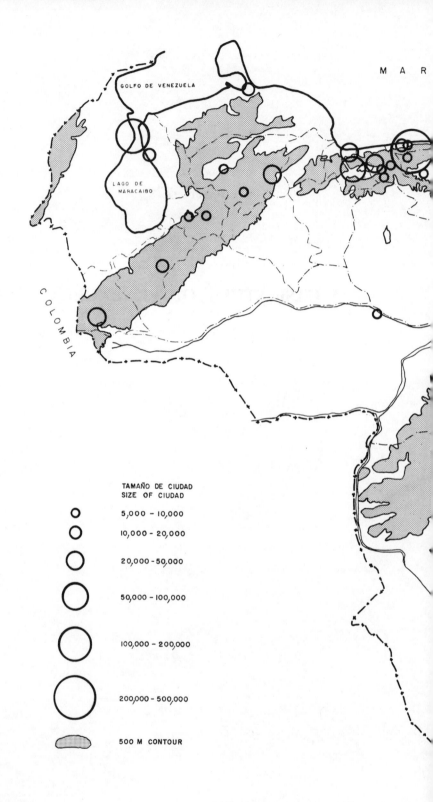

MAR

GOLFO DE VENEZUELA

LAGO DE
MARACAIBO

COLOMBIA

TAMAÑO DE CIUDAD
SIZE OF CIUDAD

○ 5,000 – 10,000

○ 10,000 – 20,000

○ 20,000 – 50,000

○ 50,000 – 100,000

○ 100,000 – 200,000

○ 200,000 – 500,000

▬ 500 M CONTOUR

C A R I B E

ISLA DE
MARGARITA

G
U
A
Y
A
N
A

B
R
I
T
A
N
I
C
A

B R A S I L

MAP 2

DISTRIBUTION OF
URBAN POPULATION, 1936

0   200   400
KMS
OCTOBER 1962   SCALE 1/4,000,000

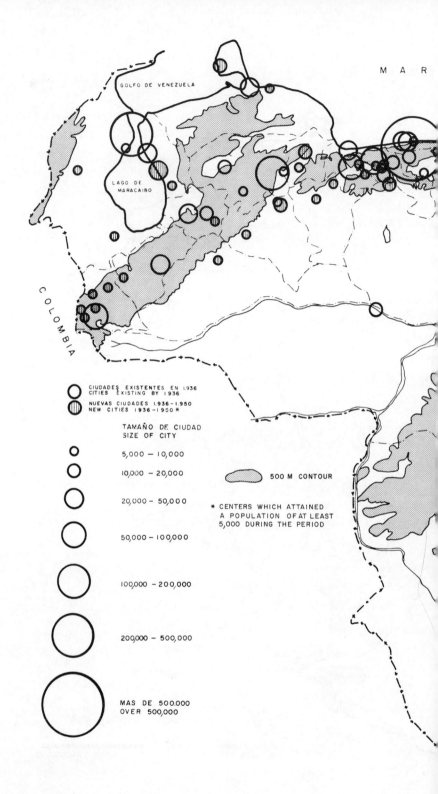

M A R

GOLFO DE VENEZUELA

LAGO DE
MARACAIBO

C O L O M B I A

CIUDADES EXISTENTES EN 1936
CITIES EXISTING BY 1936

NUEVAS CIUDADES 1,936-1,950
NEW CITIES 1936-1950 *

TAMAÑO DE CIUDAD
SIZE OF CITY

5,000 — 10,000

10,000 — 20,000

20,000 — 50,000   500 M CONTOUR

50,000 — 100,000   * CENTERS WHICH ATTAINED
                        A POPULATION OF AT LEAST
                        5,000 DURING THE PERIOD

100,000 — 200,000

200,000 — 500,000

MAS DE 500.000
OVER 500,000

C A R I B E

ISLA DE
MARGARITA

G U A Y A N A
B R I T A N I C A

B R A S I L

MAP 3

DISTRIBUTION OF
URBAN POPULATION, 1950

```
         0              200           400
KMS  |▬▬▬▬▬▬▬▬▬▬▬▬▬▬▬▬▬▬▬▬▬|
OCTOBER 1962              SCALE 1/4,000,000
```

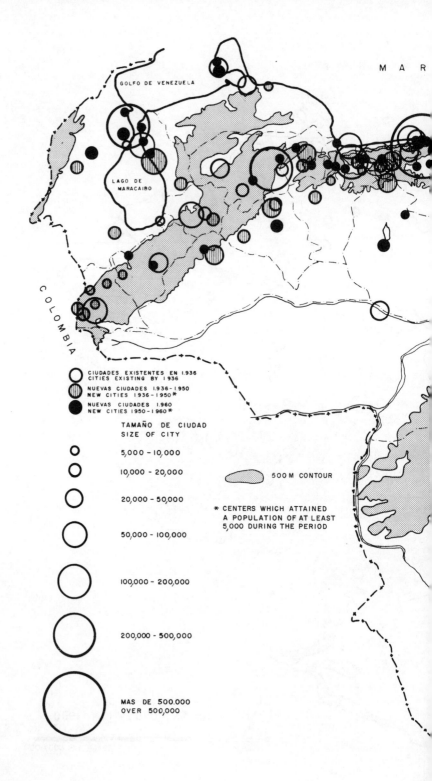

MAR

GOLFO DE VENEZUELA

LAGO DE
MARACAIBO

COLOMBIA

○ CIUDADES EXISTENTES EN 1.936
CITIES EXISTING BY 1936
◫ NUEVAS CIUDADES 1.936-1.950
NEW CITIES 1936-1950 *
● NUEVAS CIUDADES 1.960
NEW CITIES 1950-1960 *

TAMAÑO DE CIUDAD
SIZE OF CITY

○ 5,000 - 10,000

○ 10,000 - 20,000   ⬭ 500 M CONTOUR

○ 20,000 - 50,000   * CENTERS WHICH ATTAINED
                            A POPULATION OF AT LEAST
○ 50,000 - 100,000   5,000 DURING THE PERIOD

○ 100,000 - 200,000

○ 200,000 - 500,000

○ MAS DE 500.000
   OVER 500,000

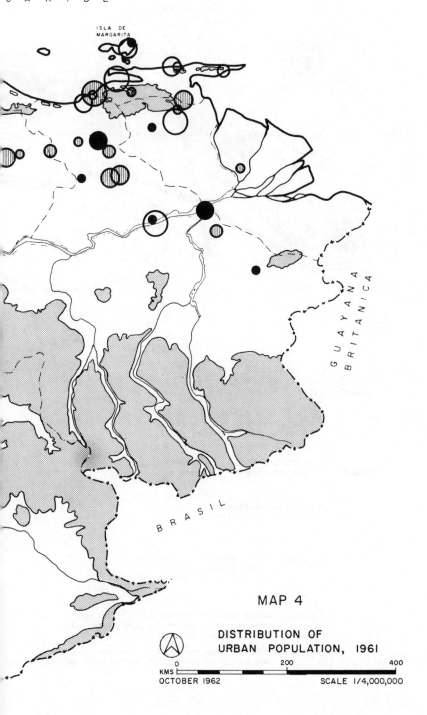

C A R I B E

ISLA DE
MARGARITA

G U A Y A N A
B R I T A N I C A

B R A S I L

MAP 4

DISTRIBUTION OF
URBAN POPULATION, 1961

0   200   400
KMS
OCTOBER 1962   SCALE 1/4,000,000

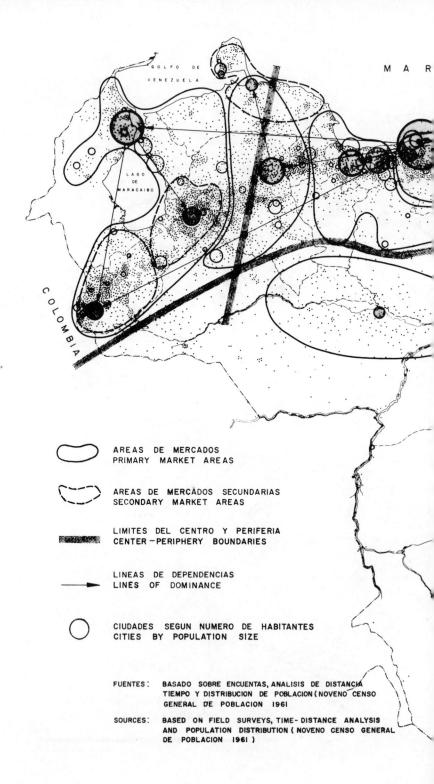

GOLFO DE
VENEZUELA

M A R

LAGO
DE
MARACAIBO

C O L O M B I A

AREAS DE MERCADOS
PRIMARY MARKET AREAS

AREAS DE MERCADOS SECUNDARIAS
SECONDARY MARKET AREAS

LIMITES DEL CENTRO Y PERIFERIA
CENTER-PERIPHERY BOUNDARIES

LINEAS DE DEPENDENCIAS
LINES OF DOMINANCE

CIUDADES SEGUN NUMERO DE HABITANTES
CITIES BY POPULATION SIZE

FUENTES: BASADO SOBRE ENCUENTAS, ANALISIS DE DISTANCIA
TIEMPO Y DISTRIBUCION DE POBLACION (NOVENO CENSO
GENERAL DE POBLACION 1961

SOURCES: BASED ON FIELD SURVEYS, TIME-DISTANCE ANALYSIS
AND POPULATION DISTRIBUTION (NOVENO CENSO GENERAL
DE POBLACION 1961)

C A R I B E

GUAYANA BRITANICA

BRASIL

MAP 5

STRUCTURE OF MAJOR
MARKET AREAS 1962

0   200   400
KMS
OCTOBER 1962   SCALE 1/4,000,000

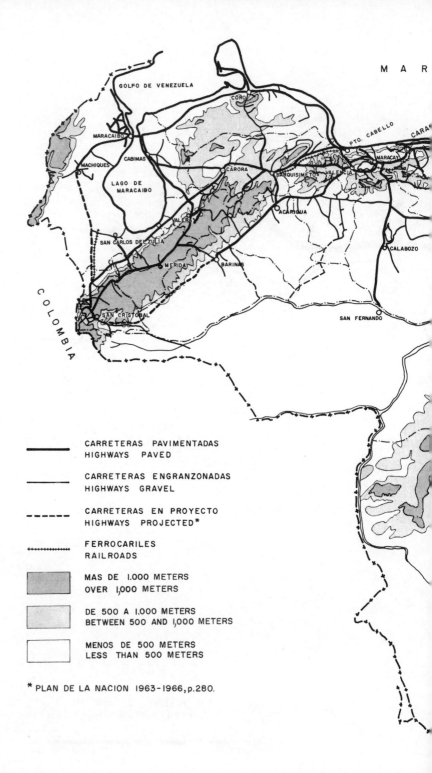

MAR

GOLFO DE VENEZUELA

CORO

PTO. CABELLO

CARA

MARACAIBO

CABIMAS

MARACAY

MACHIQUES

CARORA

BARQUISIMETO VALENCIA

LAGO DE
MARACAIBO

ACARIGUA

VALERA

SAN CARLOS DEL ZULIA

CALABOZO

MERIDA

BARINAS

C
O
L
O
M
B
I
A

SAN CRISTOBAL

SAN FERNANDO

━━━━━ CARRETERAS PAVIMENTADAS
        HIGHWAYS   PAVED

───── CARRETERAS ENGRANZONADAS
        HIGHWAYS   GRAVEL

─ ─ ─ CARRETERAS EN PROYECTO
        HIGHWAYS   PROJECTED*

+++++ FERROCARILES
        RAILROADS

        MAS DE 1.000 METERS
        OVER 1,000 METERS

        DE 500 A 1.000 METERS
        BETWEEN 500 AND 1,000 METERS

        MENOS DE 500 METERS
        LESS THAN 500 METERS

* PLAN DE LA NACION 1963-1966, p.280.

A R I B E

ISLA DE
MARGARITA

CARUPANO

CUMANA

PTO. LA CRUZ

MATURIN

EL TIGRE

SANTO TOME DE
GUAYANA

CIUDAD BOLIVAR

UPATA

EL CALLAO

G U A Y A N A
B R I T A N I C A

B R A S I L

MAP 6

PRINCIPAL ROAD SYSTEM 1963

0   200   400

KMS
OCTOBER 1962   SCALE 1/4,000,000

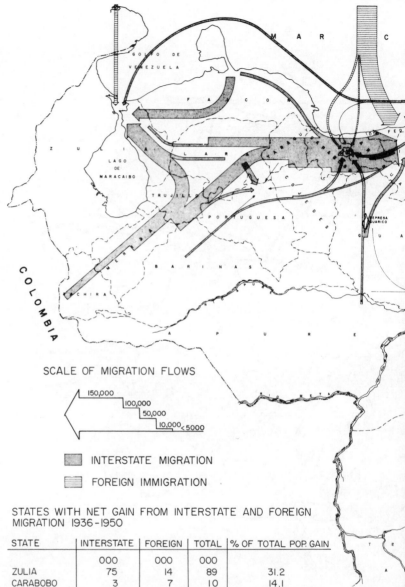

SCALE OF MIGRATION FLOWS

150,000
100,000
50,000
10,000 < 5000

▨ INTERSTATE MIGRATION

≣ FOREIGN IMMIGRATION

STATES WITH NET GAIN FROM INTERSTATE AND FOREIGN
MIGRATION 1936-1950

STATE	INTERSTATE	FOREIGN	TOTAL	% OF TOTAL POP. GAIN
	000	000	000	
ZULIA	75	14	89	31.2
CARABOBO	3	7	10	14.1
ARAGUA	10	5	15	25.0
DTO. FEDERAL	163	77	240	56.2
PORTUGUESA	20	2	22	44.0
ANZOATEGUI	38	7	45	40.2
MONAGAS	12	1	13	15.7

SOURCE: POPULATION CENSUS 1950

NOTE: MIGRANTS REPRESENT NUMBER OF NONLOCAL POPULATION
CLASSIFIED BY PLACE OF BIRTH, RESIDENT IN PRINCIPAL
RECEPTION AREAS IN 1950

B E

I B E

NUEVA
ESPARTA

ANZOA...

MONAGAS

CO

TERRITORIO
FEDERAL
DELTA
AMACURO

GUAYANA
BRITANICA

B   O   L   I   V   A   R

ITORIO

ONAS

BRASIL

MAP 7

APPARENT MIGRATORY
MOVEMENTS TO PRINCIPAL
RECEPTION AREAS UP TO 1950

0   200   400
KMS
OCTOBER 1962   SCALE 1/4,000,000

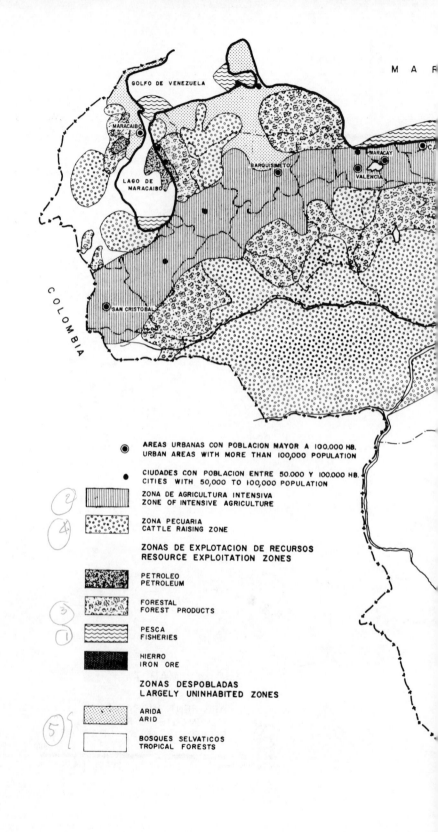

M A R

GOLFO DE VENEZUELA

MARACAIBO

LAGO DE
MARACAIBO

BARQUISIMETO

MARACAY

VALENCIA

CA

SAN CRISTOBAL

C O L O M B I A

⊙ AREAS URBANAS CON POBLACION MAYOR A 100.000 HB.
URBAN AREAS WITH MORE THAN 100,000 POPULATION

• CIUDADES CON POBLACION ENTRE 50.000 Y 100.000 HB.
CITIES WITH 50,000 TO 100,000 POPULATION

ZONA DE AGRICULTURA INTENSIVA
ZONE OF INTENSIVE AGRICULTURE

ZONA PECUARIA
CATTLE RAISING ZONE

ZONAS DE EXPLOTACION DE RECURSOS
RESOURCE EXPLOITATION ZONES

PETROLEO
PETROLEUM

FORESTAL
FOREST PRODUCTS

PESCA
FISHERIES

HIERRO
IRON ORE

ZONAS DESPOBLADAS
LARGELY UNINHABITED ZONES

ARIDA
ARID

BOSQUES SELVATICOS
TROPICAL FORESTS

C A R I B E

ISLA DE
MARGARITA

PENINSULA DE ARAYA
GOLFO DE CARIACO

BARCELONA

G U A Y A N A
B R I T A N I C A

B R A S I L

MAP 8

ECOLOGICAL ZONES
OF VENEZUELA

0   200   400
KMS
OCTOBER 1962   SCALE 1/4,000,000

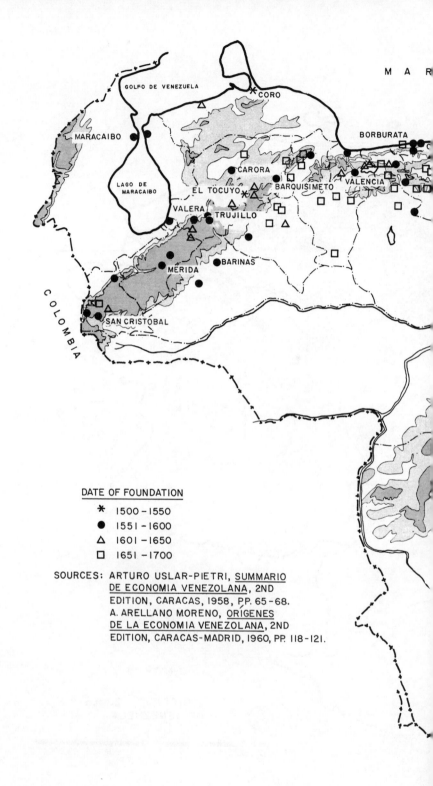

M A R

GOLFO DE VENEZUELA

�×CORO

BORBURATA

MARACAIBO

CARORA

VALENCIA

LAGO DE
MARACAIBO

EL TOCUYO

BARQUISIMETO

VALERA

TRUJILLO

MERIDA

BARINAS

C
O
L
O
M
B
I
A

SAN CRISTÓBAL

DATE OF FOUNDATION

✳	1500 – 1550
●	1551 – 1600
△	1601 – 1650
☐	1651 – 1700

SOURCES: ARTURO USLAR-PIETRI, SUMMARIO
DE ECONOMIA VENEZOLANA, 2ND
EDITION, CARACAS, 1958, PP. 65-68.
A. ARELLANO MORENO, ORÍGENES
DE LA ECONOMIA VENEZOLANA, 2ND
EDITION, CARACAS-MADRID, 1960, PP. 118-121.

C A R I B E

ISLA DE
MARGARITA

LA ASUNCIÓN

CUMANÁ
BARCELONA

SANTO TOMÁS
DE GUAYANA

G U A Y A N A
B R I T A N I C A

B R A S I L

MAP 9

FOUNDATION OF PRINCIPAL SETTLEMENTS,
16TH AND 17TH CENTURIES

KMS. 0   200   400

OCTOBER 1962   SCALE 1/4,000,000

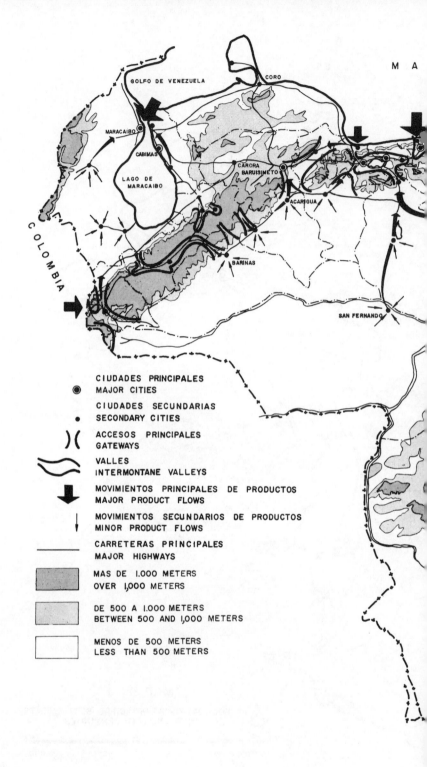

CIUDADES PRINCIPALES
MAJOR CITIES

CIUDADES SECUNDARIAS
SECONDARY CITIES

ACCESOS PRINCIPALES
GATEWAYS

VALLES
INTERMONTANE VALLEYS

MOVIMIENTOS PRINCIPALES DE PRODUCTOS
MAJOR PRODUCT FLOWS

MOVIMIENTOS SECUNDARIOS DE PRODUCTOS
MINOR PRODUCT FLOWS

CARRETERAS PRINCIPALES
MAJOR HIGHWAYS

MAS DE 1.000 METERS
OVER 1,000 METERS

DE 500 A 1.000 METERS
BETWEEN 500 AND 1,000 METERS

MENOS DE 500 METERS
LESS THAN 500 METERS

C A R I B E

ISLA DE
MARGARITA

CARUPANO

PTO. LA CRUZ

MATURIN

EL TIGRE

SANTO TOME
DE GUAYANA

CIUDAD BOLIVAR

G U A Y A N A
B R I T A N I C A

B R A S I L

MAP 10

TOPOGRAPHICAL DETERMINANTS
OF HUMAN SETTLEMENTS

0   200   400
KMS
OCTOBER 1962   SCALE 1/4,000,000

INTRODUCTION

Venezuela may in many ways be considered the perfect prototype for a study of regional policy. The spatial structure of its economy has a classical simplicity. Until recently, it was molded chiefly in the image of the center-periphery model. Political power, wealth, and population were heavily concentrated upon Caracas, while the periphery, excepting the oil regions, deteriorated out of mind of Venezuela's central decision makers.

This basic simplicity was undisturbed by political and cultural cleavages that in so many other countries (India, Canada, Nigeria) create a fierce antagonism among regions. Venezuela's government is a unitary one, and its twenty-three provinces have no independent political existence. Since they have only small resources of their own, they are unable to affect their economic welfare in any ways that are significant. To a large extent, local populations are still the creatures of central policy determination.

When Venezuela carried through its decisive social revolution in 1958, a democratic and progressive government initiated a system of national planning that quickly gained a high reputation throughout the continent. At about the same time, the government also launched an important program of regional development in Guayana. This experiment to build a new industrial city at the edge of the tropical forest set off a spate of interest in the location of new investments throughout the country. Increasingly, the government came under pressure to consider, in addition to national goals for economic growth, objectives for the spatial incidence of growth.

123

The attempt to examine some aspects of regional policy for Venezuela may be instructive for many countries similarly faced with the task of overcoming a center-periphery structure while maximizing their rate of economic expansion. In the course of this examination, it will become evident, I think, that the problem of regional development is in no sense more political than any other problem of public policy, and that decisions in this realm represent the usual admixture of intuition and objectively verified knowledge. It would be superfluous to mention all of this if it were not for the notion, widespread among economists, that intersectoral resource allocations follow a "scientific" methodology while interregional allocations must be resolved primarily on political grounds. This view is patently a myth. It probably derives from the economist's traditional preoccupation with highly aggregative models that have only a minimal degree of influence over what is finally decided. Regional policy, on the other hand, is concerned with *real* allocations on the ground. It is consequently very closely related to what people experience and inevitably involves a political reckoning. But so do all decisions that really matter. They need not, for that, become completely arbitrary. As I hope to show, the general principles developed in Part I can be successfully applied to a historical situation. There is a logic underlying the evolution of a space economy that, but for the high risk of failure, may not be violated.

The problem of a regional policy that is adequate for Venezuela's current phase of development will be approached in stages. I hope, among other things, to show how the evolution of the policy problem must inevitably influence a prescription for the future. In Chapter 6, the interplay between urbanization and national economic development is traced from the start of the colonial era. This is followed by an account of the emergence of regional development in Venezuela as a public policy issue and, in Chapter 8, of Guayana's role in this process. Major elements of regional policy are outlined in the next two chapters, with attention given to the selection of those metropolitan economies that may play a generative role as centers for economic

124

activity. In the final chapter, a number of basic problems of implementing a regional policy are taken up, and measures for building regional programming into a system of national planning are proposed.

CHAPTER SIX

URBANIZATION AND ECONOMIC DEVELOPMENT IN VENEZUELA[1]

The regional problem in Venezuela is bound up with the country's history of development and settlement. A snapshot of the space economy captures the patterns that have been frozen into the landscape as well as the dynamic processes of expansion, invasion, succession, decline, and atrophy that continuously gnaw at them. An historical approach to the study of regional order will therefore yield important information about those elements in the existing structure of locations that are viable and those that have become weak or redundant. This is vital knowledge for evolving sensible policies and programs for regional development. Historical spatial patterns display considerable inertia; they can be reformed only gradually, as increment is added upon increment.[2] In the short run, history appears largely to constrain the range of possible decisions. Only the cumulative result of many small changes may in retrospect be seen as having caused a "revolution." Thus to speak of history as a constraint is to attribute to the pattern of past changes a major role in shaping the future outcomes of decisions.

A useful approach to the study of regional development is by way of an investigation into the incremental changes in the pattern of activity locations. Unfortunately, little of the requisite data for such a study are available for Venezuela. I have therefore chosen to focus on population settlement as proxy. Demographic information is relatively abundant. Although parts of the 1961 census have not yet been published, the history of Venezuela's settlement can be sketched with rough accuracy. Urban growth, rural-urban migration, and the morphology of market

126

areas will be the principal variables in the discussion. They will be interpreted in light of changes in the structure, volume, and growth patterns of the national economy.

A start is made by presenting a model of economic change for Venezuela from pre-Columbian times onward, with estimates projected into the twenty-first century. The temerity of this undertaking is perhaps redeemed by its usefulness in clarifying some of the complexities of the structural transformation of space.

This discussion is followed by a detailed account of the urbanization process during recent decades and a review of the relevant data on interstate migration. Next, attention turns to an examination of the persistencies in the spatial structure of the economy, and this leads to an excursion into the early history of settlement in Venezuela, an analysis of the country's major ecological complexes, and a study of the topographic determinants of settlement. In conclusion, some hypotheses on the relation between urban structure and economic development are presented.

Stages of Economic Growth

Venezuela's economic history may be arranged sequentially into periods or stages that roughly correspond to the classification developed by W. W. Rostow (Table 6.1).[3] Each period will be characterized by its leading economic sector, beginning with the primitive subsistence agriculture practiced by the indigenous population prior to the Spanish conquest and ending with the "quaternary" service sector—comprising the communication and control services—more than half a millennium later.

The colonization of Venezuela began with a brief prelude of intensive mining activity. This lasted for scarcely a century. When early and exaggerated expectations about vast stores of precious metals were disappointed, the ephemeral extractive economy yielded to a more permanent settlement of the region by farmers and ranchers. The subsequent period of commercial agriculture lasted for approximately three hundred years: until about 1925, Rostow's concept of the "traditional society" can be

127

Table 6.1. Stages of Economic Growth in Venezuela

Leading Economic Sectors	Corresponding Rostow "Stage"	Approximate Dates	Total Population (millions)	Per Cent of Population		Per Cent of Active Population by Sector of Employment			
				rural	urban	primary	secondary	tertiary	quaternary
1a. Hunting, fishing, subsistence farming (Indian)	—	pre-1500	?	100	—	100	—	—	—
1b. Mining (gold, silver, copper, pearls)	Traditional society	1500–1600	?	?	?	?	?	?	?
1c. Commercial agriculture (sugar, tobacco, hides, cacao, coffee)		1600– 1920–1925	2.8	85	15	75	10	13	2
2. Oil	Preconditions for "takeoff"	1920–1925 1945–1950	5.0	60	40	45	18	31	6
3. Consumer goods (import substitution) industries; creation of a heavy industrial base (steel, petrochemicals, electric power); automobile manufacture and assembly	"Takeoff"	1945–1950 1965–1970	10.0	40	60	30	20	40	10
4. Manufacturing industries for export (producer goods; consumer durables)	Drive to maturity	1965–1970 1990–2000	20.0	30	70	25	25	35	15
5. Quaternary services	Mass consumption	1990–2000	50.0	5	95	10	20	45	25

Sources:

General: (1) For colonial era up to the 19th century, A. Arellano Moreno, Orígenes de la Economía Venezolana (Caracas-Madrid: Edime, 1960); (2) for the 19th and 20th centuries, Edwin Lieuwen, Venezuela (Oxford, Oxford University Press, 1961), IBRD, The Economic Development of Venezuela (Baltimore, Md.: The Johns Hopkins University Press, 1961), and "Economic Development in Venezuela in the 1950's," United Nations, Economic Bulletin for Latin America, Vol. V, No. 1 (March 1960); (3) On the stage theory of growth, W. W. Rostow, The Stages of Economic Growth (Cambridge: Cambridge University Press, 1961).

Specific: (1) Population: National Censuses for 1926, 1950, and 1961: values are given for the end of each period; for the final period (Stage 5), approximate terminal values are given; (2) Urban-rural distribution: all places with 5,000 or more inhabitants were defined as "urban," the remainder of the population as "rural"; estimates of urban population for 1965–1970 and beyond refer to total population living in urban and metropolitan areas; (3) Employment: 1920–1925, estimated; 1945–1950, Banco Central de Venezuela, Cuentas Nacionales, 1959; 1965–1970 and beyond, estimates based on information for 1959, Banco Central de Venezuela, Cuentas Nacionales, 1959.

Note: No sectoral breakdown for "quaternary" employment is available, and all figures shown are rough guesses of magnitude. This sector includes control and communication services, such as research, analysis, planning, decision making, finance, administration, education, and the mass media, all requiring a high level of professional education. The tertiary sector includes only trade in the sense of direct sales, maintenance and personal services, and transportation. Urban employment is counted here as part of the tertiary sector. Cf. Jean Gottmann, Megalopolis: The Urbanized Northeastern Seaboard of the United States (New York: Twentieth applied with considerable justification.[4] During the whole of this period, the technology of the predominant agricultural sector was essentially premodern. Productivity was low, and output fluctuated often violently, so that a cumulative growth process could not be sustained. Political power was in the hands of a small group of wealthy landowners, and their strength in national politics rested chiefly on regional loyalties: national unity in any effective sense was lacking.

By 1925, although the oil "boom" had already begun, Venezuela was still a rather small country, sparsely settled, and given over almost entirely to an agrarian way of life. Table 6.1 draws an abbreviated statistical profile: scarcely three million people—of whom roughly half were children—lived in an area half the size of western Europe. They were settled predominantly in small towns and isolated farmsteads; cities existed chiefly for the sake of regional commerce and administration. The manufacturing sector was still dominated by rudimentary handicrafts; and the superstructure of services did not exceed the minimum required for continued viability of the economy. Politically, Venezuela was a dictatorship. As one historian has put it, Juan Vicente Gómez presided over the nation as though it were "the private preserve of his own family and the army."[5]

The historical turning point occurred shortly after World War I, marked by the incipient commercialization of the country's wealth in petroleum by major European and American companies. The next twenty to twenty-five years covered a period that led to the establishment of what Rostow has called the preconditions for a subsequent takeoff into cumulative economic growth. The new affluence was based on oil, and prolonged and intimate contact with countries of the world metropolis "shocked the traditional society and began or hastened its undoing. . . ."[6] Population jumped by 70 per cent; cities grew from about 400,000 to two million inhabitants. While agriculture sharply declined as the nation turned its eyes to be spellbound by the miracle of oil, city populations "exploded," above all in Caracas where much of the new wealth was both invested and consumed. During this time, the government gave small thought to productive sectors other than oil, and if the cities flourished, it was less for the jobs they provided than for the lavish spending of the central government on public works. The service sector expanded rapidly, but so did unemployment, which by mid-century had risen to one tenth of the available work force in the country. If wealth had been distributed unequally prior to the oil period, the extremes in income levels now attained politically dangerous dimensions.[7] The elite of oil workers was indeed well provided for, but it made up less than 1 per cent of the total labor force. Most of those who remained on the farms as well as many who had drifted to the cities, barely managed to survive. Social injustice on an intolerable scale, coupled with the rise of the urban middle sectors, created a powerful political reform movement that made industrial diversification and agrarian reform central to its aims. When this movement finally prevailed, Venezuela was already well into the third stage of economic growth.

This period had its inception toward the end of the nineteen-forties. In referring to it as the "takeoff" stage in Rostow's sense, three comments are in order. First, the transition from the preceding stage was a gradual one: modern manufacturing industry had begun to be established somewhat earlier. The only really abrupt transition in Venezuela's economic and social history coincided with the beginnings of large-scale commercial exploitation of the country's vast petroleum reserves. All other stages are, by contrast, uncertain points of reference along a transitional path that is projected to last for about seventy-five years. Second, the bulk of the nation's output is still in petroleum, though emphasis has shifted to manufacturing as the leading sector. Third, use of Rostow's metaphorical terminology should not be interpreted to mean that economic growth henceforward may be regarded as inevitable. Continued economic progress is not so much a matter of rational choice as of political good fortune. Ultimately, Venezuela's destiny will be determined not by an act of the will but by exogenous events that are beyond the ability of any but the largest and most powerful nations in the world to influence decisively.

With these important caveats in mind, the situation during

the fifties and sixties appears to fit Rostow's criteria for the "takeoff" reasonably well.[8] A rate of net savings well in excess of 10 per cent was maintained; diversification into new industrial sectors occurred; a political group came to power that was "prepared to regard the modernization of the economy as serious, high-priority business";[9] and central economic planning was for the first time effectively applied at the national level.

Venezuela will have accomplished a remarkable transformation during this period.[10] Manufacturing activity has already begun to shift from import-substitution of consumer goods to heavy metals and industrial chemicals. Exports are increasingly in manufactured goods. At the same time, service employment and unemployment is projected to rise from a little over one third in 1950 to approximately one half of the country's labor force twenty years later. Because of large gains in productivity, manufacturing is unable to absorb but a small fraction of the additional increments to the urban labor force.

The remaining two stages—the "drive to maturity" and the age of "mass consumption"—lie still within the realm of speculation.[11] In any event, the transition from one stage to the next will scarcely be noticed. Period four will be led by an expansion of manufacturing for export, whereas the final stage will probably be given its basic impulses for further expansion by an autonomous growth (and improvement in the quality) of the service complex that includes education, research, information, management, planning, and finance. The results of this final period cannot as yet be foreseen, nor, for that matter, can it be determined whether a sixth stage might not lie beyond the era of "mass consumption." Certain "terminal" values, however, may suggest the type of society that current developments foreshadow: a population roughly equivalent to that of any of the great countries of Western Europe today—Great Britain, Germany, France; total urbanization in the sense of a spread of urban values; a reduction of agricultural and mining employment to 10 per cent or less; an increase of tertiary and quaternary services to about 70 per cent; and a decline of manufacturing employment to perhaps 20 per cent of the labor force.

131

Shifts in the Pattern of Settlement

To map out the changes that occurred in the structure of the space economy, paralleling Venezuela's forward movement to industrialism, I shall confine myself to the quarter century from 1936 to 1961. Three national censuses were taken during this period; the earlier census of 1926, unfortunately, does not contain sufficient data for a full-scale comparison. The first census period relevant for our purposes covers a good part of the "preconditions" stage of economic growth (1936–1950), while eleven years (1950–1961) are available for analysis of the period coincident with the "takeoff." Since key data can be readily projected backward and forward in time by at least a decade, an approximate reading can be obtained of the spatial shifts that occurred during the whole of the preconditions and takeoff stages as shown in Table 6.1.

This was the period of Venezuela's great urban revolution, a revolution that swept over much of South America at the same time.[12] In 1926, Venezuela's urban population had been about 400,000. During the thirty-five years following, it leaped forward by a factor of 10, while total population, though growing at one of the highest rates in the world, increased only two and a half times. Dozens of settlements, both new and old, grew to urban size by the definition employed in this study, while rural population experienced a sharp relative decline (Tables 6.2 and 6.3).

Table 6.2   Urbanization in Venezuela, 1936, 1950, and 1961 (*in thousands*)

	1936	1950	1961
Total population	3,364	5,035	7,524
Cities with 5000+ population	743	2,121	4,333
Per Cent	22.1	42.1	57.6
Nonurban population	2,621	2,914	3,191
Per Cent	77.9	57.9	42.4
Per Cent of total population in cities of			
25,000 or more	12.7	32.6	44.3
100,000 or more	9.3	20.6	25.4

Source: 8th and 9th National Censuses, 1950 and 1961.

132

Table 6.3. Urban Population and Numbers of Cities, by
Size, 1936, 1950, and 1961

Size (thousands)	1936		1950		1961	
	per cent of urban population	number of cities	per cent of urban population	number of cities	per cent of urban population	number of cities
5–10	22.5	18	13.2	40	8.2	51
10–25	19.9	11	13.6	22	14.7	42
25–50	15.5	3	18.0	14	13.8	16
50–100	0	0	15.8	3	19.0	12
100–250	42.1	2	16.1	2	16.4	5
250–500	0°	0	23.3	1	9.7	1
500–750	0	0	0°	0	0	0
750–1000	0	0	0	0	18.2	1
1000 and over	0	0	0	0	0°	0
Total Urban	100.0	34	100.0	82	100.0	128

Source: 8th and 9th National Censuses, 1950 and 1961.
°Population of the Caracas Metropolitan Area:

Year	Official	Including Maiquetía and La Guaira
1936	259,000	282,000
1950	694,000	748,000
1961	1,336,000	1,433,000

By 1961, 4.3 million Venezuelans, nearly 60 per cent of the total population, were living in 128 cities throughout the country.[13] Most of them (56 per cent) still resided in small cities of less than 100,000 inhabitants, but the numerical advantage of smallness was scarcely decisive; the long-term trend was toward a gradual convergence of the country's population upon the larger urban centers (Table 6.3).

During the period of traditional society, Venezuela's cities had been few, scattered, and small. Although the urbanization process was already well under way by 1936, Map 2 may give a sense of what the situation must have been a decade earlier, when Caracas was the country's largest city with scarcely 100,000 inhabitants.

At the time, the East Central States had already begun to assert themselves as the dominant center of urban population, initiating a trend that will almost certainly culminate in a tight intermetropolitan network extending from Valencia to Caracas.[14] Maracaibo was several days' journey away, a distant provincial capital that already in 1926 was the country's second-largest city with about 75,000 inhabitants. In the Andean Region, a number of small cities had been able to maintain themselves over the centuries as local trade centers. Of these, only San Cristóbal had attained significant size. In the East, finally, only Cumaná and Ciudad Bolívar were able to project an image of more than local importance. In sum, but for a certain cohesiveness of structure at the center, Venezuela at the beginning of the oil period consisted of a number of town-centered regional economies that had little commerce with each other and could be governed from the center only with difficulty.

This situation is reflected in the location of the larger seaports, including Maracaibo, Puerto Cabello, La Guaira, and Guanta. Extended along the Caribbean coast on an east-west axis, each concentrated upon itself a hinterland with, generally, a north-south orientation. Data for the early years are unavailable, but traces of this feature still survive (Map 5). A national transport system that would articulate the east-west grain of the country's settlement geography and consequently lead to greater urban and regional interdependency did not take shape until the early 1930's.

This, roughly, was the situation at the beginning of the period that formed the "preconditions" for sustained economic growth. By its end in mid-century, dramatic changes in the pattern of settlement could be observed (Map 3).

Emergence of Caracas as the national metropolis. The population of Caracas had risen phenomenally from 92,000 in 1920 to 495,000 in 1950, with total population of the Metropolitan Area reaching 700,000 during the latter year. The principal reason for this was the concentration of the oil wealth in the form of government revenues at the capital and the government's largesse in making splendid improvements in the city's physical appearance. In the span of only thirty years, Caracas was transformed from a sleepy colonial town into a futuristic metropolis.

Movement to the new oil regions. The oil-producing regions failed to share in the wealth extracted from their soils. Nevertheless, there were jobs to be had, and intensive exploration activity resulted in fairly large local expenditures by the oil corporations. As a result, Zulia and Anzoátegui (to a lesser extent also Guárico and Monagas) became the target for a large inflow of population from adjoining regions. Most of this migration came to be concentrated in a few cities. Maracaibo had attained a size of 235,000 by 1950 and a string of nondescript oil towns had grown up along the eastern shore of the lake: Cabimas, Lagunillas, Tia Juana, and so on. To the east, oil explorations led to the founding of new cities at Puerto la Cruz, Cantaura, and El Tigre, as well as to expansion of older centers, such as Maturín.

Descent from the mountains into the plains. The new wealth of the country brought many farm people to the country's principal metropolitan centers. Population pressure relative to arable land was so great, however, that other outlets had to be found. Between 1936 and 1950, the southeastern piedmont was rapidly colonized, and a number of earlier settlements grew to urban size in serving the expanding farm population in their surroundings. Chief among these were the twin localities of Acarigua and Araure with a combined population of 22,000 in 1950.

Intensification of agriculture in existing farm areas. The simultaneous increase in total and urban populations created a great demand for the products of agriculture. This led to intensification of farming in the Central States, especially in Lara, Yaracuy, Carabobo, and Aragua, where several new towns sprung up as rural service centers.

Barquisimeto benefited most from these developments. Its fivefold expansion from 23,000 in 1926 to 105,000 in 1950 can be ascribed to its central location in a relatively prosperous and growing farming area (Yaracuy Valley, Portuguesa), its midway position on the increasingly traveled route between Caracas and Maracaibo, its function as a traffic distributor to some of the principal regions of the country, and its physical proximity to the Andean Region, an area of heavy emigration.

Satisfactory functional integration of the national space economy was not achieved by 1950, but a beginning had been made. The several regions of the country were coming to be linked with each other and especially with the nation's capital. At the same time, as the interurban grid of highways took shape, the basic east-west structure of the country became accentuated. With the passing of time, this structure would become even more firmly ingrained. Caracas' central location in this structure is to be noted: once the basic road grid had been laid down, the city was the logical choice for the seat of government as well as cultural and business leadership. Eventually, all roads converged upon the national metropolis and contributed to its splendor.

The period of incipient industrialization came about partly in response to the external shock of World War II, but even more in consequence of the dynamics of growth in the country itself. The spatial impact of this period of rapid economic change remains to be analyzed.

The first point to be noted is that the structural pattern of cities that had begun to emerge by 1950 continued to be forcefully expressed. Most of the older cities, with some significant exceptions, about doubled in size between 1950 and 1961, maintaining annual growth rates of 7 to 9 per cent (Table 6.4).

Caracas' gain does not especially stand out in comparison with other cities. Its increase, equivalent to nearly 30 per cent of the

Table 6.4. Typical City Expansions, 1950–1961
(*in thousands*)

	1950	1961	Percentage Gain
Maracaibo	235	421	79.1
Cabimas	42	93	121.4
San Carlos del Zulia	7	14	100.0
San Cristóbal	54	99	83.3
Barquisimeto	105	200	90.5
Valencia	89	164	84.3
Maracay	64	135	110.9
Caracas Metropolitan Area	694	1,336	92.5
Acarigua	16	31	93.7
San Juan de los Morros	14	37	164.2
Puerto la Cruz	28	59	110.7
Maturín	25	54	116.0
Ciudad Bolívar	31	64	106.4

Table 6.5. Distribution of Urban Population by
Groups of States, 1936, 1950, 1961
(*in thousands*)

Groups of States	1936		1950		1961	
	number	per cent	number	per cent	number	per cent
Western Oil	145	19.5	379	17.9	801	18.5
Mountain	50	6.7	159	7.5	297	6.9
West Central	63	8.5	155	7.3	321	7.4
East Central	382	51.4	1,012	47.7	2,046	47.2
Llanos	8	1.1	115	5.4	256	5.9
Eastern Oil	17	2.3	143	6.7	319	7.4
East Coastal	57	7.7	112	5.3	160	3.6
Guayana	21	2.8	46	2.2	133	3.1
Total Venezuela	743	100.0	2,121	100.0	4,333	100.0

Sources: 8th and 9th National Censuses, 1950 and 1961.

national gain in population between 1950 and 1961, was no more than proportional to its size. In fact, the remarkable thing about urban growth during this period is its ubiquity: nearly all parts of the country shared in it to some extent, the principal exceptions being the East Coastal States of Sucre and Nueva Esparta.

Examination of the data for 1936 and 1961 shows that even states with heavy outmigration experienced high urban growth rates (Tables 6.5 and 6.6). The Center clearly gained at the expense of the Mountain, West Central, and East Coastal States, with the oil regions barely maintaining their relative position. Over the eleven years under study, the four East Central States alone accounted for over 40 per cent of the total population increase in the country.

But this tendency for demographic concentration in the Center was balanced by high rates of urban growth elsewhere, as the excess of rural population streamed everywhere to the cities. Table 6.6 shows the extent to which regional differences in the index of urban concentration became attenuated over the years.

During the decade of the fifties, forty-six places attained urban status (Map 4). One important clustering of these "new" cities appeared in the vicinity of Maracaibo as a direct conse-

Table 6.6. Index of Urban Concentration by
Groups of States, 1936, 1950, 1961°

Groups of States	1936	1950	1961
Western Oil	1.33	1.10	1.11
Mountain	0.35	0.48	0.52
Western Central	0.69	0.74	0.84
East Central	2.16	1.69	1.45
Llanos	0.10	0.54	0.57
Eastern Oil	0.35	0.81	0.88
East Coastal	0.77	0.65	0.55
Guayana	0.90	0.65	0.91

°The index of concentration is calculated by dividing the share that the region's total population represents in the nation into the share that the region's total urban population represents in the nation. An index of 1.0, therefore, means that the region has proportionately the same concentration of urban population relative to the nation as it has of total population.

quence of continued oil explorations there. The two "new" cities on the Paraguaná Peninsula (state of Falcón) were also related to the expanding oil industry, which had important refining facilities there. A second cluster of cities occurred in the vicinity of Caracas, as a sign of the physical expansion of this great metropolis. And finally, some 450 miles to the southeast, the country's third major industrial center was under construction at Santo Tomé de Guayana. By 1964, this dynamic urban nucleus had more than 60,000 inhabitants and was growing at an annual rate of 20 per cent.

The dramatic urbanization of the Central Region, 84 per cent of whose population was classified as urban at the time of the last census, resulted from a conjunction of several circumstances.

Central position. The region from Caracas to Valencia is centrally located: any part of Venezuela lies within 500 miles as measured over the existing road system from any point along the Caracas-Valencia axis. From this it follows, given the high concentration of population and income in the region, that a national market can be served most efficiently out of this central location. During the late forties and fifties, the bulk of the country's manufacturing industry did, in fact, choose this location.

Seat of the national government. Venezuela's traditional system of unitary government proved to be of exceptional advantage for the further growth of the central region. Not only did public investments almost continuously favor the central area, particularly Caracas, but many private entrepreneurs found proximity to government offices a decisive factor in location decisions.[15] A cumulative growth cycle was thus set in motion. Government expenditures, location of commercial and industrial enterprise, foreign immigration, and expansion of the banking system created a pattern of economic and social linkages that with each passing day became more attractive to potential investors. A start was made with the creation of a mass market for the tastes of a metropolitan society. More than one half of the national consumer market was, in fact, developed at the Center: outlying provinces shared to only a limited degree in national progress.[16]

Traditional entrepreneurship in Valencia. The industrial expansion of Caracas—physically constrained as it was by the topography of the city's site—eventually spilled over into adjacent regions. When industrial land in the city itself became scarce, the cities of the Valencia Basin began to compete effectively with the capital. They not only had the land but also a tradition of enterprise and the necessary surplus of wealth and family connections to take the lead in bringing manufacturing industries to their areas. Today, the Valencia Basin and its adjacent coastal areas have become a serious industrial rival of Caracas and are able to display one of the best organized promotional programs in the country.[17] A toll road linking the basin with Caracas is forging strong linkages among all of the cities in the East Central States, none of which is now further than two hours' driving distance (four hours by truck) from the hub of national power.

The takeoff then has clearly been marked by the upsurge of industry: basic metals in Guayana, petrochemicals at Morón, consumption goods and automobiles at Valencia. Oil explorations had slowed down as foreign companies shifted drilling activities to more promising areas outside of Venezuela. Oil still dominated the economy by the early sixties but was ceasing to be the main driving force in economic growth. By the end of the takeoff period in Venezuela's economic development, this shift from

139

one leading sector to another will have led to a patterning of the space economy that may be characterized by

1. the creation of major industrial areas in the Valencia-Maracay urban region, the Caracas Metropolitan Area, and at Santo Tomé de Guayana;

2. the emergence of a rapidly growing and highly urbanized Center or *core region* simultaneously with the actual or threatened relative decline of a periphery that includes the traditional oil-producing areas in addition to the Mountain, West Central, and East Coastal States (Map 3);

3. the development of a national hierarchy of central places with respect to tertiary functions, showing an increasing degree of interdependency in the structure of market areas (Map 5); and

4. the completion of an efficient nationwide network of transport linkages (Map 6) that will facilitate the complete integration of the national space economy during the period of industrial maturation.

The Direction of Interstate Migration

The structural transformation discussed in the preceding section was accompanied by large-scale internal migration and by a considerable influx of foreign populations. Data for the most recent decade are not as yet available, but an analysis of interstate migration during the first part of the "preconditions" period, from 1936–1950, is nonetheless instructive. A summary of findings is given in Table 6.7 and Map 7, and in the analysis below.

Magnitude of internal migration. Between 1936 and 1950, more than half a million people had changed their residence from one state to another.[18] This corresponded to more than one fifth of Venezuela's total population at the beginning of the period.[19] In the chief inmigration areas, the gains were remarkable. Of Portuguesa's population increase during this period, 40 per cent was from interstate migration, the corresponding ratio in the Federal District was 38 per cent (and

Table 6.7. Internal and Foreign Migration, Venezuela, 1936–1950
(*in thousands*)

Province and Region	Out-migration (1)	In-migration (2)	Net Internal Migration (3)	For-eign Immigration (4)	Total (3 & 4) (5)	OM₁ (6)	TM₁ (7)
Western Oil States	57	95	38	17	55	11.6	11.2
Zulia	15	90	75	14	89	5.4	25.7
Falcón	42	5	−37	3	−34	−20.0	−15.0
Mountain States	119	17	−102	16	−86	18.6	−13.5
Táchira	32	7	−25	13	−12	14.8	−4.8
Mérida	32	4	−28	1	−27	17.8	−13.9
Trujillo	55	6	−49	2	−47	22.6	−17.8
West Central States	76	14	−62	6	−56	18.3	−13.5
Lara	48	12	−36	4	−32	16.4	−9.6
Yaracuy	28	2	−26	2	−24	22.5	−18.8
East Central States	112	274	161	106	268	14.0	33.5
Carabobo	21	24	3	7	10	12.2	4.1
Aragua	18	28	10	5	15	13.8	10.8
Miranda	45	30	−15	17	2	20.8	0.8
Federal District	28	192	164	77	241	9.8	63.1
Llanos	45	43	−2	8	6	12.7	1.7
Barinas	7	7	0	1	1	12.5	1.5
Portuguesa	4	24	20	2	22	5.5	18.0
Cojedes	7	1	−6	1	−5	14.5	−10.0
Apure	11	2	−9	2	−7	18.9	−9.8
Guárico	16	9	−7	2	−5	13.3	−3.7
Eastern Oil States	29	79	50	8	58	13.0	26.1
Anzoátegui	11	49	38	7	45	8.4	28.8
Monagas	18	30	12	1	13	19.3	10.5
East Coastal States	69	2	−67	1	−66	20.6	−19.7
Sucre	55	0	−55	1	−54	21.3	−18.2
Nueva Esparta	14	2	−12	0	−12	19.1	−17.3
Guayana	25	8	−17	3	−14	23.8	−13.3
Bolívar	18	7	−11	1	−10	21.6	−10.6
T.F. Delta Amacuro	6	1	−5	1	−4	30.0	−14.2
T.F. Amazonas	1	0	−1	1	0	50.0	0
VENEZUELA	532	532	0	165	165	22.5	4.9

Source: 8th National Census, 1950.

$$OM_1 = \frac{\text{outmigration 1936–1950}}{\text{population 1936}}$$

$$TM_1 = \frac{\text{total migration 1936–1950}}{\text{population 1936}}$$

141

47 per cent if only indigenous growth is taken as a base). In Anzoátegui one third and in Zulia one fourth of the total gain was from migration. These focal areas of economic activity grew at the expense of other regions; they acted as magnets, concentrating population upon themselves.

Increase in mobility. Whereas only 11 per cent of Venezuela's population resided outside of the state where it was born in 1936, 18 per cent did so by 1950.[20] Mobility has undoubtedly increased since then. In general, the available data support a widely shared impression that the people of Venezuela are not strongly attached to place but respond readily to the appearance of economic opportunities wherever they occur. This basic conclusion, however, needs to be modified in several respects. First, the movement to some of the principal growth points may have been due to the promise of better living conditions as much as to the objective existence of opportunities for employment. This is clearly borne out by estimates of unemployment that during the economic crisis in 1959 reached a high of 20 per cent in Caracas alone, and still continues to be high.[21] Second, the main stream of migration to a center of inmigration occurred invariably from adjacent or at least from nearby states (see Map 7). For instance, 86 per cent of Zulia's out-of-state population in 1950 had been born in the three Mountain and two West Central States; in Monagas, four neighboring states accounted for 93 per cent of out-of-state population; in Anzoátegui, the ratio was 90 per cent from six contiguous states; and in Portuguesa, the ratio was 88 per cent from four contiguous states. Even the Federal District, which traditionally receives population from all parts of the nation, obtained 54 per cent of its nonlocal population from only six states lying within a radius of about 200 miles.[22] Third, the "intervening opportunity" of Caracas, given the central location of the city and the basic linear structure of Venezuela's settlement pattern, effectively prevented significant east-west movements of the population.[23] Oil developments in Zulia, for instance, attracted chiefly westerners; those in Anzoátegui and Monagas, chiefly easterners. The only significant exception to this pattern is Nueva Esparta (Island of Margarita), whose people—mostly fishermen—

have long been known for their sea-migrations along the whole of the Caribbean coast.

Foreign immigration and its incidence. Venezuela gained 165,000 immigrants of foreign birth during the period 1936 to 1950 and as many again during the following decade. Nearly 60 per cent of the foreigners came to live in the Federal District and in those portions of the Caracas Metropolitan Area which extend into Miranda.

Direction of interstate migration. Many states lost the equivalent of a rather substantial portion of their population to the principal inmigration centers (Table 7). The index OM, which measures outmigration as a percentage of total population in the initial year, stood between 19 and 24 per cent for the Mountain, West Central, and East States, as well as for Guayana. With the exception of the last named region whose economic and demographic fortunes have in recent years been reversed, these regions have undoubtedly remained heavy losers of population during the decade of the fifties.

Data for the chief centers of inmigration are presented in Table 6.8.

The importance of the oil explorations, the movement from the mountains into the plains, and the rising importance of the Valencia Basin are all reflected in these figures.

Patterns of Structural Persistence

The structural transformation of space is molded by underlying patterns of stability that tend to change only gradually

Table 6.8. Net Gains from Migration, 1936–1950

	Internal Migration	Foreign Migration	Total
Federal District	164,000	77,000	241,000
Zulia	75,000	14,000	89,000
Anzoátegui	38,000	7,000	45,000
Portuguesa	20,000	2,000	22,000
Monagas	12,000	1,000	13,000
Aragua	10,000	5,000	15,000
Carabobo	3,000	7,000	10,000

Source: 8th National Census, 1950.

and over relatively long periods of time. Discovery of spatial persistencies follows upon a change in the scale of observation. The focus so far has been mainly on the details of structure; it will now be necessary to look beyond this detail to the basic scaffolding. Two major configurations can be discerned: the pattern formed by major ecological complexes and the hierarchy of cities. Each will be examined in turn.

Basic Pattern I: Ecological Complexes. The present order of ecological complexes—a series of five roughly parallel bands extending from east to west—was laid down during the sixteenth, and seventeenth centuries. In a general way, these complexes correspond to the outstanding physiographic features of the country (Map 8).

Each complex may be identified by its dominant activity: (1) offshore fisheries, (2) intensive agriculture, (3) forest products, and (4) cattle raising. A final complex (5) includes the largely uninhabited and arid regions of Falcón and the tropical forests of Zulia and Guayana. Soil, climate, topography, and relative location contributed to establish the characteristic activity of each complex. These natural conditions were sufficiently strong to imprint a pattern on the landscape that would survive five centuries of colonization and development.[24]

This proposition can be supported by data summarized on Map 9 which shows the location of early settlements in Venezuela. The first phase, lasting until 1550, saw the founding of a handful of rather haphazardly located towns. None of them would ever play more than a peripheral and local role in the nation's development history.

On the east coast, three cities were started during the first half of the sixteenth century, chiefly as a base to exploit the local pearl fisheries. Cubagua was destroyed after a few decades by an earthquake and was never rebuilt. La Asunción on the island of Margarita lost out to the more favorably situated neighboring town of Porlamar. Of the three, only Cumaná achieved some distinction as the capital of the state of Sucre. Its potentialities for expansion were limited, however, and 540 years after the initial settlement was founded, the city still had only 70,000 inhabitants, many of whom were housed in shantytowns on the swamp-infested outskirts. Further to the west, two more coastal settlements appeared. The hill town of Borburata, however, was soon overtaken by Puerto Cabello, which was situated directly on the coast. And Coro, although it continues today as a provincial capital, would have been reduced to a very minor role, indeed, had it not been for the decision, about 1950, to build an oil refinery on the Paraguaná Peninsula nearby. Construction of this refinery helped to revitalize the community which long before had ceased to perform its role as a significant commercial entrepôt. The last of the early cities, El Tocuyo, was the only inland settlement and important initially as the principal staging area for the further conquest of the country. Its site, however, was poorly chosen, and the center of gravity soon shifted to the more advantageously situated city of Barquisimeto.

The second and decisive settlement phase lasted from 1550 to about 1600. During this interval, some of the most important of Venezuelan settlements were founded, cities which worked themselves to the top of the urban hierarchy and there remained: Caracas, Maracaibo, Barquisimeto, Valencia, San Cristóbal, Valera, Mérida, Puerto Cabello. Even tiny Santo Tomás de Guayana was counted among them. Though it had lingered for a long time on the edge of civilization, it is now, under a slightly changed name, on the way to becoming one of the country's leading industrial cities.

Most of these towns were established either as ports or as mining communities. But they also served as administrative centers and were used as instruments of colonization. Established by political authority as subcenters of administrative control, they were bases from which to take possession of the land.[25] Their strategic location aided in the development of centralizing functions. Until the beginning of the nineteen-twenties, however, most of them remained rather small and isolated from one another. Their primary influence was local, extending over the political, legal, and religious realm, while the country's wealth was controlled by the landed gentry who lived on their estates and came to town only infrequently. Except for Santo Tomás de Guayana, all new cities were founded in the western

145

half of the country, and the majority of the cities—ports excepted—were situated in the mountains. The dense population in the mountain regions today had its inception during the sixteenth century and even before then, in the pattern of preconquest Indian settlement.

Occupancy of the mountain regions was greatly accelerated during the seventeenth century. The great adventure of mining for silver and gold had proved largely ephemeral, and interest soon turned to agriculture and to the export of such crops as sugar, cotton, tobacco, and cacao. The richest agricultural soils were sought out, and new towns were created at the principal points of access. This period saw the conquest and settlement of the Yaracuy Basin (San Felipe, Chivacoa); the Valencia Basin (Maracay); the Upper Llanos (Acarigua, Araure, San Juan de los Morros); and the fertile valleys on the eastern coastal range. Most of the new towns never grew to be more than local service centers, however, and remained tributary to the larger cities established scarcely a century earlier. In any event, by the time the seventeenth century was drawing to a close, the basic outlines of the effectively occupied space of Venezuela had emerged.

Basic Pattern II: The Urban Hierarchy. The concept of an urban hierarchy is meaningful only when applied to a system of cities.[26] In Venezuela, systemic interrelations among urban centers on a national scale probably did not occur until the start of the period of tooling up for sustained economic growth. Since 1926, however, the four top cities of the hierarchy have remained dominant despite the many changes that had occurred in the intervening years. With somewhat more qualification—because of changes in rank order—one can point to the fact that of the first ten cities in 1926, nine were still on the list by 1961. However one chooses to read this hierarchy, one cannot fail but be impressed by the remarkable stability in the general order of relative dominance of cities (Table 6.9).

Greater mobility could be observed in the lower ranks, but in view of the large number of cities of middling to small size, this is well within the range of normal expectation.

This stability of the urban hierarchy should not be construed

146

Table 6.9. Rank Order of Cities, 1926, 1936,
1950, and 1961

Rank	Cities			
	1926	1936	1950	1961
1	Caracas, M.A.	Caracas, M.A.	Caracas, M.A.	Caracas, M.A.
2	Maracaibo	Maracaibo	Maracaibo	Maracaibo
3	Valencia	Valencia	Barquisimeto	Barquisimeto
4	Barquisimeto	Barquisimeto	Valencia	Valencia
5	C. Bolívar	Maracay	Maracay	Maracay
6	Cumaná	S. Cristóbal	S. Cristóbal	S. Cristóbal
7	S. Cristóbal	Cumaná	Cumaná	Cabimas
8	Maiquetía	C. Bolívar	Cabimas	Maiquetía
9	Coro	Pto Cabello	Maiquetía	Cumaná
10	Maracay	Cabimas	Pto Cabello	C. Bolívar

Rank	Population (in thousands)			
	1926	1936	1950	1961
1	168	259	694	1336
2	75	110	236	422
3	37	49	105	200
4	23	36	89	164
5	23	30	64	135
6	19	22	54	99
7	15	22	46	93
8	12	21	42	76
9	11	21	38	70
10	11	19	34	64

Sources: 5th, 8th, and 9th National Censuses.

as a statistical oddity, a somehow curious but irrelevant phenomenon. Among the major reasons for its relative invariance
is the influence of physiographic features on the location, functional role, and expansion of urban settlements in Venezuela
(Map 10).

Two major patterns are discernible: city locations in intermontane valleys and "gateway" locations. It may be argued
that topographical structure of the country has made these
patterns unavoidable, has contributed to the emergence of a
stable hierarchy of cities, and has inhibited the development of

major centers that failed to conform to this general structure. Exceptions to this rule are few.

The principal intermontane cities in the central range are Caracas, Valencia, and Maracay, and in the Andean States, the cities of Mérida and San Cristóbal. As already observed, these valleys were preferred by the early settlers for reasons of their soil fertility and the salubrious quality of their climates. Moreover, the central location of the Caracas and Valencia Basins gave a natural advantage to cities which grew up in them, particularly during the recent industrial phase. The proximate position of the two basins with respect to each other reinforced their early tendencies for expansion. At the same time, the emergence of a center-periphery structure reduced the distant Andean cities to a subordinate role.

Among the "gateway" cities, ports must be mentioned as a distinct subcategory. In contrast to the intermontane valley cities, the country's major seaports were all built in a hot, humid, and malarial climate. They achieved their early eminence because the country's economy was fundamentally oriented to exports, and all external trade had to be channeled through them. However, only ports with a productive hinterland, responsive to changes in the international market place, attained a size of any consequence (Puerto Cabello, La Guaira, Puerto la Cruz).

Maracaibo deserves special comment for maintaining its position as Venezuela's second-largest city for many decades.

By discovering the straits leading to Lake Maracaibo in 1499, Alonso de Ojeda initiated an outward orientation of this region that was to persist for centuries.[27] The first serious colonization came by land from the city of Coro. After reaching the Indian settlement of Maporo on the lake, the Spaniards constructed two ships and proceeded to the present site of Maracaibo. Here, in 1571, they founded Ciudad Rodrigo which was later renamed after a local Indian chieftain whose name the present city and the lake retain.

By the end of the nineteenth century, Maracaibo had developed as an important transport focus that drew its sustenance from a major portion of the mountain region. A sandbar blocked the entry of oceangoing vessels into the lake, and commodities had to be transferred to and from lake boats at the mouth: hence, the traditional transport-orientation of the city. "The city of Maracaibo," according to the National Census of 1890, "is today one of the principal commercial centers of the Republic. As it has an ample and protected port, all the agricultural products of the Basin converge upon it, as well as the totality of the crops from the state of the Andes and part of Santander in the Republic of Colombia."[28]

During the twentieth century, Maracaibo benefited from the development of the region's oil resources. But as active exploration for oil declined toward the end of the 1950's, the traditional commercial families of the city began casting about for new opportunities, especially in agriculture and cattle raising. The recently completed bridge across Lake Maracaibo will undoubtedly assist in this search for a new economic role for the city by improving the efficiency of land communications to other regions of the country.

The "gateway" location of cities is not confined to seaports, however. Cities in the southeastern piedmont and along the central coastal range in the Llanos are invariably situated at the point of entry to a major pass leading into the main population centers in the mountains and, beyond them, to the coast. Barinas, Acarigua, San Carlos, San Juan de los Morros, and Altagracia de Orituco are the cities of principal access through which traffic to and from the Llanos has to pass.

Other important "gateway" cities include San Felipe in the Yaracuy Valley, Barcelona, Cumaná, and Ciudad Bolívar. However, a detailed analysis of their location is not feasible here.

The urban pattern which has emerged in Venezuela has thus a double rationale in the stratification of major ecological complexes and the topographical advantages of city location. This pattern may be considered basic and, with the passing of years, has been reinforced by a secondary pattern of trade linkages, including roads between the major centers and their respective tributary areas. This secondary pattern has rarely departed from

149

the fundamental structure suggested by the country's physiographic features and, in every instance of significant departure, has managed to produce centers of only local significance.

Conclusions

The preceding analysis has traced the relation between Venezuela's economic growth and spatial structure to the end of the current period of development. The principal conclusions may now be briefly stated. Although pertaining to Venezuela in the specific case, they may be advanced as hypotheses for testing in other national contexts.

1. Every major period of economic growth has its characteristic structure in space as defined by the location of activities and population and the interactions among them. The transition from one period to the next creates serious problems of adjustment, however, as areas which had formerly experienced rapid expansion become locationally obsolescent.

2. As the economy evolves from its preconditions stage to takeoff into cumulative growth, it will typically experience

   a. the appearance of a small number of urban-industrial areas having a high potential for further development and leading to the focalization of demographic and social energies upon themselves;

   b. economic stagnation and decline in locationally obsolescent areas on a "periphery" that is structurally related to the dynamic urban-industrial centers and is the principal source of migrants to these centers;

   c. progressive integration of the space economy through (1) a multiplication in the number of urban centers; (2) the emergence of a functional hierarchy of cities; and (3) the organization of the economy into a system of interrelated market areas.

3. The evolving form of the space economy will be shaped, to an important degree, by its basic structural persistencies which include

   a. the distribution of major resource complexes and the economic activities that are based upon them;

150

b. the hierarchy of cities, particularly of the urban centers at the top which, once established, tend to perpetuate their relative position and functional role in organizing the pattern of economic growth in its spatial dimension.

In time, however, both of these structural patterns may be transformed.

CHAPTER SEVEN

REGIONAL DEVELOPMENT AS A POLICY ISSUE

Ideology and Revolution

Early in 1958, the Democratic Action Party, in alliance with dissident elements within the armed forces and with overwhelming public support, brought down the brutal dictatorship of Colonel Marcos Pérez Jiménez. This was no ordinary palace revolution of the type so frequently associated with Latin American politics. In raising to a position of effective power the principal spokesmen of the urban middle sectors, it represented instead a genuine turning point in Venezuelan history. The conservative coalition of army officers, landlords, financiers, and import merchants was broken or, at any rate, reduced to impotence. A new mentality took hold of the country, became everywhere dominant, and found expression through new social formations and new institutional arrangements.

Against this background, it was perhaps inevitable that regional development should emerge as a major policy issue. Political and economic circumstances combined to favor a lively public debate of the "where" of economic development.

Since the middle twenties, Venezuela had enjoyed a steady, unprecedented growth of certain sectors of her economy. The driving force behind this expansion was, of course, petroleum. Though originating in the great oil fields on the far western and eastern peripheries, much of the country's newly found wealth terminated in Caracas. To a generation of governments, this steadily swelling tide of "black gold" appeared as a virtually inexhaustible treasury in comparison to which all other economic opportunities shrank to insignificance. This was the predominant attitude and it would prove nearly disastrous. A perceptive study of recent Venezuelan history comments:

The fact that the process of economic change was initiated by foreigners, with imported techniques, capital, and organization, made unnecessary the creation of socio-political and cultural prerequisites. It was not necessary to break down a power structure, create entrepreneurs, increase knowledge, create a favorable attitude towards saving, work and, in general, economic rationality, nor to create new formal institutions. It was neither necessary to develop agriculture to the point where it would leave a surplus for the development of other activities. Even today a large percentage of the agricultural labor force does not know the use of the plow and of animal traction.[1]

Pursuit of a policy that staked the nation's development on the recovery of oil and on its placement in world markets prepared the stage for major structural reforms. A vast proletariat of rural and urban workers lived in abject ignorance and poverty, while a small minority of city dwellers came to enjoy a rapidly rising level of living whose principal components were imported from overseas. The impression of luxury created by conspicuous consumption, reinforced by a policy that favored urban areas in the allocation of both public and private investments, led to a massive dislocation of population to the cities and especially to Caracas. Within a quarter of a century, urban population increased from 743,000 to 4.3 million. At the beginning of the sixties, nearly one fifth of the country's population was living in the metropolitan area of the capital city. Urbanization brought with it a dramatic rise in the number of professionals, technicians, administrators, businessmen, and white-collar workers. They were a vocal, literate minority, but their collective interests failed to gain adequate expression in the policies being pursued by a succession of governments in collusion with the "Caracas Oligarchy."[2] The relatively new phenomenon of urban middle sectors, oriented to the modern values of liberalism and social democracy but thwarted in their aspirations by the prevailing feudalistic power structure, led to first stirrings of discontent as early as 1928. Rapidly gathering momentum, this discontent erupted in revolutionary violence seventeen years later. Led by Rómulo Betancourt, a provisional govern-

153

ment achieved some notable reforms but was unsuccessful in consolidating a democratic form of government. The counter-revolution in 1948 imposed a dictatorship upon the country, which, in its general incompetence to govern except by force, stands without parallel in the nation's history. Within a decade, the government of Pérez Jiménez had succeeded in alienating nearly all important sectors of the population. In 1958, a popular uprising deposed the Colonel, silenced the forces that had supported him, and swept the Democratic Action Party into power.

The revolution of the middle sectors had triumphed. Yet, as late as 1961, the population census had counted only 326,000 workers among those whose occupation might suggest a middle-class background. This was less than 14 per cent of the total labor force, and nearly one half of this number was living in the metropolitan area of Caracas.[3] To consolidate its claim to power, therefore, the new leadership had to seek a wider basis of support. It did so by proclaiming itself the vanguard of a progressive social movement of peasants and workers.[4]

But as the multiclass party it claimed to be, Democratic Action had to legitimize its leadership by winning a popular national election. Because it was certain of its *de facto* control of cities, the party courted primarily those regional forces that had always been latent in Venezuelan history. It was the development of provincial resources rather than further accumulation of wealth and power in Caracas that constituted its chief promise. The results of the 1958 elections bore out the wisdom of this theory. The Democratic Action Party gained an overwhelming victory, but its weakest showing was precisely in Caracas itself.

The party's ideology may be summarized in the key slogans of nationalism, economic development, and planning.

As a multi-class organization, the Party's militant membership is united in the common task of building a fatherland liberated from the foreign forces that presently subjugate our lives; of creating our own economy; of transforming the social environment of our country; of stimulating the immense productive capacities of the nation; of overcoming the cultural backwardness of large sectors of the population; of improving the levels of living of the majority of the people; of speeding the development of industry and of agriculture; of modifying the feudal system of rural land ownership; of dignifying our public administration through the honest exercise of its duties; and of giving full expression to the popular will.[5]

By nationalism the party understood the liberation of the nation from foreign economic domination and from the debilitating dependence upon a single industry; by economic development it understood the utilization of all the potential resources of the nation; and by planning it understood the marshaling of all available instrumentalities for achieving a new social order. Democratic planning was to be a system of collaborative efforts held in an appropriate balance by a conception of the national interest as expressed in a development plan. According to President Betancourt:

To plan is the unavoidable slogan of our time. In our days, responsible administrative work is inconceivable without a proper articulation of objectives, coordination of efforts, and projections into the future. Autarchic action on the part of the several branches of government without attempting to align their efforts according to a common orientation and a common set of goals . . . is a practice incompatible with the idea of a modern State.[6]

It was by focalizing economic decisions upon a national planning agency—CORDIPLAN was created in 1958—that the location problem and by implication the broader issues of regional development came to be posed.

The revolution of the middle sectors was to be a revolution according to a plan! It would occur, therefore, not by decree imperiously imposed but through a process of dialogue and accommodation among competing interests of vocation, class, and region in which the central planning agency was to perform a catalytic role. Enrique Tejera Paris, an economist, and subsequently Venezuela's Ambassador to the United States, was the person chiefly responsible for the original conception and organization of Venezuela's system of national planning. According to him, planning was to be primarily a process of collaboration:

Experience seems to demonstrate that the simple insertion of a planning unit does not by itself produce the results one might be led to expect, no matter how many documents and programs are presented which, from a technical standpoint, are irreproachable. In addition to such a planning unit, we must look for its acceptance by the entire structure, as well as for a tradition of collaboration in the formulation of the plans. These conditions require strong presidential support, and a mechanism of constant consultations, supported by adequate legislation.[7]

This philosophy was to guide CORDIPLAN throughout the years of its existence.

The heart of what might be called the ideology of the middle sectors was stated in a government pronouncement on May 22, 1962. According to this important declaration, the fundamental goals of the nation were conceived to be

1. The greatest possible welfare for all Venezuelans, to be achieved through full employment of the labor force and through an equitable distribution of wealth, using the expanding resources of the several regions of the country in the most efficient way possible; and

2. Economic independence, through an adequate diversification of the economy and an optimal growth of the national product, especially on the basis of the best possible utilization of the income obtained from the just participation of the nation in the extractive industries.[8]

All the major ideological themes are echoed in these lines. Regional development turned out to be listed among them, appearing as a critical phase in the evolution of policy during the first few years of the democratic government. In a way it was odd that the urban middle sectors should have proposed a course of regional development. But the logic of their position left no other choice. Not only did their political aspirations require the support of provincial populations but their fundamental aim of industrializing the country and of establishing a society without distinct class differences and distributing equitably the wealth produced by the nation led them to propound the complementary principles of diversification in resource use and decentralization of economic activities away from Caracas

156

itself. To build a nation was to think first of the contribution that the several regional economies might make.

The Role of the Guayana Program

In the Guayana program, the new government took up the challenge it had flung down for itself. Here, in a distant part of southeastern Venezuela, a major effort at coordinated resource development was to take place. Focused upon a new city, this region was to become the country's principal center of heavy industry. Newspapers called it the Pittsburgh on the Orinoco.[9]

A beginning had been made a few years earlier by putting into operation two iron-mine concessions under the management, respectively, of the United States and Bethlehem Steel Corporations. At about the same time, the government had undertaken the construction of an integrated steel mill and a 350,000 kw hydroelectric plant on the Caroní River. But these had been treated as only isolated projects. Though they related to each other—the steel mill would be a major consumer of both the iron ore and the electric energy produced in the region—the manner in which the Guayana scheme would relate to national economic development was only vaguely understood. It was left to the democratic government to define a new image in which the development of Guayana's resources was seen integrally as part of a national program for industrialization and the region itself as a permanent, structural element of an expanding inter-regional system. Economic, social, and physical components were to be fused in planning for the region so that a unitary conception might take shape. The new task was to go beyond industrial production to the creation of a new region deep in the interior of the country where but a few years earlier had been a virtually unpopulated geographic space.

The new city of Santo Tomé de Guayana was to be the focal point for the series of interrelated industrial complexes that would, in time, transform the region's potential wealth of natural resources into a steadily rising level of living for the local population. At the same time, it would contribute to the long-term strategy of national development in the form of diver-

157

sified foreign exchange earnings and intermediate product supplies to an expanding national market.

Five such complexes were found to be potentially suitable to the area: iron and steel products, electrometals, electrochemicals, heavy machinery, and pulp and paper. In addition, the region was to become the principal supplier of electric power to the rest of the nation. Related to these ambitious prospects, heavy investments were to be undertaken in mining, construction materials, agriculture, forestry, and tourism. Projection of the region's economic base appeared to favor a possible expansion of the city to more than half a million inhabitants before the end of the century.

This vast enterprise posed a series of issues for spatial organization whose resolution was essential to programming for the region. Guayana was the first and most daring example of the government's new policy for decentralizing economic development. How would its implementation affect the spatial organization of the national economy? The program was placed in a unique geographical matrix. How would sustained heavy investment in this matrix affect the fortunes of other areas within the country? Or, for that matter, how would shifts in spatial organization elsewhere affect the planning of Guayana itself? These were not rhetorical questions but basic information needed for the exacting task of regional programming. They were the kind of questions that might be asked in connection with any major investment project anywhere and demonstrated the critical importance of locational considerations in national economic policy. For instance,

• With what areas would Guayana have its principal intercourse at successive stages of its development?

• What transport and communications linkages would be most suitable for relating Guayana's growing economy to other national centers of development?

• What complementary investments outside of the immediate operational area of Guayana would be needed in order to reach the full potential of development within it?

• In what ways, positively or negatively, would the Guayana

project affect economic opportunities in other areas, specifically by its impact on interregional migration, potential shifts in the spatial distribution of urban functions, cheapening the costs of basic material inputs, creating a strong regional center of consumption and, in a general way, stimulating a new awareness of local development opportunities?

To answer these and related questions, the elements of a national policy for regional development would have to be formulated. Given a basic conception of an evolving space economy—the system of development areas, core regions, development axes, central places, and zones of urban dominance—the specific issues raised by the location of heavy industrial complexes at Guayana might begin to be discussed in realistic fashion. For, clearly, an approach was called for in which all parts of the interregional system might be considered simultaneously.

While theory pointed to the need for a regional policy, implementation of the Guayana program had a powerful practical effect in demonstrating the efficacy of the regional approach to development. The immediate result was an intensification of regional consciousness in many parts of Venezuela, a new awareness of the potentials for regional development, widespread support for a variety of regional planning efforts, and a growing concern on the part of national policymakers, especially at the Central Planning Agency, with ways to harness the energies, so suddenly released, to the guiding conceptions of national planning. At the time of this writing (1964), this problem has not been satisfactorily resolved.

The Guayana program had created a deep awareness of the effects of interregional competition in Venezuela. To contain the consequences of "decentralization" to just one area was proving an impossibility. Other areas soon discovered that they would have to "catch up" and forcefully to present their claims in the choice of new investment locations. The Guayana program had turned the thinking of regional leaders to a consideration of the place of their own communities within the national economy, had made them poignantly aware of the problems and opportunities for local development, and had challenged them to the

159

same kind of hard-headed planning for which the Guayana Development Corporation had earned an enviable reputation. The importance of a planning approach was quickly grasped. While political pressures, good connections, and other traditional means for prevailing on the central government had by no means lost their efficacy, the *style* of politics had subtly changed. The Guayana program had given a dramatic demonstration of the usefulness of technical reasoning for mobilizing financial resources on a large scale. After Guayana, it was no longer possible to base one's claims for consideration on grounds of public righteousness alone. Proof had also to be shown that appropriated funds would be spent wisely, and that projects were well conceived from a technical standpoint and would fit into the larger framework of a regional development plan. The political process had to be made effective through a correlative process in which futurity and technical norms would be explicitly related to subjective wants. Emphasis was to be placed on systematic surveys, rational diagnosis, strategies for goal achievement, and programming of specific project investments. This was the important lesson learned.

Results followed quickly. By mid-1963, the fever of regional development had spread to nearly all parts of the country. The widely respected newspaper, *El Nacional*, went so far as to call it the "new doctrine of Venezuelan economic development."[10] Abetted by official policy for reasons outlined earlier, regional development had in fact acquired some of the characteristics of a surging social movement. The province was at last to play a vital role in Venezuelan life. The movement itself foreshadowed far-reaching transformations based on a decentralization of political power.

A Study Commission for the Andean States was created in 1962, chiefly in response to local initiative and a skillful manipulation of political forces.[11] Within a year from its inception, support was being rallied in the Congress for its reorganization as an autonomous institute, a Development Corporation along the lines of the Guayana Authority. A similar effort on the part of the eastern provinces had failed to rally sufficient support in 1962 but will undoubtedly be made again. Meanwhile, state planning organizations were being established in Táchira, Sucre, Anzoátegui, Bolívar, and Zulia. Even municipal districts, long languishing in a stupor of inactivity, were coming alive. The city of Valencia had formed its own development foundation in 1962 and helped finance a comprehensive study to guide its future efforts in coping with the expected rapid growth of industry in that important center.[12] Its example in creating a well-managed industrial estate was being widely copied in other cities.

Regional interests began to be reflected in the activities of the national government itself. The Ministry of Development inaugurated a special program, *Industria para la Provincia*, to stimulate the decentralized development of industry. Under this program, a number of regional meetings were held.[13] At the same time, offices of the Ministry's Department of Industries were established in a number of cities throughout the country.

A recent Annual Report justifies the Ministry's program in a manner that neatly reflects the new thinking:

. . . the industrialization of the Province is not simply a sentimental movement, but an action with a well-defined economic and social rationale. Its purpose is to reduce the costs of production, to achieve a greater utilization of natural resources, an improved income distribution for all Venezuelans, and a reduction in the internal migration to the capital of the Republic.[14]

The Ministry of Development was not alone in its concern with regional issues. The Public Works Ministry created a new division of regional planning for the coordination of all public construction within the country. The Ministry of Agriculture was financing special consultant reports on regional development prospects and had been the first to give attention to the mapping of natural resources on a country-wide basis.[15] CORDIPLAN itself had established a section to deal with the problems of project location. The final part of its most recent Four-Year Plan was given over entirely to regional planning. As yet in many ways deficient, especially in its more systematic aspects, this emphasis on the spatial component of economic development is, indeed, noteworthy. A way was urgently being sought to integrate spatial with sectoral planning and to provide an adequate organizational structure that would permit the process of regional planning to be integrated more closely into the process of national planning. A press release on the Operational Plan for 1964 gives further proof of this concern:

A clear tendency for the proliferation of regional organisms has been observed. In the future, this may well create serious problems for planning. The majority of these new organizations fail to maintain close coordination with agencies of the central government. For this reason, it is necessary to define a policy at the following levels:

    a. Regional organizations, such as the Guayana Corporation, the Commission for the Andes, etc.; and

    b. industrial zones, such as Valencia, Maracaibo, etc.

This policy should define:

    a. the manner of coordination with central government agencies;

    b. integration with the National Plan;

    c. clear attribution of the functions to be performed by the several regional organizations; and

    d. definition of regional development objectives with respect to industry, agriculture, public works, and other services.[16]

In Search of a Policy

Whether these were, indeed, the most pressing problems with which a regional policy should be concerned will be left unanswered for the moment. The existence of a national planning system had brought them into focus. The next step would clearly have to be the policy itself.

In the original planning legislation, the concept of regional planning had been mentioned as part of a national planning system. In principle, therefore, CORDIPLAN favored the decentralization of decision making. But in actuality, its viewpoint was ambiguous. Objections to regional planning were raised on a number of grounds. First, CORDIPLAN itself claimed no particular competence in the subject. None of its own staff had been trained in the techniques of regional development, and precise investment criteria were lacking. Second, the shortage of experts in regional development was advanced as a major

162

argument against the extension of planning below the national level. Third, it was feared that regional planning would strengthen the bargaining position of local areas while reducing the ability of CORDIPLAN to assert its presumably more comprehensive national viewpoint. The agency feared that the delicate balance between politics and planning that it had taken great pains to build up and maintain might be destroyed by rash adventures into regional planning. Finally, CORDIPLAN was aware of the political implications of any move toward decentralization in decision making in the sense that this would eventually lead to a revitalization of regional politics and a general strengthening of the periphery's decision power over that of the center. And this, strictly speaking, was a matter lying outside its sphere of responsibility.

Subject to intensive pressures for regional development, however, CORDIPLAN could not simply remain a passive and essentially critical observer. Subsequent to 1962, the agency slowly evolved a positive viewpoint. In the section of the National Plan devoted to regional questions, two contradictory allocation criteria were proposed. According to the first, investments were to be allocated according to a system of priorities that would frankly favor the most backward regions, so that, within a reasonable period, they might attain to living levels "compatible" with those prevailing in the rest of the nation. The very backwardness of an area would, by this formula, entitle it to special treatment. The more developed regions would be asked to forego a measure of their own potential growth in the interest of a more equitable distribution of income.

The second criterion stated that resources should be allocated in conformity with the principle of marginal productivity. Priority would therefore be given to those areas that promised the highest social return per unit of capital invested. According to this principle, the less developed areas would begin to benefit in due time, not only from the more rapid expansion of the economy as a whole but also from an eventual decline in the marginal productivity of capital at the first centers of growth.[17]

A growth principle was thus confronted with a principle of

equity and social justice. Lacking an Archimedean reference point outside the system, CORDIPLAN found it impossible to resolve the conflict which, in a sense, it had brought upon itself. It opted instead for the simultaneous application of both criteria in what it called a "just balance." There was, in addition, the thought that regions might somehow be identified as "economic unities" whose internal development could be set into motion successively to achieve a "takeoff" into cumulative growth.

CORDIPLAN's principal conclusion on the problem of re-source allocation in space was to recognize the need for some sort of interregional "balance." What was missing, however, was a conceptual framework for working out such a balance on rational principles. In its absence, the conflict between equity and growth criteria would be transferred onto a political plane, where the issues could only be resolved by the relative strengths of competing interests in moving central allocative decisions in their favor.

More important than investment criteria, however, was the question of organization. This would have a direct bearing on the manner in which decisions would be made and on the important problem of coordination. Tentative and somewhat confusing steps were taken by the establishment of regional planning divisions within both CORDIPLAN and the Ministry of Public Works. Neither was adequately staffed nor had a clear conception of its purposes.

In July 1963, CORDIPLAN helped establish the Zulia Planning Council as possibly a model for future regional planning organizations. The administrative scheme of the Council is an interesting one and essentially in line with the basic planning philosophy that CORDIPLAN had been trying to promote. Represented on its Board of Directors (Conselho Directivo) are all principal interests active in the state, including government, military, church, business, industry, labor, and farmers. The five-man Executive Committee is headed by the governor of the state and is serviced by a Technical Secretariat headed by CORDIPLAN technicians. Central to the organization, however, are its Working Groups which are concerned with specialized problems in agriculture, industry, public works, and services, and whose membership includes government officials as well as interested representatives from the private sector. Coordination with national planning would be achieved principally through the Secretariat.

The Council has its offices in Maracaibo, the state capital, and its area of competence includes primarily Zulia. Its establishment had been urged on the government by local civic groups. If successful, it would reproduce at the state level what CORDIPLAN had been trying to do at the national level. Private interests would join the government in a corporate endeavor at developmental planning. The political process would be improved by a more rational assessment of development possibilities and presenting investment projects for consideration at the national level in a more professional manner than had been customary. Emotional regionalism, especially prevalent in Zulia, would thus be transformed into a more functional, objective attitude and, through CORDIPLAN representation on the secretariat, some coordination with national planning efforts would in principle be assured. In accepting regional planning, therefore, Zulia concurred in the proposition that its own planning and development efforts should in some sense be subordinated to the national interest. Whether the Zulia Planning Council will actually work in this manner remains to be seen. But the intention, at least, is clear.

CORDIPLAN appeared once more to be moving toward a middle ground where a continuing dialogue could be maintained. It was drifting from its earlier position which had opposed the regionalization of economic development planning on grounds that decentralization would slow down the rate of economic growth. It was also drawing away from the alternative proposal to establish for each major region a special, independent development corporation. In place of these extreme and contradictory positions, CORDIPLAN was beginning to assert a form of regional planning that would establish a framework for local-national coordination in development planning and extend to the several regions of the country the principle of participant planning somewhat along the lines of recent French experience.[18]

Recapitulation of the Argument

How, then, in retrospect, did regional development get put on the agenda for public policy consideration? Why did it become a genuinely popular issue, accorded wide play in the daily press and finding almost always, everywhere, responsive audiences? An obvious reason is that regional development calls attention to the material, visible manifestations of national development. The average citizen experiences no difficulty in understanding roads and irrigation projects; he is left confused and basically unmoved by the intricacies of central banking and trade balances. The concrete project on the ground will affect him directly, more directly, he thinks, than all the mysterious doings in Caracas. It therefore matters a great deal to him who gets what share, as investment funds are distributed around each year.

But this, in a sense, is the superficial answer. It might indeed be true anywhere. A more specific, historical explanation has been provided in this chapter.

The regional issue in Venezuela arose as a consequence of three decades of sustained economic development. By the late 1950's, the economy had reached the "takeoff" stage and could look forward to an extended period of intense industrialization. During the preceding generation, the central region from Caracas to Valencia had been built up to impressive proportions. But the periphery, except for specific investments in the petroleum sector, had been badly neglected and far outstripped by the glamorous wild pace of modernization at the center. Population movements readily responded to the ever-widening gap of economic opportunity. The great majority of the migrants sought their fortunes in Caracas; smaller but substantial numbers poured from surrounding regions into the oil encampments. And with the clear emergence of a "center," the stage was set for another act in the drama of social transformation. All that was needed now was opportunity for the provinces to press their claims for a fair share in the growing prosperity of the nation.

The long-awaited moment was the revolution of January 1958, which passed the reins of government to the leaders of social formations to whom effective political power had previously

166

been denied. The Democratic Action Party spoke for the urban middle sectors and propounded a liberal democratic philosophy that in economic affairs stood for rapid industrialization, agrarian reform, and national planning. The party also advocated a new nationalism that was intended to lead to greater autonomy in all matters of national determination and, more specifically, to the full development and utilization of national resources. This implied some form of *regional* development and in the specific case of Venezuela a concentration of development efforts away from Caracas itself. To the extent that Democratic Action politicians sought support for their program in the provinces—and the majority of the voters lived *away from* the national capital region—the regional issue came to be regarded as a godsend.

The first concrete measures to give substance to the new philosophy was a redoubled effort to create in distant Guayana a major industrial complex based on local iron ore, hydroelectric power, and natural gas. For Venezuela, this was a gigantic undertaking, involving the solution of many extremely complex problems. Not the least of these was the accommodation in a new city of the tens of thousands of migrant workers who continued to arrive each year. The task of building Guayana was entrusted to a government corporation.

Soon the logic of Guayana's development posed difficult questions of development policy—with regard, for example, to the location of new industry, transport connections, and urbanization —that had to be resolved by Venezuela's national planners. If a "regional policy" had not been thought of in explicit terms before, it now came to be recognized as inevitable.

Still, these issues might have been resolved at a high technical level had not the successful implementation of the Guayana program demonstrated to all the country the material advantages of "regionalism" in the administration of development programs. Hundreds of millions of dollars were being invested in Guayana. By copying the example of the Guayana Corporation, every region might hope to gain for itself equally favorable consideration. Regional planning became all the rage. State governors demanded it; private organizations supported it; and local leadership organized to demand of the central authorities better coordination of development activities within their own areas and funds especially earmarked for regional investments.

The government responded to this eruption of public interest with something less than spontaneous enthusiasm. Its evident reluctance derived partly from a recognition that institutionalizing regional development might lead to far-reaching changes in the country's political structure, as political power became displaced from a single national center to be reconstituted around a number of regional loci. Regionalism was clearly a useful platform for those who clamored for municipal reform and the revitalization of urban government. Political careers could be advanced by taking a strong stand on regional issues. And political organizations might be built up at local, state, and regional levels—where none now existed—capable of catapulting obscure regional personalities into national prominence. Indeed, the existence of a functioning system of planning at the national level left little choice in the matter. Planning had served to put a brake on the traditional game. Access to the central government had been reduced from the time when government was run, as it were, for the exclusive benefit of a few stockholders, and "connections" were used to obtain personal consideration for oneself. Special favors had now to be presented as "projects," and projects had to be justified on economic grounds, that is, on the planners' own terms. Thus, planning engendered more planning. And a marriage was contracted between politics and expertise.

It is clear that the existence of an institution for national planning not only allowed the regional policy issue to be posed but also created the political circumstances that would make it difficult to formulate and carry out a national policy for regional development. This dilemma has led to a restless search for a working relationship between the processes of regional and national planning in which conflicts of interest might increasingly be resolved on technical, objective grounds.

CHAPTER EIGHT

GUAYANA: DEVELOPMENT OF A RESOURCE FRONTIER REGION

The Guayana program represents the major effort of Venezuela's present generation in regional development. This vast public undertaking, scarcely a decade old, is already having a profound impact on the national economy. It is creating a new region on the edge of the effectively settled space in the eastern part of the country; it is expanding the productive capabilities of the nation by bringing new resources into play; it is building the principal base of heavy industry for the further industrialization of the country; it is stimulating economic expansion in other parts of Venezuela; and it is serving as a powerful example of the possibilities of programming for regional development.

Guayana's role in stirring national interest in questions of investment location, settlement, urbanization, and transportation is so crucial, its implications for regional change are on so vast a scale, that a closer look at some of these aspects seems justified. Guayana serves, moreover, as an exemplary case of resource frontier development. The general issue that has had to be faced is how a remote but richly endowed region may be harmoniously woven into the fabric of the national economy.

The dimensions of the project taking shape at the confluence of the Orinoco and Caroní rivers are, by any standard, impressive and afford a critical test of some of the theories of regional development. Population for the new metropolitan areas is expected to grow in excess of half a million within a generation; 20 per cent of total manufacturing production and total exports may be generated by the regional economy; the capacity of the projected power system may reach ten million kilowatts; and total investment requirements between 1963 and 1975 have been estimated at four billion dollars.[1] Such magnitudes speak for the great complexity of an undertaking that is destined to become one of the major engines of economic transformation in the country.

History of the Guayana Region

The region of Guayana has an ambiguous connotation. *Geographically*, the name refers to the extensive highlands area—almost an island—that is bounded by the Atlantic Ocean on the one side and is cut off from the mainland by the waters of some of the largest streams in Latin America: the Orinoco, Casiquiare, Negro, and Amazonas. The *traditional Venezuelan concept* of Guayana generally includes all of the national territory to the south of the Orinoco River. But the new *legal concept* of Guayana, embodied in the decree establishing the Guayana Development Corporation, delimits only a narrow "development zone" on the lower Caroní.[2] At the core of this zone lies the new city of Santo Tomé de Guayana.

It is a "remote" region in the sense referred to earlier. Santo Tomé de Guayana is roughly 250 miles distant from the metropolitan region of Barcelona–Puerto la Cruz, which is not only the largest urban complex in the eastern part of the country but the major trade and service center for the entire area. The existing roads to the industrial heartland and the principal seat of political and administrative power in the country run for about twice this distance, or nearly five hundred miles. Much of the "traditional" Guayana remains still unexplored.[3] This is the area that gave rise to that entrancing fable of El Dorado, the city, in search of whose glittering wealth many adventurers went forth and lost their lives. Sir Walter Raleigh's description of the region—he had made a foray into the area in 1595—still echoes in the minds of many people. Landing his ship near the present site of San Félix, he ascended to the top of one of the gentle hills on the plain adjoining the river and beheld

. . . that wonderful breach of waters which ran down Caroni . . . . And there appeared some ten or twelve waterfalls in sight, every one as high over the other as a church tower which fell with such fury that the rebound of waters made it seem as if it had been all covered over with a great shower of rain.

He writes that he never saw a more beautiful country nor more lively prospects,

. . . hills raised here and there, over the valleys; the river's winding into divers branches; the plains adjoining, all fair, green grass, without bush or stubble; the ground of hard sand easy to march on, either for horse or foot; the deer crossing on every path; the birds towards evening, singing on every tree a thousand several tunes; cranes and herons, of white, crimson, and carnation, perching on the river's side; the air fresh with a gentle easterly wind; and every stone that we stooped to take up promising either gold or silver by his complexion.[4]

Three hundred years later, that same area presented to the eye of another explorer a quite different impression. In a fascinating account of his travels, Eugène André describes his disillusionment in language no less picturesque than Sir Walter's.[5]

The veil of enchantment which has shrouded the unexplored interior of Guiana has been torn aside. In place of the fair city gleaming with gold and precious stones, with a vast population revelling in luxury, we now know that there is an immense stretch of impenetrable forest interspersed here and there with open savannas, with mountains of fantastic shapes and surpassing grandeur, rising abruptly from the surrounding country—a region of abundant rains and rapid rivers, thinly peopled by small tribes of Indians who for centuries have carried on a series of cruel blood-feuds with their neighbors—a region rich in bird, insect, and vegetable life, but difficult of access, and deadly in climate.

And in the very spot where Sir Walter heard the birds at eventide sing a thousand different songs, Eugène André, writing in 1904, describes the city of San Félix as

. . . a straggling, ill-kept place. One looks in vain for some vestige of wealth which passed through it during those prosperous days when the Callao yielded its millions, and when it was believed that the numerous mines in the interior would produce even greater quantities of the

171

metal we adore than had ever been obtained from the goldfields of California and Australia.[6]

Guayana is an extremely complex region, and generalizations about it are hazardous. The best scientific study of its geography is found in the monumental work of Pablo Vila, the country's outstanding geographer. Unfortunately, only the first of his planned series of three volumes is currently available.[7]

Viewed in the traditional way, Guayana encompasses all the national area of Venezuela south of the Orinoco River, a vast territory extending over nearly half the country's land area. The eighth parallel, together with the great Orinoco, defines its northern boundary; in the south it reaches into the equatorial belt. The region, therefore, lies entirely within the tropics. Yet despite the vastness of its physical size, it is almost totally uninhabited. The 3 or 4 per cent of the national population who reside in Guayana are chiefly concentrated upon Ciudad Bolívar, Santo Tomé de Guayana, and a scattering of towns, villages, and farmsteads in the Upper Cuyuní Basin.

In addition to the Cuyuní, a stream running due east into British Guiana where it meets the Essequibo near its mouth, three major river systems drain the region; the Caura, Aro, and Caroní. Of these, the Caroní is the largest, with a course of almost 600 miles and a drainage basin of approximately 37,000 square miles.

The topography of the region is varied, ranging from near sea-level elevations in the plains along the lower Orinoco to altitudes of more than 3,000 meters in the Federal Territory of Amazonas. The outstanding physical feature of the region is the imposing tablelands of the Gran Sabana, which rise vertically for better than half a mile above the surrounding forests in the southeastern corner of Guayana. This is an area of stark beauty, but its economic potentialities are almost totally unknown.

Although eight major climates have been described for Guayana, the region may, in general, be classified as hot and humid. Rainfall is fairly evenly distributed and varies according to area, from 40 to 160 inches; temperatures hover about the middle eighties throughout the year. Tropical savanna and forests cover

172

the full extent of the region. A distinct dry season is known only in the vicinity of Ciudad Bolívar whose climate is more akin to that of the Llanos—the great inland savanna of Venezuela—than it is to the more tropical-humid areas to the south. There is no compelling evidence that the climates typical for Guayana are, in fact, generally suitable for intensive, large-scale population settlement. Most of the existing population is clustered in those parts of the region that are subject to the Llanero and Atlantic climates. More moderate than those that prevail in the rest of Guayana, these climates are, on the whole, more suitable for supporting large populations at a relatively high standard of living. But the problems of settlement in the tropics have by no means been solved. From the standpoint of economic development, areas such as Guayana will continue to be "regions of lasting difficulty" (J. H. Fleure).[8]

For centuries, Guayana languished in tropical torpor, with only few historical interludes to interrupt the monotony of its existence. Its population growth was unimpressive. The first penetrations, around 1500, proved to be totally unsuccessful, taking their heavy toll in lives, and leaving behind no permanent settlements. At that time, the region's treasures lay still hidden from view, and the *conquistadores* had still great empires to despoil.

The Province of El Dorado was created by Royal Decree in 1568, but for almost a century thereafter the only European settlements were a few fortified strongholds along the lower course of the Orinoco. Between 1628 and 1721, Catalan Capuchin monks made four separate attempts to establish a beachhead in the region, but all efforts were doomed to failure because of the rigorous climate, inadequate health care, and lack of adequate logistical support. All these attempts at colonization started in the general area of Santo Tomé de Guayana. A successful "invasion" and consequent exploration of the lower Caroní and upper Cuyuní basins did not take place until the middle of the eighteenth century. The friars were interested in the conversion of the Indians and in bringing them under Christian and European civilizing influence. Most of the settlements subsequently established in the region had predominantly Indian populations. Upáta, founded by civil authorities in 1762, was the only truly Spanish community in the area. Still, after three decades of relentless colonization effort (1744–1777), the number of inhabitants in the region is reported to have been only 8,000, and it is not clear whether this estimate includes Indians as well as European settlers.[9] For 1825, Marco Vila gives a figure of 21,000.[10]

A new development cycle began with the first commercial mining of gold in 1829. But scarcely a half century later, the great Callao mine closed down, and the census of 1890 reports the region's population as only 56,000. Its growth continued to be slow in the succeeding decades. Nevertheless, by 1941, Guayana had nearly doubled in size, and twenty years later the official census gave 232,000 as the population of the region. Prospects are for over a million people by the end of this century.

The lack of spectacular history did not prevent a regional consciousness from developing that would periodically call upon the nation to remind it of its great and unexploited future in Guayana. The recurrent dream of the regionalists was the settlement of this enormous region, a "taking possession" of its virgin lands.[11] It was felt that in the development of Guayana the true national spirit would somehow be discovered and a sense of national identity be gained. Proponents of this view would resort to quasi-poetic language to describe their vision:[12]

In Guayana will be realized the amalgamation of our diverse and almost antagonistic regional types, and the genuine Venezuelan will emerge. Our independence will not be assured until the day when our patriots will dominate the Orinoco. That Venezuela which will recover and increase manifold the heritage left to us by those marvellous men of a century ago. Our hope is that one day there will arise the first nation of tropical America, brought into being by the genius and civilizatory force of their descendants. In short, the Venezuela of our dreams will not come into being until we have populated Guayana and have incorporated it into the fatherland.

The urge of an indigenous development, non-European, non-cosmopolitan, in the conquest and colonization of national space, constitutes an element of frontier mentality that is frequently

174

encountered. Turner stated a similar theme for the United States; it is to be found in the history of other countries as well.[13] The frontier, it is argued, will create the national type. But the frontier lies in the interior of the continent, and its conquest represents a turning away from the metropolitan centers of the coast. The destiny of the country is seen to be entwined with its "continentalization." It was this thought that justified the great expenditure of effort that went into the creation of Ankara and Brasília at a great distance from the main avenues of commerce and the old centers of political life in the rude interior plains of Turkey and Brazil. It is also difficult to dissociate this thought from the continuing fascination of the average Venezuelan with Guayana. But the new Guayana was to rise not on an ephemeral base of gold and diamonds nor on the fields and pastures wrested by fire and axe from the tropical forest but on the firm foundation of modern industrial enterprise which would come to the region attracted by the real wealth in iron ore and water power that it had to offer.

A New Conception

Commercial mining of the rich iron ore deposits at El Pao and Cerro Bolívar was begun in the early fifties. The concessionaires were subsidiaries, respectively, of Bethlehem and U.S. Steel Corporations.[14] At about the same time, the government reached a decision that would mark a significant departure from earlier policies and signal a new stage in the history of Venezuela: an integrated steel mill was to be built in Guayana, and the vast power potential of the Caroní River was to be harnessed not only to furnish the essential energy for the mill but also to meet a rapidly growing demand in the rest of the national territory. Implementation of the program was entrusted to the Venezuelan Development Corporation. As the years went by, the main components of what was to become a major national effort at regional development took shape: the foreign mining concessions, the first of a series of major hydroelectric dams, the nationally owned steel plant on a site overlooking the Orinoco River, the dredging of a deep channel for oceangoing vessels

175

through the delta of the Orinoco, and narrow-gauge railways leading separately into each of the two mining areas. Thousands of workers and their families moved to the region.

Under President Betancourt, the revolutionary government decided to continue the program which had been started during the dictatorship. But both its objectives and the means for reaching them were to be changed. Its main purpose would now be the comprehensive development of the Guayana region and its resources. The program would have a strong welfare orientation and would be carried out within the context of a national development plan. Commensurate with this vision, the Corporación Venezolana de Guayana (CVG) was created as an autonomous agency in 1960, modeled in some fashion after the Tennessee Valley Authority. Responsible for the over-all planning and coordination of the scheme, the CVG was given far-reaching powers to do the job.[15]

The Guayana program fit well into the goals and ideology of the new era. Guayana was to become the showpiece of a new regional emphasis in the design of government policy. Hence, the focus of the project was to be the economic and social development of the traditional Guayana, and the new city, Santo Tomé de Guayana, was to become the principal "gateway" to this region, although direct development activities were initially to be confined to the narrow zone that had been specified in the basic act establishing the corporation.[16] *Sembrar el petroleo* —to sow the oil—was a key slogan of the new government, and the development of other indigenous resources, such as iron and water power, was intended as a concrete demonstration of this policy.

Favorably located with respect to the resources that were to be brought into the ambit of the national economy, Guayana was to become the country's principal base for heavy industry. The newly proclaimed ideology of nationalism was another reason for the strong interest the new regime displayed in the future of the region. For as long as Guayana was simply an exporter of ore concentrates, it would remain an essentially colonial economy, an exclave, dominated by foreign interests and almost completely at the mercy of foreign markets. The Gua-

176

yana program, on the other hand, was to be a national effort, conceived and carried out by Venezuelans.

The new Guayana was therefore to be more than the ephemeral resources frontier as which it had begun, just as the country's economy had to be put on a basis more stable than petroleum. The pace of exploring for new oil was, in fact, greatly reduced after 1958, and a decade of rapid industrial development was grinding to a halt. Guayana was to be fully integrated into the life of the nation as a permanent element. The goal was to be self-sustaining, cumulative growth and a gradually improving level of living for the people of the region. It was logical, therefore, that the new orientation gave emphasis to the design and construction of a new city as the vital center of the region: Santo Tomé de Guayana was founded amidst great ceremony on July 2, 1961. The option of merely getting by on a temporary group of construction camps or a few isolated company towns, such as Puerto Ordaz, was rejected. "Ciudad Guayana," states the *Annual Report* of the CVG for 1961, would be a "center for a region rich in natural resources, the focal point for the development of the southeast region of Venezuela. It will have urban attractions competitive with those in other large cities in the country, so as to inspire and gain the loyalty of its citizens."[17] The city was to be a lever for transforming a traditional resource frontier into a new settlement region. To achieve this purpose, a suitable environment for attracting industry had to be created.

The city's future would depend almost entirely on its ability to attract outside capital in basic industry. Its service functions would initially be few. Creation of a new core region meant to bring into existence a "location matrix" on the outer edge of settlement in eastern Venezuela, a matrix able to compete effectively for new industrial investment with other national centers, such as Caracas and the cities of the Valencia Basin. All this was known, and the program was consequently to be carried out as a coordinated enterprise. The basic elements were present, but they would have to be brought together into a single conception.[18]

The genuine strength of the region derived from its considerable potential for the development of low-cost power (up to 10 million kilowatts), its very large high-grade iron-ore deposits (1.3 million tons), its vast petroleum (*ca.* 2.2 billion barrels) and natural gas reserves (*ca.* 300,000 million cubic meters), its extensive hardwood forests (*ca.* 44 million cubic meters), unlimited supplies of fresh water, and a location which, though peripheral to the country's main centers, was readily accessible by air, sea, and land.[19] If properly combined and developed in a strategic sequence, these resources would be capable of providing the basis for a major industrial complex and of making a significant contribution to the economic development of Venezuela.

The new city was to be a key feature in the program. It would serve the obvious purpose of creating the external economies that characterize any urban environment and constitute one of its chief attractive forces. But the strategic decision to concentrate investments at Santo Tomé de Guayana had additional consequences that would favor the growth of the whole region.

Powerful symbolic forces were brought into play. The achievements in Guayana were visible and dramatic, and they created a strong image in the public mind. This, in turn, fostered a sense of progress that would have a positive influence on Guayana's ability to mobilize resources. The scale of the undertaking and its exclusive administration by a single authority created a highly favorable situation. It enabled the CVG to hold politics at bay and to cast its decisions chiefly in technical terms; it induced first-rate technicians to work for the corporation and made it possible to contract the prestigious M.I.T.-Harvard Joint Center for Urban Studies as consultants to the program. All of this made the corporation less vulnerable to opposition within the country so that it might attend to its work rather than engage in political infighting. It also facilitated dealings with international organizations, such as the World Bank, which might be more inclined to support an integrated operation than a series of isolated projects scattered over the country, each one of which, taken by itself, might conceivably appear to be a doubtful economic proposition. Finally, the Guayana program could be presented as a truly national effort, a rallying

178

point for the nation's energies, and thus contribute to political
stability within the country.

Public criticism of the program has, in fact, been remarkably
restrained. The image that had been created fitted well into the
popular mystique of Guayana—the El Dorado, the true Venezuela—and big dams and a steel plant were the visible evidence
that all had not been idle speculation but was at last to turn
into reality. Santo Tomé de Guayana, the city in the wilderness,
rising on the very spot where General Manuel Piar had defeated
the Spanish forces a century and a half earlier, was the magnif-
icent symbol of this vision, linking a great event in the history
of Venezuela to the new forces that were reshaping the face of
the nation.

A dispersal to other parts of the country of the individual
projects that make up the Guayana program would have left
the region as it was during the early fifties, a typical resource
frontier, dominated by foreign interests, an exclave on the far
periphery of the national space economy. The mobilization of
resources for individual components of the program would have
been far more difficult. Internal political forces might have been
set into motion that, in the end, could have fought each other to
a mutual standoff, with the result that no development at all
would have occurred. A new core region would not have been
created, and possibly fewer natural resources would have been
incorporated into the stream of national production. All this is
speculation, but it suggests that very considerable advantages
were probably gained as a consequence of the decision to concentrate developments around a single point. It may be true—as
some have argued, though without convincing demonstration—
that individual components of the program might have been
located elsewhere to better advantage. But such an argument
would overlook the decisive externalities of integrated development. Maurice Dobb, for example, writes:

When the matter is placed in the context of externalities, the whole
notion of [external economies] acquires both a wider and more crucial
significance as something integral to the process of growth; as a necessary condition for growth to occur, and not just an incidental factor
that happens to be ignored in the market-equilibrating process. It

179

appears as nothing less than the interdependence of different elements in an organic process of growth: an interdependence that defines an essential balance without which growth may be impossible or once it starts it may be quickly halted. Thus the growth potentiality of the whole system will not be a simple sum of the growth-potentialities of its constituent sectors or industries separately viewed (with appropriate adjustments for scale): it will vary with the structural pattern according to which the system as a whole grows.[20]

The political and social intangibles of concentrated development form an important part of the external effects of the program. But this should not be taken as an argument for inefficiency. It merely extends the framework within which efficiencies have to be measured.

We are now in a position to summarize the foregoing discussion and, in so doing, show the significance of this new conception for the future of Guayana.

When the government decided to build its steel plant, Guayana was well along to becoming a classical example of a resource frontier environment. It was, indeed, a remote region. Foreign investors had moved in to develop some highly profitable mining concessions and ship the ore by boat to destinations overseas, principally in the United States. Three small company towns had been built to house the numerous mining personnel, many of whom were foreigners. But nearly everything the region needed was imported, and none of the new towns served any regional functions whatever: the service sector was a strictly local affair. Living costs were consequently high, but this mattered little to the elite of engineers and foremen who received premium pay for working in an isolated environment devoid of cultural amenities. In any event, they had not come to stay. High prices were a burden chiefly to the migrants who had come to the region in the hope of finding employment with the foreign corporations or as servants in the homes of the elite. A dualistic social structure was thus established from the start. The companies looked out for their own people, but they claimed no responsibility for the well-being of the population at large nor for the development of regional resources other than some of the properties they owned. As long as world demand held out, Guayana might fare reasonably well. But the inevitable fluctuations in world demand for iron ore put the region at the mercy of impersonal forces beyond any measure of local or even national control. It might have been predicted then that population would eventually level off and, within a matter of a few decades, start to decline, leaving behind no more than memories of former promise.

The conception of a steel mill and power plant changed all this to some extent, but these investments were initially treated as special projects, quite unrelated to a development program for either region or nation. Moreover, little attention was paid to economy in their design. In 1958, the new government had to renegotiate the original construction contract as a result of which several million dollars were saved.

It was only with the revolution in 1958 that a new conception replaced this fragmented approach. The intention was to transform an ephemeral resource frontier into a permanent part of the national economy. A new identity for the region was created by the founding of Santo Tomé de Guayana as a municipal district, encompassing the many smaller communities and towns that stretched out over a fifteen-mile strip along the Orinoco, from the old center of San Félix to the steel plant at Matanzas. The city would be planned to last, with the full range of service facilities that any large and rapidly growing town might have: schools, hospitals, hotels, a stadium, and parks; a general port; a lively and sophisticated city center; and, later, perhaps, a jet airport and a technical university.

• The city must have diversity and a wide choice for its citizens and yet have unity. It must offer the opportunity for social interaction and for privacy.
• It must have compactness, to further urbanity, to make best use of the services, to strengthen public transit—and to create a clear distinction between "city" and "country," creating tension between the man-made structure and the wide-open llanos. This will strengthen the image of the city.
• It must have a strong center, a focus as an integral part of a clear, articulated and differentiated structure of movement. This must coincide with and enhance the natural focus.[21]

These were to be the primary goals for urban development. High priority was also given to the housing question.[22]

But the city was meant to be not only a permanent place for living a full and dignified life but also an attraction for potential investors in the industries that were to form its economic backbone. Any new firm that might come to Guayana would find there a full complement of urban services, a number of well-equipped industrial estates, facilities for training labor, and assistance (proferred by the CVG) in mobilizing capital funds. It would thus need to make only a minimal commitment of its own resources to investment in social and economic overhead facilities. More than fifty new investment possibilities were identified in manufacturing, construction, housing, transportation, and commercial services. A *Portfolio of Investment Opportunities* was prepared as the first stage of a concerted promotional program. And by the end of 1964, the following heavy industry projects were under active consideration:

1. iron-ore reduction to produce a sponge-iron type of synthetic scrap
2. primary aluminum ingots
3. elemental phosphorus
4. heavy machinery
5. pulp and paper

Meanwhile, intensive efforts were being made to lower the costs of local food consumption by developing new farming opportunities in the region. Early investigations included a small irrigation system near Upáta, a land reclamation and flood control project in the Amacuro Delta, and a citrus development north of the Orinoco River.

The general strategy in all this activity was to maintain a momentum of expansion—economic, social, and physical—that might carry the region beyond its critical minimum size into an era where pump-priming might yield to a self-generating process of growth.

As these lines are being written, the former monopoly of foreign interests has been broken by the CVG, and the region is being developed under the leadership and guidance of Venezue-

182

lans. Most of the land in Santo Tomé de Guayana is owned, controlled, and managed by the CVG. National capital has come to predominate in regional investment. And ways are being explored for strengthening the local administration so that the people of the city might increasingly assume responsibility for their own destiny. Tables 8.1, 8.2, and 8.3 give an idea of the magnitude of the works that have been proposed.[23]

Some Issues Posed

Guayana's rise to national importance unloosed potentially dramatic changes in the network of interregional relations in Venezuela. These effects, which might have been foreseen but were not, posed two critical, related policy questions for the planners of both the CVG and CORDIPLAN. The first concerned ways in which this new core region, hundreds of miles distant from the traditional centers of the country, might be

Table 8.1. Preliminary Production Goals for Guayana,
1964 and 1970
(*value in millions of bolivares at 1962–1963 prices**)

	1964	1970
Resource Development	493	887
A. Hydroelectric energy	19	71
B. Gas	—	20
C. Minerals	470	788
D. Agriculture	4	8
Industrial Development	563	4,398
A. Heavy Industry	419	3,897
1. Metals	405	3,051
2. Chemical Products	—	76
3. Heavy Machinery and Equipment	—	637
4. Construction Materials	14	31
5. Pulp and Paper	—	102
B. Light Industry	30	239
C. Construction Industry (value added)	114	262

*The conversion rate of bolivares to dollars was approximately 3.2 to 1.

Table 8.2. Estimated Guayana Employment, 1964 and 1970
(*thousands of workers*)

	1964	1970
Total	26.0	82.3
Resource Development	5.8	8.8
A. Hydroelectric Energy and Gas	0.1	0.5
B. Minerals	4.1	5.8
C. Agriculture	1.6	2.5
Industrial Development	10.9	41.4
A. Heavy Industry	4.2	25.1
1. Metals	4.0	13.9
2. Chemical Products	—	1.6
3. Heavy Machinery and Equipment	—	8.6
4. Construction Material	0.2	0.4
5. Pulp and Paper	—	0.6
B. Light Industry	0.6	5.3
C. Construction Industry	6.0	11.0
Housing and Infrastructure	9.2	32.0

Table 8.3. Preliminary Percentage Estimates of
Total Public and Private Investment
Requirements, 1964 to 1970

Total	7.857 billion bolivares (= 2.45 billion dollars)	100.0
Resource Development		24.4
A. Hydroelectric energy		10.1
B. Gas		0.6
C. Minerals		10.4
D. Agriculture		3.1
Industrial Development		34.3
A. Heavy Industry		31.7
B. Light Industry		1.0
C. Construction Industry		1.7
Housing and Infrastructure		41.3
A. Housing		16.1
B. Public Services and Communications		2.7
C. Government and other Services		5.0
D. Commercial Installations		6.4
E. Urban Transportation		2.1
F. Regional Transportation		8.9

incorporated as a stable element into the national space economy. The second question related to Guayana's impact on the eastern provinces and, in particular, on the depressed agricultural areas along the coast.

In approaching these questions, the planners had to gain some knowledge of the manner in which the Guayana program would affect economic conditions in other parts of the country. The interregional effects of the development of a new core region in Guayana had to be measured. Although sophisticated models and precise calculations are impossible in view of the paucity of reliable economic data, some guarded qualitative statements may be made.

Guayana as a target of migration. Most of the existing population of Santo Tomé de Guayana has been born elsewhere. At the projected rate of growth for the city—to 115,000 in 1966, 415,000 in 1975, and more than 600,000 in the late eighties—this situation is bound to remain without much change for at least a generation though, of course, the proportion of the population born locally will gradually increase.

For the most part, migrants have been coming from poverty-stricken rural districts within a two-hundred mile radius of the new city.[24] Guayana is thus helping to relieve the pressure of population in areas that have limited prospects for development in addition to diverting some of the flow of migrants from the central region of the country. Nothing is known, so far, about the localized effects of this migration, except that a disproportionately large share of males of working age is involved.[25] There is no question, however, that the impact upon their communities of origin of the tens of thousands of workers and their families moving to Guayana will be significant. Futhermore, in the absence of the Guayana program, a significant part of this migration movement might not have taken place. This would have rendered any adjustments in the regional structure of farming more difficult.

Creating a new center of urban demand. The reconcentration of migrant populations in a dynamic center of new industry is creating in Guayana a strong and rising demand for raw materials, semifinished products, and consumer goods. It has been estimated that community purchasing power by 1975 may reach between 400 and 500 million dollars annually. While a substantial portion of this demand will be met locally, up to one third of the city's needs may eventually need to be imported from other parts of Venezuela and from overseas.[26] Thus, a substantial demand effect will be transmitted internally to other regions. Current efforts to develop new areas for food production near the city are an early response to the anticipated increase in consumption. And in the years to come, major service and distribution centers such as Barcelona and Ciudad Bolívar can look forward to capturing a good share of the increased business with Guayana.

Shifts in the regional distribution of urban functions. Continued expansion of Santo Tomé de Guayana may bring about important shifts in the economic base and service functions of some of the cities in the Eastern Provinces. Small rural service towns may be abandoned as their inhabitants seek a more promising future in Guayana. Other centers, by contrast, may be strengthened as the result of agricultural development in their immediate vicinity and in response to the demand effects described above. Among them may be such regionally important towns as Upáta, Maturín, and Tucupíta. On the other hand, a city such as Ciudad Bolívar, only sixty miles distant from the new core region, may eventually lose a good deal of its current regional preeminence as a trade center—though not until some initial gains have been made—as more and more businessmen will shift their operations to Santo Tomé de Guayana in response to an expanding local market.

Reducing the cost of production inputs. The effects of concentrated regional resource development may also be transmitted across space by way of reducing the cost of certain inputs for production. This may encourage industry outside of the immediate region. In the case of Guayana, the principal cost reduction is likely to be in electric energy that will be distributed throughout the Eastern Provinces as well as to the central region. Although energy is only a minor cost component in most forms of production, the availability of low-cost power *in conjunction with other favorable conditions* may call forth a wave of new

186

investments at a few favored locations. In a more diffused, symbolic way, the construction of the gigantic Guri Dam on the Caroní River and the physical visibility of high-tension transmission towers will almost certainly call attention to as yet undeveloped opportunities, particularly in eastern Venezuela, and stimulate the interest of potential investors in that region, even outside of Santo Tomé de Guayana itself.

The reader will note that all of the examples chosen fall into the Eastern Provinces. This is no accident. For the impact of the Guayana program in that region will be felt in almost undiluted form. Though Guayana may come to have quantitatively more intense relations with the central region, the economic development of the country's center will be subject to more varied influences, and reduce the relative importance of the Guayana program. Quite the opposite will be true of the peripheral eastern region which—not only because of its predominately rural character but also because of its greater proximity to Guayana itself—will be strongly affected by developments in neighboring Guayana. This relationship will now by examined in greater detail.

Fragmentation: the Regional Pattern Prior to 1958

Only a few years ago, the Eastern Provinces displayed many of the characteristics of a preindustrial order. The region was divided into a number of small, localized economies which had little commerce with one another. With the export of a few primary commodities to urban centers in the central region and to foreign countries, its external relations were chiefly of the colonial type. Materials left the region generally in semiprocessed form, with most of the profits made by traders, while price fluctuations were transmitted directly to the region with no opportunity for mediating their effects. The people themselves were among the poorest in Venezuela, subsisting chiefly on maize and tubers. And the limited development potential of the area encouraged young people to leave for other parts in search of work. The few investments that did occur were used primarily to expand the region's export base, but did not

187

lead to multiplier effects of any consequence. As a result, those parts of the region that had been settled were sliding into a downward-transitional phase. Poor, undernourished, untutored, sick, with very high dependency ratios, the people of the Oriente and the Guayana lacked the means to help themselves. Successive waves of resource discovery—gold, oil, iron ore—did little to assuage the general condition of hopelessness. Yet, despite sustaining heavy migration to other areas for over a generation, the Eastern Provinces still accounted for 17 per cent of Venezuela's total population in 1961. They had become one of the major problem areas of the nation.

A quick review of some aspects of its economic conditions may help to deepen the perspective on this area. The East Coastal States of Sucre and Nueva Esparta were among the earliest to be settled in the seventeenth century. Three centuries later, the local economy gave little evidence of having undergone a major transformation. If anything, living conditions had deteriorated.[27] The population was engaged primarily in subsistence agriculture and fisheries. The technologies used were of the most primitive kind, and total productivity was therefore low. A good part of the economy was altogether removed from commercial relations. The principal contribution of the East Coastal States to national development—other than sheer manpower—was a specialization in export crops such as cacao and copra; the production of salt and canned fishery products for urban markets; and dried fish, mostly for the poorer population. But only a fraction of the 500,000 people in the two states shared significantly in the proceeds of this production.

Cities, on the whole, were minor provincial centers, each controlling a small hinterland of little economic consequence. Cumaná, the largest city in the region, had a population of 70,000 in 1961. Although local unemployment statistics are unavailable, the rate of joblessness must have been high. The equivalent of nearly 20 per cent of the area's population in 1936 had migrated to other parts by 1950. Total population nevertheless continued to expand.

The oil boom in the adjacent Eastern Oil States (Anzoátegui, Monagas) began in the mid-thirties and undoubtedly helped to ameliorate the brutal misery in which the coastal population was living. The nascent oil economy was superimposed upon the traditional economy based on extensive cattle raising. For the Eastern Oil States, despite the name which has been given to them in this study, are, ecologically speaking, a continuation of the great interior plains of Venezuela. But ranching was able to support a population at only a low density. In 1936, just at the onset of the period of intensive oil exploration, Anzoátegui's population was only 130,000 and its main city, Barcelona, barely attained 10,000. The demographic situation in Monagas was not very different.

Intensive oil explorations during the late thirties brought about dramatic changes. New cities suddenly appeared and many older centers expanded. By 1961, the two states had fourteen cities over 5,000 population, dominated by the Barcelona–Puerto la Cruz conurbation, which by that time exceeded 100,000 inhabitants. The process of urbanization had affected Anzoátegui to an exceptional degree. In 1936, only 8 per cent of the state's population could be classified as urban; only twenty-five years later, this proportion had risen to 60 per cent. A great many of the urban migrants had come from within the state itself; but adjacent depressed areas in Sucre and Nueva Esparta had also contributed, and this wave of emigration probably eased their economic conditions somewhat.

The heart of the oil-producing region was connected to the coast by road and pipeline. The coastal cities of Barcelona and Puerto la Cruz grew as a reflex of the developmental activities in the oil fields. However, when exploration activities declined, as they did during the late fifties, these cities were left stranded and a good part of their populations became "surplus." For little of the wealth produced from the subsoils of Anzoátegui, Monagas, and Guárico had remained in these states; it had been either exported or transferred to Caracas. And no compensatory public expenditures had taken place. Thus, beginning in 1958, the Eastern Oil States reverted to their former economic base in cattle.

This situation was radically changed with the decision to create at Santo Tomé de Guayana a new core region based on

189

heavy industry. A strategy now became feasible that would link the several states with each other into a total subsystem of the national economy and exponentially raise the development prospects of the entire region. The downward-transitional character of large parts of the East could be reversed and its productive base diversified. Resource development, institutional innovation, and regional-national integration could become the means for raising the Eastern Provinces to a level equal with the rest of the nation, not only sharing in national progress but making a major economic contribution of their own.

Guidelines for Integration

In identifying major elements of this strategy, it will be useful to begin by sketching the pattern of development zones that might be brought into existence over the next few decades. The schema is strongly related to the resources and ecological conditions of each area as it begins to take shape under the impact of the Guayana program.

For each zone, three aspects will be emphasized: the main economic contribution the zone is capable of making within the total pattern of Venezuela's space economy, the principal urban foci through which its economic life will be organized, and the range of specialized functions that may be performed by each city. In describing these zones, I shall proceed, geographically, from the Guayana region northward to the coast. Boundaries are not clearly demarcated, however, nor do they need to be (see Maps 11 and 12).

1. *Guayana Development Zone.* This area extends chiefly to the south of the Orinoco River, but also includes portions of the delta. Its principal contribution will be as a supplier of metallic minerals, steel and steel products, electrometals, electrochemicals, heavy machinery, forest products, and hydroelectric energy.
Principal focus: The Santo Tomé de Guayana Metropolitan Region, whose chief function will be as a major center of heavy manufacturing in Venezuela. The city's economic base may eventually include a technical university having national

and even international status, together with associated research and development activities.

Subsidiary foci:

a. Ciudad Bolívar, serving as the administrative capital of the State of Bolívar, and as a subdominant trade center for the Guayana region.

b. Tucupíta, serving as the administrative capital of the Federal Territory of Delta Amacuro, and as a subdominant trade center for the delta region.

2. *Central Development Zone.* This extends approximately from the Orinoco River northward to the watershed of the coastal range; its western boundary coincides roughly with the Barcelona-El Tigre-Ciudad Bolívar highway. Its principal outlet includes crude oil and natural gas, as well as agricultural, livestock, and forest products.

Principal focus: Maturín, as an agricultural trade and service center, state capital of Monagas, and a focus of light processing and labor-intensive industry in the zone.

Subsidiary focus: El Tigre, as administrative center for the oil and natural gas industry of the zone, and as a trade center, subdominant with respect to Barcelona.

3. *Coastal Development Zone.* This includes, in addition to the States of Sucre and Nueva Esparta, the Barcelona-Puerto la Cruz Metropolitan Region. It will serve as a major supplier of marine products, nonmetallic minerals (coal, salt, limestone), consumer products, and tourist facilities and services.

Principal focus: the Barcelona-Puerto la Cruz Metropolitan Region as the main trade, financial, service, and administrative center for the Eastern Provinces, also as a center of light manufacturing and as the state capital of Anzoátegui.

Subsidiary foci:

a. Cumaná, as a university city, state capital of Sucre, and subdominant trade center. Tourist services and manufacturing (especially food processing) will be significant elements in the city's economic profile.

b. Porlamar, as a national-international tourist and subdominant trade center.

c. Carúpano, as a subdominant trade center and naval base.

191

The scheme just described implies a certain polarization of the regional economy. Santo Tomé de Guayana would act as a point of resource concentration, reaching far into the interior of Guayana for its raw materials. Most of its manufactured products, in addition to electric energy, would be of the intermediate type for final assembly or transformation in other parts of Venezuela, including the Coastal Development Zone. That zone will presumably have been brought into closer contact with the East Central States, especially the Caracas Metropolitan Region, as the result of substantial improvements in the connecting highway system. Should this be done, the Barcelona-Puerto la Cruz area may begin to compete effectively with Caracas and Valencia as a production center for the national market as well as for the Eastern Provinces. In addition, the Coastal Development Zone will specialize in essential services to the region, including recreation, business, finance, and government.

The Central Development Zone would have close relations with regions both to the south and north. It would supply natural gas and oil to both adjacent zones as a source of energy and industrial raw material in addition to becoming a major source of food products for the Eastern Provinces and, possibly, for the nation as a whole, specializing in grains from the delta, truck crops from the coastal range, and meat products. By focusing the economic life of the zone on Maturín (except for the capital-intensive oil economy which will be based chiefly on El Tigre), the weight of gravity within the zone is shifted to the east. This shift promises to be of major significance for the future spatial organization of the Eastern Provinces.

What is still missing from this description is reference to the pattern of flows that will bind the three zones into a tight economic subsystem of the national economy. Once established, these linkages can be expected to encourage intensification of economic activities along their principal axis. The intensity of development between two core regions will tend to be related to their sizes, the distance separating them, and the character of the resources in the intervening area. A *development corridor* can therefore be expected to come into existence along the highway connecting the Santo Tomé de Guayana with the Barcelona-Puerto la Cruz core regions, leading through Maturín.

This assertion requires further explanation. The present land connection runs from Santo Tomé de Guayana to Ciudad Bolívar, and thence northward to the coast. A bridge across the Orinoco River at Ciudad Bolívar is currently being built. The main road, however, passes through largely barren land whose agricultural promise in considerably less than for areas further to the east. Along its entire extent, little spontaneous development is likely to occur. Yet the road distance, via Maturín, is approximately the same, and the final highway link to Santo Tomé de Guayana will be completed within a few years. It is therefore reasonable to expect that most of the north-south traffic will eventually choose to go over the new route which passes through the economically most active portion of the Central Development Zone. According to a study prepared by Richard Soberman, the average daily flow between Santo Tomé de Guayana and selected points to the north and west may rise from 200 trucks (and nearly a half million tons in commodities) in 1966 to 1,500 trucks (and 3.5 million tons) by 1980.[28] This last figure represents a substantial volume. The convenience of the Ciudad Bolívar bridge may initially divert a good part of this traffic to the western route, but during the 1970's pressure is likely to build up for a *second* bridge across the Orinoco at Santo Tomé de Guayana.[29] The city's national and regional preeminence will make it difficult to resist these pressures, especially in view of the agricultural and other developments that will by then have taken place in the urban field of Maturín. It is therefore difficult to escape the conclusion that, within a generation, the major traffic flow between Santo Tomé de Guayana and the coast will go by way of Maturín. The communications effect of this shift would be expected to lead to an intensification of investment along the route, raising to new heights the economic potentialities not only of the development corridor itself but also of the metropolitan poles that it connects. The economic unity of the Eastern Provinces will thus become a reality.

A possible time sequence may be suggested for the realization of this ultimate pattern. Rather than prescription for a program, it is a prediction of the timing of certain events on the assumption that the events themselves will come to pass. By about 1965, the road connecting Santo Tomé de Guayana with Maturín may be completed, coinciding with the probable opening of the Orinoco River Bridge at Ciudad Bolívar. The ferries now shuttling back and forth between the latter city and Soledad on the opposite bank of the river will then move east to continue plying their trade at the new steel capital of Guayana. Toward the end of the present decade, the industrial growth of Santo Tomé de Guayana may well have become self-sustaining. During the early seventies, intensive agricultural development should be well under way in the delta, which will have become an important inmigrant area. An industrial estate will have been established in the Barcelona area and will begin to attract manufacturing industry. Meanwhile, political pressure will be exerted for the construction of a second Orinoco bridge and the improvement of communications from Barcelona to the capital region and Valencia. The rising economic importance of the Eastern Provinces is likely to make the case a rather persuasive one, and both the bridge and a toll road or freeway to the west may be constructed toward the end of the 1970 decade. Once completed, traffic will be diverted from Ciudad Bolívar to pass over the new route; developments in eastern Monagas will be stimulated, and Maturín itself will begin to emerge, consolidating its subdominant position within the region as a major trade and service center.

By the late eighties, the Eastern Provinces would be dominated by three large metropolitan centers. Barcelona-Puerto la Cruz, with its diversified economy, may have grown to within 900,000 in population; Santo Tomé de Guayana to about 600,000; and Maturín to perhaps ten times its present size, or to 500,000. All three of these metropolitan regional economies would have reached the "takeoff" stage. The role that Barcelona will have performed over the preceding generation as the region's capital will begin to be challenged by Santo Tomé de Guayana, as a larger share of the regional market will have shifted into the area over which Santo Tomé de Guayana exerts a predominant influence. The new bridge will permit that city to expand its service functions down into the delta and into the northern portions of Monagas and Anzoátegui. Its economy will gradually be diversified, especially in the tertiary and quaternary sectors, as many firms formerly established in Ciudad Bolívar (and even Barcelona) will establish major branches in Santo Tomé de Guayana or possibly transfer the head offices to that city. For the center of Guayana's market will be there, and greater customer convenience will strongly suggest these moves.

As a result, Ciudad Bolívar may find it difficult to maintain earlier rates of expansion. With commerce flowing along the new development corridor in the east, the city will become stranded unless it should succeed in the preceding twenty-five years to consolidate its economy so as to render it less vulnerable to shifts in the spatial organization of the region. Its actual destiny appears to be that of a small provincial capital, that will be bypassed by the main thrust of progress, as Venezuela enters the stage of a postindustrial, mass consumption society toward the end of this century.

The economic fortunes of El Tigre may be similarly threatened by these developments. The city's eventual decline may possibly be stayed, however, by the construction of a direct highway link to Maturín by about the time that the second Orinoco bridge comes into operation.

In the meantime, the coastal states of Sucre and Nueva Esparta will have experienced a renascence of their own. The rise of metropolitan centers along their perimeter, together with expansion of their own cities (Cumaná, Carúpano, Porlamar) will have absorbed a large part of their population. Their farming population may increase only slightly and may, in fact, decline. Nearby urban markets can be expected to exert a generally positive influence and lead to gradual adjustments in agriculture, including heavier capitalization. The tourist industry will be stimulated as the region and the country as a whole become more opulent, leading to a sharp rise in the demand for recreation and tourist facilities. Improvements in transportation would further enhance the prospects of the region's tourist industry. In brief, the fortunes of this area, appearing bleak and hopeless now, may well begin to be reversed before the end of the century.

If these projections are reasonably close to the truth, the whole complex of the Eastern Provinces will have been successfully integrated into the national space economy by the late 1980's. The measurement of integration presents analytical problems of great complexity, and no quantitative projections will be attempted. Yet, intuitively, it would seem that, by whatever index that may be used, the Eastern Provinces will have become a functional part of the total space economy. One would expect returns to the principal production factors in the region to be more equal with factor remuneration in the rest of the economy, and especially at the center. Its economic structure, tightly bound to national markets, would be more similar to that of the central region than it is today, chiefly with regard to the share of agriculture and industry in regional income. The Eastern Provinces would have become a major producer of minerals, agricultural materials, producer and consumer goods, and recreational services. The region would thus be no longer wholly dependent on outside influences but a generator of influence on its own part. Its system of cities would be well articulated functionally and tied directly into the national system through the structure of trade and capital markets. And in *per capita* income and other pertinent welfare indices (education, health, housing), the Eastern Provinces should be able to stand muster in comparison with the great metropolitan economies of the central region.

The Challenge to National Planning

The achievement of a state of affairs that will in some measure be congruent with this description in neither automatic nor, to a significant extent, within the range of capabilities of the Guayana Corporation. Certainly, the corporation can in some ways assist the eastern states in planning for transition to a new type of economy in response to changes within Guayana itself. It can promote research, a wider exchange of information among interested agencies, and it can sponsor training courses for development experts in different subject fields. In a wider sense, too, it can assume some functions of leadership within the region, though this might substantially alter its character as an agent of the national government.

Important as such activities would be, their effectiveness must be gauged, on the one hand, against an institutional structure that is inadequate to support development activities at the regional level and against the extreme centralization of effective decision-making power in Caracas, on the other. The phenomenon is an extremely complex one in which cause and effect are intricately mingled. But whatever the explanation, the following judgment made six years ago still stands: "The Venezuelan local unit of government, as a class and with limited exceptions, is at present completely unequipped financially, administratively, or otherwise to serve a useful role in modern government."[30] This condition of helplessness is endemic across the total spectrum of institutions on the periphery. In place of active local enterprise, one encounters a pervasive fatalism, a clinging dependence on the national government for solving local problems, and widespread ignorance of actual development possibilities and rational means for their realization.

But there are reasons additional to local impotence that push responsibility inevitably upward. Preoccupation with regional development is, after all, a nationwide phenomenon, and the network of interdependencies has grown so extensive that a decision to invest in one locality can have substantial repercussions on many other parts, as well as on the general course of progress of the national economy. Indeed, there are many ways in which the space economy might be organized, each of which would result in a different combination of welfare and growth and in a distinct living environment. Regional policy must therefore be cast in light of national objectives, just as it is bound to be influenced by national political forces that are concerned with the spatial allocation of resources and the distribution of political power. A pronounced shift of investments to the Eastern Provinces might adversely affect the western periphery and step up the rate of migration to central and western cities greatly in excess of their ability to absorb new migrants. Priority attention to the problems of depressed and backward areas would divert critical resources from regions of spontaneous growth where they might be used to greater *economic* advantage. Whatever the decision made, it will affect the lives of millions of people who are vocal, who can vote, and who can bring to bear effective pressures on the government. As with other vital issues, the nub of the problem here is political, but planning analysis can do much to clarify the choices that are made. In the remaining chapters, I shall suggest a framework for such an analysis as well as some guidelines for regional policy that may help Venezuela to resolve her problems of spatial organization satisfactorily.

CHAPTER NINE

ELEMENTS OF A REGIONAL POLICY FOR VENEZUELA (1)

The need for systematic thinking about locational aspects of economic development in Venezuela has become widely acknowledged. The Guayana experience has roused interest in regional questions throughout the country and has posed some knotty issues for national planners. But how should they, or anyone else, think "systematically" about the relation of location to development? Where does one start? In this and the following chapter I hope to suggest a potentially fruitful approach. Practical problems of organization, programming, and information will be left for a concluding chapter.

Locational Requirements as a Policy Constraint

Regional policy is not so unencumbered that it can dispose over the location of activities at will without jeopardizing their efficiency. Where markets serve as the principal mechanism of allocation, the propensities of activity location, guided in the main by the desire to make profits, must be respected. Conditions affecting locational choice may be modified through measures such as resources development, investment in urban facilities, subsidies, tax exemptions, and similar direct incentives. They cannot be completely overturned, however. Every attempt at modifying these conditions has for its background the normal interaction pattern of locational forces. It is primarily by acting on this normal pattern through changes in the parameters of choice that regional policy seeks to attain its ends. A knowledge of the locational forces that are likely to be generated by Venezuela's economy must therefore be regarded as essential to formulating an effective regional policy.

Some Elements of Structural Change

Among the chief influences acting on location will be changes in total population, production, technology, and employment. Assumptions regarding each of these variables are stated below.

Total population. An average annual growth rate of between 3.0 and 3.5 per cent can be assumed to persist for the generation in view. This would allow for further improvement in the death rate, a proportionately smaller reduction in the birth rate, and moderate immigration from overseas. For purposes of this study, population will be assumed to reach a level of 20 million during the decade 1985–1995. Our policy model will therefore be geared to a population about 2.5 times its present size.[1]

Rate of economic growth. Production will have to expand more rapidly than population if national objectives are to be met. As a secular trend, to prevail steadily over a generation, a yearly increase in the gross product of the nation of from 5 to 7 per cent will be projected. At this rate, per capita income would slightly more than double within the stated period.[2]

To achieve this over-all rate of growth, several allocation patterns are feasible. But any decision will have to recognize that the future growth of Venezuela's economy will have to come increasingly from the manufacture of basic metals, industrial chemicals, and consumer durables (automobiles, refrigerators, and so on). Alexander Ganz, chief economist for the M.I.T.-Harvard Joint Center for Urban Studies Group in Caracas, has stated the case persuasively:

Latin American industrial development has virtually exhausted the stage of easy expansion of non-durable goods and consumer durable manufacture in substitution of finished consumer goods imports . . . . In fact, Latin American economic development is at a pause . . . . The next stage of economic development for Latin American, and for Venezuela as well, centered on metals, chemicals, and productive machinery in the framework of an integrated Latin American Common Market, signifies a turning-away from the existing urban-industrial centers and the establishment of new industrial complexes in resource and energy-rich regions. In effect, Latin America and Venezuela are entering upon an era of regional programming of industrial complexes as the new phase of accelerated economic development.[3]

For the limited objectives of the present study, detailed estimates of the changing structure of manufacturing is unnecessary. Instead, trends will be projected for each of the principal economic sectors.

Implicit in the over-all growth rate is the development of manufacturing industry on a large scale. To achieve the projected rate for gross national product, total value added in manufacturing will have to rise by better than 10 per cent annually. However, the new export-oriented industries referred to by Ganz will have to expand at a rate substantially higher than that for the production of nondurable goods, most of which would be consumed at home.

Agricultural production can probably be made to grow at a long-term rate somewhat greater than that for population. The country's soils and climate do not suggest, however, competitive advantage in crops other than cacao, coffee, and possibly some starches (sugar, rice). A few other products of farming may eventually reach the export stage but would be unlikely to alter much the present situation in which the agricultural sector contributes less than 7 per cent to the nation's product. Over the period of a generation, this share can be expected to decline.[4]

The long-term outlook for petroleum production is one of both absolute and relative decline. In this critical area, no independent projections will be attempted. The Central Planning Agency of Venezuela has recently prepared a graph of two hypothetical long-term production curves.[5] They show that a level of maximum production may be reached around 1970, followed by a rather steep decline. By 1990, the curves show an annual rate of production roughly equivalent to that which prevailed between 1955 and 1960, with further reductions being projected beyond that date. By 1975, CORDIPLAN expects that petroleum production together with mining will account for only 14 per cent of the gross national income.[6]

201

Value added in commerce and services will rise approximately parallel to the average long-term growth in national product, perhaps slightly below it, within a range of 4 to 6 per cent a year. Within this broad sector, however, unusually high rates of expansion will be registered in financial services, communications, education, and scientific research.

The impact of technology. Venezuela's drive to industrial maturity is taking place during the era of automation. The country will therefore be unable to exercise significant choice with respect to the technology that will provide the material means for the income and employment growth projected in these pages.

Several conditions combine to render practically worthless most of the recent literature on the subject of an "optimum" technology for capital-short economies.[7] To begin with, most of the production machinery for Venezuela's industrialization will be imported; but the only machinery available on the international marketplace is likely to be the same highly automated equipment which is increasingly coming into use in the more advanced countries. One item of capital equipment may be a little less productive, a little less completely "programmed" than another, but this is unlikely to influence the correctness of the over-all judgment that Venezuela has no effective choice but to "automate" along with everybody else and hence achieve very high productivities of labor in specific sectors. Market availability will be reinforced by the preferences of engineers and technicians who, regardless of whether they are Venezuelan or foreign, will be strongly inclined to favor exciting late models whose properties they have studied at the university and discussions of which fill the professional and trade journals. Moreover, the character of much of Venezuela's potential industrial park—metallurgical and chemical—lends itself superbly to automation, and many other products will eventually be produced in fully or partially automated factories. Competitiveness in export markets will impose its own productivity requirements. Since even unskilled factory labor is not inexpensive in Venezuela, partly because of the pace-setting high wages of workers in the petroleum industry, the installation of automated equipment will be generally profitable, especially if scale of plant is brought into consideration.

Even now, automation is by no means a stranger to Venezuela. The country's largest petrochemical complex is being operated by three shifts of one hundred workers each. A brewery in Maracaibo with branch plants throughout the Andean region has procured the latest equipment from the United States and has initiated automatic data processing for all of its payroll data in Caracas. The country's gigantic petroleum industry, producing 28 per cent of the national wealth, employs only 36,000 workers out of a total labor force of over 2.3 million. Examples could be multiplied.

This pervasive trend will have profound consequences for the development of Venezuela's economy. At the projected annual rate, the modern manufacturing sector will be unable to absorb a proportionate share of the new labor force coming on the marketplace each year. Since agricultural possibilities are restricted, and even many types of office work are subject to modernization, a significant portion of Venezuela's potential labor supply will become redundant and will terminate in retail trade and personal service occupations where excessively low productivities will reduce millions of urban workers to a condition of endemic "underemployment," that is to say, to poverty.[8] At the same time, the skewed distribution of income resulting from capital-intensive production will lead to increasing government participation in industrial and perhaps commercial enterprise—as an alternative to excessive taxation on profits—as well as to vast income redistribution schemes in favor of the poor. Thus, inevitably, Venezuela will evolve into a version of the service state in which a very large number, perhaps even a majority, of the population will, in one form or another, be dependent on government support. The political and sociopsychological consequences of this trend are as yet difficult to foresee.

The structure of employment. In order to have some quantitative estimates available, the employment model in Table 9.1 was constructed. Although it must not be taken too seriously in

Table 9.1. Estimated Active Population by
Major Industrial Sectors*
(*in thousands*)

Sector	1950		1960		1990±5		1960–1990±5
	number	per cent	number	per cent	number	per cent	absolute gain
Agriculture, Forestry, and Fishing	705	41.3	842	31.9	1,610	23	768
Mining	6	0.3	12	0.5	70	1	58
Petroleum	43	2.5	40	1.5	50	1	10
Manufacturing	207	12.1	259†	9.8	1,100	16	841
Construction	91	5.3	153	5.8	560	8	407
Utilities	5	0.3	12	0.4	50	1	38
Commerce	150	8.8	259	9.8	1,000	14	741
Transport and Communications	52	3.1	95	3.6	600	8	505
Services	342	20.0	547	20.7	1,680	24	1,133
Total Employment	1,601	93.7	2,222	84.2	6,720	96	4,498
Unemployment	106	6.3	416	15.8	280	4	−136
Total Active Population	1,707	100.0	2,638	100.0	7,000	100	4,362
Ratio to Total Population	34		35		35		

Sources: For 1950, Central Bank of Venezuela, *Memória 1959*, Table 17.6. For 1960, Central Bank estimate in "Breve Analisis Comparativo Entre las Cifras Provisionales del IX Censo de Población y Las Estimaciones del S.I.M. del D.C.N. Sobre La Población Activa," Typescript, n.d. (Central Bank, National Income Accounts Department).

*Statistical data for employment in Venezuela are contradictory and, for historical series, accurate, at best, to the nearest 100,000. Some idea of the discrepancies among published data may be found in the table on "Active Population" on the following page.

all of its detail, the magnitudes shown are suggestive of what the achievement of national production goals might mean in terms of the sectoral distribution of jobs. Data for 1950 and 1960 were estimated by the national income staff of the Central Bank; the projections to the decade 1985–1995 represent an informed judgment regarding the outcome of the production trends discussed and of foreseeable changes in labor productivity.

In agriculture, a continued relative decline of employment is shown, though at a lower rate than during the past decade. A major reason for this retarded rate is the virtual inability of the urban sector to absorb more population than is implied by the model without, at the same time, increasing unemployment. Thus, by about 1990, Venezuela may still have as much as a quarter of its active population in farming, for a total increase

	1950		1951		1959		1961
	census of population	Central Bank	Central Bank	CORDI-PLAN	Central Bank	CORDI-PLAN	census of population
Agriculture and Fishing	704	705	722	789	833	777	730
Mining	6	6	4	5	12	12	10
Petroleum	44	43	44	38	43	37	38
Manufacturing	168	207	208	227	261	304	250
Construction	91	91	94	96	187	157	81
Utilities	5	5	5	6	12	20	22
Commerce	150	150	158	164	249	260	271
Transport and Communications	52	52	57	57	86	79	86
Services and Others	361	342	358	368	522	505	599
Total Employment	1,599	1,601	1,650	1,750	2,205	2,151	2,088
Unemployment	n.a.	106	127	127	252	251	328
Total Active Population	n.a.	1,707	1,777	1,877	2,457	2,402	2,416

Active Population, 10 Years or More, by Sectors (*in thousands*)

Sources: Central Bank data are from *Memória 1959,* Table 17.6; CORDIPLAN data are from "Datos Fundamentales del Plan de la Nación, 1963–1966," mimeographed 1962, Table III.1.7.

It is evident that Central Bank estimates in 1950 were based on the results of the 1950 Census of Population, with major discrepancies in manufacturing and service employment. Estimates for later years show increasing divergence (e.g., the CORDIPLAN estimate for agriculture in 1951 is *greater* by 67,000 than the Central Bank estimate but *less* by 56,000 in 1959; for manufacturing the CORDIPLAN estimate is greater by 19,000 in 1951 and by 43,000 in 1959). Census data for 1961 refer to February and may be compared with the December 1960 Central Bank estimate in Table 9.1.

†Of this total, 96,000 jobs were reported to be in handicrafts (artesenato). Manufacturing employment in modern industrial plants increased from about 92,000 in 1950 to about 164,000 in 1960.

205

of nearly 800,000 new jobs outside the urban sector. Since the existing agricultural regions of the country are, for the most part, overpopulated, the additional increment and, preferably, an even larger number, will have to be resettled on new land.

Because of what has been said concerning automation, manufacturing employment is shown to increase only slightly, or from 10 per cent in 1960 to 16 per cent at the end of the period, for a total absolute gain of about 840,000. Taking a straight-line average, this would mean an annual increase of nearly 30,000 industrial jobs. Yet even for this relatively modest goal, there is nothing in Venezuela's recent past to suggest that it can, in fact, be achieved. A doubling of industrial production during the entire decade of the fifties yielded a net gain of only 35 per cent (70,000 workers) in industrial employment which, on an annual basis, runs to about one fourth of future requirements in the model.[9] For the 4 per cent registered gain in manufacturing output between 1960 and 1961, there was a corresponding (reported) increase in manufacturing employment of only 5,000 workers.[10] The majority of those seeking work either drifted into low-level services (for example, domestic) or remained unemployed.[11] In short, even a modest employment target may be difficult to reach.

These comments may suffice to show the character of the projections and their precariousness as forecasts. It might be added that in making them, "total active population" was first derived as a control figure; should the participation rate of labor force rise above the estimated 35 per cent, the absolute burden on the agricultural and tertiary service sectors would be markedly increased.[12]

Active Locational Forces

As the result of the new structure of industries, as measured by employment, three major propensities can be expected to influence the pattern of activity location in Venezuela over the next generation.

Decentralization by which is meant a relative diminution in the importance of the Caracas Metropolitan Area as a center for economic activity and the simultaneous convergence of productive investments upon new locations on the periphery. In the early sixties, Caracas was responsible for two thirds of all industrial production in the country.[13] With decentralization, this ratio would decline.

The government is deeply concerned with promoting decentralization. But unless the *objective* conditions of Venezuela's industrialization support a policy of decentralization, it is doubtful whether it will ever be effective. The locational requirements of some of the new industries are altogether different from those of the import-substitution, consumer-oriented enterprises that have been dominant until now. More than that, new industry is a great consumer of space, and attractive industrial sites in the Caracas area are becoming scarce and are situated farther and farther from the center of the city.[14] The space problem explains a good deal about the recent upsurge of industry in the Valencia Basin, which is coming to rival the national capital region as a major industrial center.

Focalization: the search for decentralized activity locations, however, does not occur at random. Investors will seek out locations which, among other things, will have the following characteristics:

a. good accessibility to regional, national, and/or international markets;

b. a wide range of diversified, specialized services and the possibility of establishing functional linkages to already existing firms in the locality;

c. organized industrial estates including basic utility and transport facilities; and

d. a high level of urban service facilities, including schools, research centers, hospitals, recreation facilities, housing, and public administration.[15]

Good access to markets and availability of technical services will be decisive, however, for a majority of firms. A few very large enterprises will not conform to these location criteria, and I shall comment on these later. But from 70 to 80 per cent of the new industrialization—measured in terms of employment, less in terms of investment—can be expected to be predominantly based on cities. They will be distributed among the half dozen or so important core regions that enjoy a comparative advantage in their accessibility to both markets and material inputs.[16] For these reasons, coastal cities in the central belt from Barquisimeto to Barcelona are most likely to be favored.

Dispersion refers to a loose pattern of activity distribution within the confines of a focal area. External economies are becoming increasingly mobile so that any plant location within a distance-radius of from thirty to sixty minutes by automobile travel from the central city can be reasonably considered as part of that city's metropolitan economy and will normally have considerable interaction with businesses throughout the entire area and particularly with those located within the central city.[17]

The basic spatial form that emerges from this pattern of activity location may be called the *metropolitan regional economy.* Its boundaries are delimited by studying the flows of interaction as they are traced by the movement of people, goods, and information. Although its land-use pattern will be a patchwork of mixed and overlapping activities, including truck gardening, dairy farming, and outdoor recreation, its population will follow predominantly urban modes of living. Metropolitan regional economies will be regarded by potential investors as meaningful location matrices, that is, as coherent units for comparison in location decisions.

As mentioned earlier, a number of large industries will not be oriented primarily to markets, but have locations in proximity to raw materials and low-cost energy, preferably with good access to the ocean for overseas export. This complex of location needs underlies the Guayana program with its iron mines, hydropower plants, steel mill, and potential projects in aluminum reduction, electrochemicals, manganese, and paper. But in the aggregate, it is unlikely that more than 10 per cent of the total industrial employment—though somewhat more of total investment and production—will fall in this category.[18] Some additional employment will be linked to these industries because of external economies. Combined with the earlier estimate, total resource-linked employment may, therefore, reach 20 to 30 per cent of the total industrial labor force, or from 200,000 to 300,000 workers by about 1990. The remaining employment, however, will be strongly influenced by a desire to be close to the bulk of the country's urban consumers.

The same location pattern holds for nearly all other activities as well. Trades and services will proliferate in the large metropolitan regions rather than on the isolated frontier or in rural areas. This seems like an obvious point, but it is frequently forgotten in statements on the "philosophy" of decentralization. The national capital will inevitably house a very large proportion of the communications, research, and control services of the economy. Its future expansion will be largely a consequence of increasing concentration of administrative, financial, decision-making, planning, and information functions for a society whose organized complexity, spreading at a geometric rate, is demanding a nearly vertical increase in those skills by which society can retain some mastery over its own destiny.

Agricultural production will be strongly influenced by the location of major core regions and metropolitan populations in the space economy. Most of the crop production in Venezuela will be for the domestic, which is to say, the growing urban market. Studies have shown the close correlation between commercial farming, agricultural prosperity, and urban centers.[19] Soil fertility cannot be considered a major determinant of agricultural location. It is one of the conditions for agricultural development and may stimulate or retard agricultural production; but, as Chisholm points out, the quality of soils is rarely a decisive criterion in agricultural location.[20] Some extremely capital-intensive farming will be found within the metropolitan regions themselves and somewhat less intensive, commercial farming adjacent to the belt of urban population. Accessibility to markets is, on balance, as important a criterion for the location of agricultural activities as for most industrial firms.

Determinants of Population Distribution

Population is expected to follow in the wake of economic opportunity. This has been the normal pattern. And since the several emerging metropolitan regional economies promise to be the principal foci of economic activity in Venezuela, population can be expected to converge on them in large numbers. But another force deserves consideration. In a society whose rural areas are overpopulated, migrants will often drift into cities in the hope of improving their economic situation and well-being, *whether or not objective work opportunities exist there.* Services such as water, electric light, schools, cinemas, soccer stadiums, and hospitals which are found only in cities are said to form one of the chief attractions for rural migrants in Venezuela.[21]

The quality of a place for living may consequently become increasingly significant in decisions on residence locations. This is likely to hold as true for the poor as for the managerial and professional groups. Since as much as one third of Venezuela's labor force, and an even larger proportion of the urban workers, may be seriously underemployed over the period defined by these projections, provision of urban amenities—whether in rural or urban-metropolitan areas—promises to become one of the major instruments for settlement policy, irrespective of economic considerations.

Can the future urbanization of Venezuela be quantified? In Table 9.2 an attempt is made to derive some bench-mark figures on the basis of the employment model sketched.

A dramatic increase of urban population, from 4 to 14 million, is projected. In the next three decades, approximately, provision will have to be made for about 10 million new urbanites—more than the present *total* population of the country! But rural population will also be increasing, and small-town life is far from disappearing in the era of the metropolitan regional economy. Nearly 3 million people will have to be absorbed outside the major centers.

Policy Objectives

An effective regional policy must be consistent not only with the major forces that influence the location decisions of firms and households but also with the overriding purposes of national life. These will apply to public activity in general; reformulated, however, they may also be used as criteria for judging the performance of the economy in its spatial dimension.

Table 9.2. Estimates of Urban and Nonurban Population, 1950, 1959, and 1990
(*in thousands*)

	1950		1960		1990±5		Increase 1959–1990±5
	number	per cent	number	per cent	number	per cent	number
Nonurban Jobs	754	44.3	854	32.4	1,680	24.0	826
Urban Jobs and Unemployment	952	55.7	1,784	67.6	5,320	76.0	3,536
Total Active Population	1,706	100.9	2,638	100.0	7,000	100.0	4,362
Total Population	5,035	100.0	7,524°	100.0	20,000	100.0	12,476
Total Nonurban Population	2,914	57.9	3,191°	42.4	5,800	29.0	2,609
Total Urban Population	2,121	42.1	4,333°	57.6	14,200	71.0	9,867

° Data for February 1961.

Sources: Employment data for 1950 and 1960 from Table 9.1. Nonurban employment includes agriculture, forestry, fishing, and mining. Population data for past years are from the 8th and 9th National Censuses. Urban and nonurban population projections are based on job-population ratios for 1959.

The main ends of public policy are stated in the *Plan de la Nación.*[22] In language that departs from the original, but not, it is hoped, from its essential spirit, the nation's purposes may be explained as follows:

A democratic social order. Adherence to a government that is grounded in constitutional forms and dedicated to upholding the principles of a democratic social order.

Social and political stability. Creation of the conditions necessary for social and political stability by maintaining minimum essential balances in the components and rates of social and economic change.

Economic independence. Development of a national economy capable of self-sustaining cumulative growth and sufficiently diversified in the structure of its industries successfully to withstand and adapt to the vagaries of behavior in the international marketplace.

Adequate living levels. Provision of education, housing, medical, and other basic social services to all the people at levels of adequacy consistent with the productive capabilities of the nation and the requirements of economic growth.

Social equality. Achievement of a system that provides for the equal access of all the people to existing social and economic opportunities; for the full employment of those who wish to work at the prevailing standards of hours and wages; for the progressive reduction of income differences among the population; and for rising levels of disposable family income.

These comprehensive goals are capable of interpretation in purely spatial terms. If regional policy is regarded as an instrument for achieving the highest public good through an appropriate ordering of activities in space, its basic norm will be an order capable of sustaining an efficient path of economic transformation. At the present juncture of Venezuela's development, this means, first, the gradual elimination of the periphery on a national scale, and second, the progressive integration of the national space economy. (See Chapter 4.)

These are the general principles. They may be further reduced to the following policy guidelines:

1. Reduce differences in the marginal rate of return to factors of production.

2. Assure economically efficient locations for every enterprise.

3. Concentrate public investments in areas of maximum growth potential.

4. Maintain the degree of regional balance in major components of the level of living that is regarded as essential to political stability.

These goals do not depict a precise end-state for the spatial system as a whole; they do provide an orientation. The first goal states a general criterion for a more nearly perfect spatial integration of Venezuela's economy. All other goals are in a sense subsidiary to this overriding purpose. Goals 2 and 3 are complementary: the former suggests the desirability of regarding the profitability of enterprise as a suitable criterion; the latter urges the advantage of agglomeration economies that may accrue by piling up investments on a small number of core regions. The goal of regional balance, finally, modifies the impact of the preceding ones and suggests that political objectives deserve an equal standing with economic ones.

All of the goals presume a pricing policy for services, especially for energy and transportation, that will truly reflect their marginal costs of production. Subsidies granted for indefinite periods to support enterprise in what would otherwise be regarded as uneconomic locations would vitiate most of the intentions of regional policy as they have been stated here.

A Strategy for Regional Development

How may these goals be translated into a strategy for action? Four principles appropriate to this task may be suggested.

First, concentrate public infrastructure investments in key metropolitan regional economies (core regions) and development corridors.

Second, break down the existing center-periphery structure of the country's space economy by strengthening major and subsidiary core regions on the periphery.

Third, relieve the pressure of population in downward-transitional areas by encouraging outward migration and assisting in adjustments to less intensive, more commerically oriented forms of resource use.

Fourth, reduce the rate of urbanization by undertaking large-scale agricultural resettlement programs, drawing population from poor mountain districts to new communities on the agricultural frontier.

The basic strategy, therefore, recommends the activation of a number of new core regions, some of them located on the periphery and, simultaneously, the resettlement of rural population and land reclamation on an extensive scale to relieve the poverty in depressed agricultural areas and to ease the costs (and social strains) of new urbanization.

Though it might be done, I am not here concerned with a precise detailing of this framework into operational programs. What I propose to do instead is to comment on a variety of policy aspects that, if left unexplained, might cause misunderstanding.

213

Location policy. The location of every project investment must be determined individually in a cost-benefit analysis. But the net contribution of a single project can be fairly judged only where its effects are measured within the context of a *program* of related projects. This practice will lead to some accounting problems in attributing benefits to specific investments, but these are not insurmountable. The logic of investment location decisions therefore suggests the desirability of programming the economic development of selected core regions and development corridors. The activation of new core regions means creating environmental conditions so favorable that they will induce individual firms to choose, on purely economic grounds, a location within one of them. In this way, direct location subsidies can be avoided.

Urbanization policy. A basic principle of urbanization policy, given Venezuela's actual stage of development, is the desirability of reducing the flow of people to cities and especially to the larger centers. The problem of urban-bound migration will become especially severe if a strategy of core region development should be adopted. The visibility of concentrated investment will tend to make core regions the preferred targets of migration. Although this cannot be avoided, the process can be retarded by making alternative migration goals attractive. This is the subject for resettlement policy discussed in the next section.

On the other hand, it would be a mistake to encourage scattering infrastructure investments in middle-sized cities because of the supposedly excessive costs of metropolitan development.[23] The dysfunctions of the metropolis—its chaotic appearance, its perennial traffic congestion, its massive slums, its polluted air, its want of open space—are not inevitable. Through careful spatial planning and adequate provision of services, a life-enhancing environment can be created in urban clusters of practically any size. Therefore, concurrent with programming for economic development, large-scale spatial planning efforts should be undertaken to assure that the new urban forms which emerge and in which most of the country's population will eventually

be concentrated will also offer a superior setting for family living and for the vibrant drama of communal life.

Resettlement policy. The policy of resettlement that has been
proposed does not regard an increase in agricultural production
as its primary objective. Its economic effects are rather indirect:
reduced urbanization costs and greater ease for accomplishing
necessary land-use changes in the older agricultural regions. The
policy should consequently focus on ways for resettling the
largest possible number of farm families in new rural communities. With this focus on people, it is clear that the program
intended here should rely on labor-intensive methods for land
clearance, settlement, and irrigation. It will be sufficient if
worker productivity is at first higher by only a small increment
from what it was in the migrants' former home communities.
Gradually, over the years, productivity can be built up by plow-
ing back farmers' savings into new capital equipment, better
irrigation facilities, increased fertilizer use, and improved storage. To be successful, however, resettlement programs must be
carefully planned from agronomic, social, and economic stand-
points, and technical assistance should be made available to the
new settlers on a sufficient scale.

*Resource development policy (except for petroleum and natu-
ral gas).* The main emphasis here should continue to be on the
coordinated development of the Guayana region and of Santo
Tomé de Guayana as a new core region, with special attention
to the relation of Guayana to the remainder of the Eastern Provinces. In other respects, programs for resource development
should, in the main, be guided by the evolving demand for specific resources or resource-related services, such as tourism. In
connection with the proposed resettlement program, thought
may be given to the possibility of incorporating within the areas
set aside for national forests or national parks all regions of very
low economic potential.

Agricultural adjustment policy. Two problems are presented
in dealing with adjustments to new conditions in the older areas
of rural settlement. For downward-transitional areas, the main
problem is to shift out of subsistence farming to more commer-

215

cially profitable operations and to remove from production areas that from an ecological standpoint are unsuited to continued cultivation. For upward-transitional areas, situated along the margins of major cities, desirable adjustments include increasing farm capitalization, improved distribution systems, and production for a predominantly metropolitan market. Agricultural planners should work closely with the planners of resettlement programs in order to take advantage of the opportunities for change created by extensive outmigration. Near metropolitan regions, they should coordinate their efforts not only with programs for economic development but also with the physical planning of core regions if competing demands for land are to be satisfactorily resolved.

Transportation and communications policy. The basic aim of policy in this area should be to facilitate geographic mobility and the interchange of information. To put it another way, policy should aim at reducing the marginal costs of transportation and communications in terms of money, time, and convenience. In accomplishing this purpose, priorities should be derived mainly from the strategy for the activation of core regions with improvements in the internal networks of metropolitan regional economies, intermetropolitan transportation and communication, and relation between metropolis and its hinterland receiving attention in approximately that order.

To complete discussion of the strategy for regional development, the spatial framework within which specific policies will be effective must be established. But before proceeding to this topic, a major conclusion may be stated: regional policy at the national level is closely related to programming for metropolitan regional economies, resettlement projects, and agricultural adjustment areas. In this context, regional programming refers to the identification of specific project investments leading to a set of program goals for a given area and related to each other through efficient sequences in time and space. It leaves open the question of coordinating the implementation of investment programs, though a measure of such coordination would be desirable.

CHAPTER TEN

ELEMENTS OF A REGIONAL POLICY FOR VENEZUELA (2)

Criteria for the Selection of Core Regions

Core regions may be defined as metropolitan areas which have a high propensity for economic growth and for filtering this growth to other parts of the space economy. For Venezuela, core regions were identified by applying two criteria. First, a given metropolitan economy had to show high promise for development as measured by the usual indices of investment, production, and employment. At issue here was a judgment regarding the qualities of an existing urban center, or cluster of such centers, as a "matrix" likely to attract productive investments, particularly industry, without extensive subsidy. This judgment required an evaluation of the region's accessibility to future markets and to sources of raw material; the possibilities of resource development across the field dominated by the central city; and such run-of-the-mill location factors as the quality of the potential labor supply, the adequacy of fresh water within economic distance, and the supporting service structure of the area.

The present size of potential central cities was used as a preliminary index in the identification of core regions. This choice biased the outcome in favor of the existing pattern of cities. Because of the remarkable stability in the order of dominance of cities, however, this bias is probably not too much of a distortion. By virtue of its size, a leading metropolitan regional economy will have brought into being both a service structure and a potential market that is attractive to investors. In Venezuela's case, for instance, it would seem odd if Maracaibo, the country's second largest city and powerful state capital of Zulia,

217

should fail to be included in a list of future centers of development. Maracaibo has retained its relative position in the urban hierarchy at least since 1926. Strong arguments would have to be advanced to show why this city, together with its metropolitan economy, should not continue to maintain approximately its relative position in the future. It must be added, however, that present city size is by no means an infallible predictor of economic performance. Large cities may stagnate, and even decline. In every case, therefore, the proposition was tested against the city's recent economic history and its geographic location with respect to markets and supplies.

The potential of a metropolitan economy for influencing the development of other areas was employed as a second criterion. As an initial approximation to an adequate measure of this variable, I chose the extent and character of the potential urban field over which the central city could be expected to extend its influence. With certain qualifications, I assumed that the size of the urban field was roughly proportional to the relative position of the metropolitan regional economy in the hierarchy of urban clusters. The higher it ranked in the hierarchy, the larger would be its field of dominance and, consequently, the wider would be its ultimate capacity for transmitting growth impulses across space.

This view of urban fields suggested the possibility of arranging core regions into a hierarchy, as follows:

Rank Order of Core Region	Descriptive Name
First	National metropolis
Second	Regional capital
Third	Subregional center
Fourth	Local service center

First-order regions would be those that, because of their unchallenged preeminence, are judged to be vital for the achievement of national objectives. They will normally include the nation's capital city (except for artificially created government centers, such as Brasília or Canberra), as well as major manufacturing and commercial centers.

Little need be said about second- and third-order core regions.

Local service centers, on the other hand, might be better regarded as important central places (growth points) whose expansion will be derivative from the development of higher-order regions, than as core regions in their own right. Their ability to generate economic growth independently of progress in higher ranking regions will be small.

This ordering of core regions does not conform to the so-called nested hierarchy which has been proposed by some writers as a model for fully matured urban systems; rather, it suggests the "weak" or "partial" hierarchy described by Duncan and his co-workers.[1] A city such as Barquisimeto, for instance, is not "contained" within the urban field of the next higher order but has an independent area of influence, subdominant only with respect to the national capital. In this case, the extent of the urban field as a criterion of choice becomes secondary to the potentialities for growth of the central city itself.

Results of applying these criteria to Venezuela are summarized in the paragraphs that follow (as well as in Map 11).

Three first-order core regions were identified, including the Caracas, Valencia-Maracay, and Santo Tomé de Guayana metropolitan regional economies. All three have an unchallenged national importance. The capital region, as the main center of national decision and control, is an obvious choice. All the evidence suggests that this region—plan or no plan—is fast growing into one of the great cosmopolitan centers on the continent, with an eventual population of several million in its immediate environment.[2]

The several cities of the Valencia Basin, together with related urban areas along the coast, form a second incipient metropolitan economy distinguished by a burgeoning industrial sector (chemicals, tires, cement, household appliances, containers, automobile assembly, shipyards, livestock feed, glass, and so on) and specialized agricultural production (tobacco, sugar, dairy products, poultry). Its location near the center of the national market, proximity to the national capital, and general access characteristics suggest for it an important national role. The Caracas and Valencia-Maracay regional economies are, in fact, so closely related through banking, management, and distribution func-

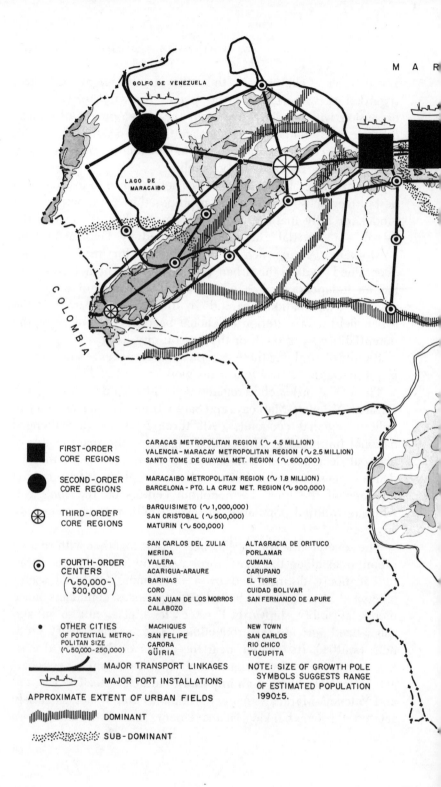

MAR

GOLFO DE VENEZUELA

LAGO DE
MARACAIBO

COLOMBIA

■ FIRST-ORDER
CORE REGIONS

CARACAS METROPOLITAN REGION (∿ 4.5 MILLION)
VALENCIA - MARACAY METROPOLITAN REGION (∿ 2.5 MILLION)
SANTO TOME DE GUAYANA MET. REGION (∿ 600,000)

● SECOND-ORDER
CORE REGIONS

MARACAIBO METROPOLITAN REGION (∿ 1.8 MILLION)
BARCELONA - PTO. LA CRUZ MET. REGION (∿ 900,000)

⊛ THIRD-ORDER
CORE REGIONS

BARQUISIMETO (∿ 1,000,000)
SAN CRISTOBAL (∿ 500,000)
MATURIN (∿ 500,000)

◉ FOURTH-ORDER
CENTERS
$\left(\begin{smallmatrix}∿50,000- \\ 300,000\end{smallmatrix}\right)$

SAN CARLOS DEL ZULIA
MERIDA
VALERA
ACARIGUA-ARAURE
BARINAS
CORO
SAN JUAN DE LOS MORROS
CALABOZO

ALTAGRACIA DE ORITUCO
PORLAMAR
CUMANA
CARUPANO
EL TIGRE
CUIDAD BOLIVAR
SAN FERNANDO DE APURE

• OTHER CITIES
OF POTENTIAL METRO-
POLITAN SIZE
(∿50,000-250,000)

MACHIQUES
SAN FELIPE
CARORA
GÜIRIA

NEW TOWN
SAN CARLOS
RIO CHICO
TUCUPITA

━━ MAJOR TRANSPORT LINKAGES

⛴ MAJOR PORT INSTALLATIONS

APPROXIMATE EXTENT OF URBAN FIELDS

▒ DOMINANT

⣿ SUB-DOMINANT

NOTE: SIZE OF GROWTH POLE
SYMBOLS SUGGESTS RANGE
OF ESTIMATED POPULATION
1990±5.

C A R I B E

ISLA DE
MARGARITA

G
U
A
Y
A
N
A

B
R
I
T
A
N
I
C
A

B R A S I L

MAP 11

ELEMENTS OF REGIONAL POLICY:
THE SYSTEM OF CORE REGIONS
1960 – 1990

KMS. 0   200   400

SEPTEMBER 1963   SCALE 1/4,000,000

tions, that one may think of them as an emergent bipolar urban region.

The third core region of national significance is Santo Tomé de Guayana, which has already been described. It is expected to become the country's principal base for heavy, export-oriented industry.

Inasmuch as the successful economic growth of these three centers must be regarded as a matter of national survival, the country does not have the option of shifting basic investments to alternate locations. First-order core regions must be regarded as fixed elements in the determination of Venezuela's future spatial order.

Both the Maracaibo and Barcelona–Puerto la Cruz metro-politan areas were identified as regional capitals. Their selection was influenced by the need to move toward a fuller integration of the space economy, liquidate the periphery, and maintain minimum interregional balances in living levels. The desire to solve the structural problem of poverty in downward-transitional areas through the activation of dynamic core regions on their perimeter also played a role in the selection process. Choice finally narrowed to these particular regions because of their character as potentially efficient matrices for industry and the extent and character of their respective urban fields. Both cities exert an influence over wider areas than any competing centers, reaching out over major portions of the downward-transitional and potential growth regions of the present periphery. Together with first-order core regions, Maracaibo and Barcelona–Puerto la Cruz will be able to impose a basic structure upon the effec-tively settled space of the nation.

Each of the third-order regions was identified for rather spe-cial reasons. Barquisimeto has ranked among the top four cities of the nation for nearly half a century and has shifted to third place in population size within the last two decades. The city is an important trade center—though clearly of less significance than Maracaibo—and offers some, if not spectacular, possibilities for industrial expansion.[3] Barquisimeto is likely to feel the direct impact of these changes in adjacent areas, especially the pro-posed settlement of the southeastern piedmont, from Barinas to Acarigua. Its location is a splendid one for serving as the "capital" of one of the most rapidly expanding agricultural regions in the country.

San Cristóbal is Venezuela's most important border city (with Colombia). It was the logical choice to "shore up" the furthest southward extension of the Andean periphery, partly for reasons of its location, not only as a border city but also as the center of transition between the Mountain States, the Zulia Basin, and the Llanos. In the past, it has shown a strong propensity for growth, and its future role as a central place near the top of the urban hierarchy would seem to be assured.

The choice of Maturín was determined by a judgment that this city would eventually become the center of a productive agricultural region in the east, fulfilling a role very similar to that of Barquisimeto in the western part of the country. The buildup of Maturín as a third-order pole would also help in shifting the center of demographic gravity from the downward-transitional zone in Sucre and Nueva Esparta to a series of dynamic urban regions on their perimeter, including Santo Tomé de Guayana and Barcelona–Puerto la Cruz.

Fourth-order centers, finally, were selected on the basis of their future role in regional development. For the most part, they are local service centers that may successfully respond to upward shifts in production within their respective hinterlands. In order to be included in this category, a city had to show reasonable prospects of reaching a size of at least 50,000 by the end of the projected period. In addition, an effort was made to space fourth-order centers at fairly regular intervals along the intermetropolitan peripheries.

A Sequence of Development

Coordinated programming for the activation of new core regions will mean a heavy commitment both of trained man-power, such as programming specialists, and of financial resources. Although it is unlikely that Venezuela will have the ability to activate all new core regions simultaneously, it is polit-ically unfeasible to withhold public investments from some of

223

them simply because "their turn" has not yet come. Any formal activation sequence can consequently be no more than a statement of *relative emphasis* in investment allocation. If we assume that total requirements are greater than the resource capabilities of the nation for any given period, the problem is one that is familiar to all budget planners: where to cut excess demand.

On the premise that impulses of economic change are transmitted in order from higher to lower centers in the urban hierarchy, the development of core regions in Venezuela should generally proceed in a downward sequence. In this way, the maximum "transfer effect" is likely to be realized. Core regions having national importance should be activated first, followed by second- and third-order cores in due succession. Emphasis in development expenditures will shift from one to the next lower order of core region whenever sustained growth has been achieved for the preceding order. The critical point will be reached when the core region is no longer dependent on massive income transfers for the success of its development program. Since clear-cut priorities, however, cannot be established, the final decision on resource allocation should be made to depend on the opportunity costs of proposed investment projects, wherever they are located.

In Venezuela, first-order regions are, with the exception of Guayana, well entrenched in their position. Before the end of the present decade, even Guayana, however, should be sufficiently advanced to permit attention to shift to the second-order regions of Barcelona–Puerto la Cruz and Maracaibo. The intensive development of these regions should, in turn, stimulate expansion of lower-order core regions and local service centers within their fields of influence. Before an interdependent economy focused on discrete centers of development is achieved, however, an entire generation may pass by.

A System of Development Areas

In a preliminary form, Map 12 shows the proximate arrangement of all potential core regions in the context of a general

224

system of development areas for Venezuela. These areas were defined in a gross way by the development problems they were expected to present over the next generation. A key judgment here involved an estimate of their prospective economic growth.

As the arrows on Map 12, indicating the probable direction of migration, suggest, regional development characteristics are closely interrelated. The emergence of zones of intensive tourist development in the Andes, along the eastern coast of Falcón, and in the vicinity of Cumaná and Porlamar is thus envisioned coming as a response to industrial-commercial developments focused on major metropolitan regions. Resource frontier regions are delineated in order to meet rising new demands for food, raw materials, and heavy industrial products, no less than to draw population from the poor and culturally backward areas along their peripheries.

Looking more closely at the structure of development areas, the map appears to be significantly at variance with the pattern of ecological zones depicted earlier in Map 8. Although a point-for-point comparison is not feasible—the maps were designed with different purposes in view—a number of significant contrasts may be drawn.

The map of development areas, for instance, throws into clear relief the projected relative decline of the traditional agricultural and oil regions on the periphery. A maturing industrial economy assumes a new face whose most striking feature is a relatively small number of new metropolitan centers. In Venezuela's case, they would include the Caracas-Maracay-Valencia development corridor, Guayana, and subordinate agglomerations focused on Barcelona–Puerto la Cruz, Maracaibo, Barquisimeto, and San Cristóbal.

Despite rapid urbanization, several new agricultural and resources regions may attain major importance on the frontiers of present settlement. They will be found in the Zulia Basin, the southeastern piedmont, and the traditional Oriente, divided into the resource-based complex of Santo Tomé de Guayana and promising agricultural areas, chiefly to the south and east of Maturín. The implied scale of rural resettlement by far sur-

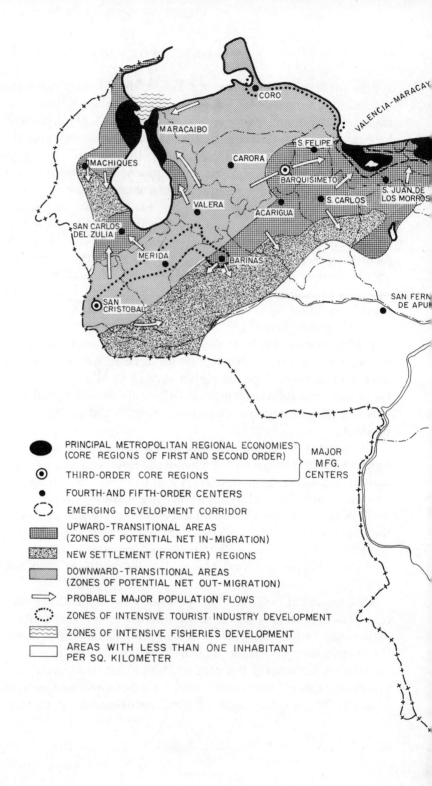

PRINCIPAL METROPOLITAN REGIONAL ECONOMIES
(CORE REGIONS OF FIRST AND SECOND ORDER)

THIRD-ORDER CORE REGIONS

MAJOR
MFG.
CENTERS

FOURTH-AND FIFTH-ORDER CENTERS

EMERGING DEVELOPMENT CORRIDOR

UPWARD-TRANSITIONAL AREAS
(ZONES OF POTENTIAL NET IN-MIGRATION)

NEW SETTLEMENT (FRONTIER) REGIONS

DOWNWARD-TRANSITIONAL AREAS
(ZONES OF POTENTIAL NET OUT-MIGRATION)

PROBABLE MAJOR POPULATION FLOWS

ZONES OF INTENSIVE TOURIST INDUSTRY DEVELOPMENT

ZONES OF INTENSIVE FISHERIES DEVELOPMENT

AREAS WITH LESS THAN ONE INHABITANT
PER SQ. KILOMETER

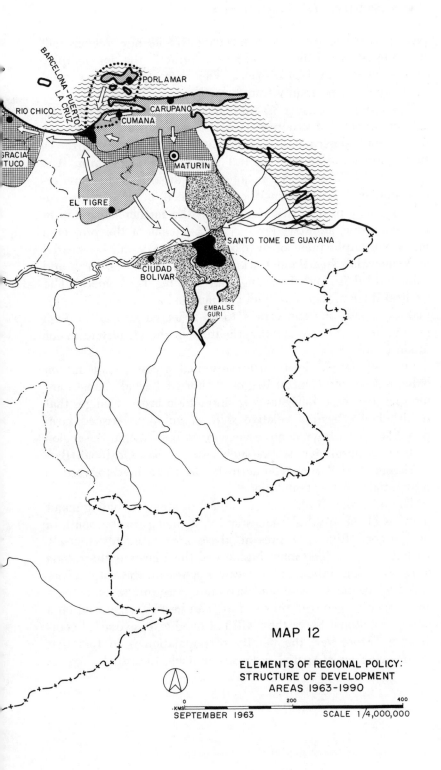

BARCELONA-PUERTO
LA CRUZ

RIO CHICO

GRACIA
TUCO

CUMANA

PORLAMAR

CARUPANO

MATURIN

EL TIGRE

SANTO TOME DE GUAYANA

CIUDAD
BOLIVAR

EMBALSE
GURI

MAP 12

ELEMENTS OF REGIONAL POLICY:
STRUCTURE OF DEVELOPMENT
AREAS 1963-1990

0   200   400
KMS
SEPTEMBER 1963   SCALE 1/4,000,000

passes any program as yet conceived. Whole new regions will be stamped out of the ground where formerly the demographic map showed only blank spaces. The character of the natural landscape will be totally transformed.

These massive changes should not detract from the fundamental persistencies of structure. A significant feature of the map—in view of a determined government policy to decentralize—is the maintenance of the Central Region, stretching from Barquisimeto to Caracas, as a major growth area. Its very considerable potentialities for growth can be traced, in large degree, to the excellent prospects it suggests for the further expansion of manufacturing industry. Possibly 60 per cent of the projected industrial employment of over one million may still be located in Venezuela's heartland toward the end of the century, and value added in manufacturing may not lag far behind.[4] The Central Region, therefore, will continue to be Venezuela's major market, a fact one can expect to be reflected also in the high performance of commercial agriculture in the vicinity of major urban centers.[5]

Overpopulated, downward-transitional areas spread out on either side of the Central Region. Major ecological changes are foreseen for these long-standing, intractible areas, changes that result chiefly from a relative shift of an impoverished farm population to a town-centered economy, both within the region and on its perimeter, where such cities as San Cristóbal, Barquisimeto, and Barcelona–Puerto la Cruz can look forward to substantial gains in population.

The map also displays large unmarked areas, including major portions of the Central Llanos and vast regions to the South of the Orinoco River. At present, these areas are only sparsely settled, if at all. The main business of the Llanos is the raising of cattle, while much of the leftover space on the map is convered by tropical forests and savannas. Any programs in these areas, such as geologic prospecting, had best be organized on a purely functional basis; they will not need extensive areal coordination. Moreover, the density of population is so thin that major questions of spatial order are unlikely to arise.

Quantitative Implications of the Proposed Development Strategy

On the assumption that a dynamic policy for the activation of the selected core regions will be forcefully pursued, together with resettlement and agricultural adjustment programs, what will be the results for the distribution of population and employment? An attempt to quantify these critical variables may help in judging both the feasibility and desirability of the strategy propounded in these pages.

It would have been desirable to measure the effects for regional income as well. But regional income data for Venezuela are wholly unreliable.[6] And not only this; it would have been foolhardy to attempt an income projection by regions extending over several decades, regardless of how sophisticated the techniques applied.[7]

The same thing might be said for other kinds of data as well. The choice of graphic techniques for presenting some of the conclusions of this study is not accidental but was dictated by the roughness of the data and the very large margins of error that bedevil all long-term projections. Maps are less likely to convey an image of precision where none is justified. The present effort to provide numerical correlates to the map statement should therefore be interpreted not as a means for reaching greater precision in measurement but as a way of expressing much the same ideas and to convey a sense of volume and relationship.

Population. Projecting population into the decade from 1985 to 1995 leads to a number of significant conclusions concerning the evolution of Venezuela's spatial structure (Appendix Tables A.1–A.5).[8]

a. There will be no major structural shifts from the present distribution of total population. No change for any group of states will exceed 5 percentage points (Table A.1).

b. Although the East Central States will remain nationally dominant, their share of total urban population will gradually decline, from 47 per cent in 1961 to 45 per cent, a relatively small change over a single generation, but significant in view of the long-term objective to decentralize the economy (Appendix Table A.4).

c. Since only 20 per cent of the total population and 17 per cent of urban population will be residing in the Eastern Provinces by about 1990, the national market will continue to lie predominantly in the west, with its center of gravity along the Caracas-Valencia axis (Appendix Tables A.1 and A.4).

d. Approximately 2 million nonurban people will have to be settled over a period of three decades in the promising agricultural regions of Zulia, the Llanos, and eastern Monagas. They will be engaged in farming or be otherwise tied to the rural economy through local service activities (Appendix Table A.3). The scale of this dramatic new development can be appreciated by comparing it to the growth of nonurban populations in the three settlement regions during the past twenty-five years. This was only one fourth of the projected rate (Appendix Table A.3).[9]

e. Notwithstanding the very considerable effort that this implies for reducing population pressure in the overcrowded and impoverished regions, the Mountain and East Coastal States will still experience an absolute rise of nearly one million in total population, of whom one third will be residing in rural areas (Appendix Table A.5).

f. The next thirty years will continue to be a period of major urban expansion. By the end of this period, Venezuela will have five metropolitan regions with over one million inhabitants, and the Caracas metropolitan region, with 4.5 million, will by itself account for one third of the country's urban population (Appendix Table A.3). A significant portion of total investment—between 35 and 45 per cent—will have to be devoted to servicing the minimum needs of metropolitan populations for housing, utilities, and transportation. This enormous task will require the most careful husbanding of the available resources as well as detailed physical planning at the metropolitan scale.

Employment.

a. Urban employment. As used here, urban employment includes all economic sectors, except for agriculture, forestry, and fishing. A total increase of 3.7 million urban jobs is projected for the country as a whole (Appendix Table A.8). The regional distribution of these jobs will not depart in a major way from the existing structure. The principal projected changes in urban employment are a relative decline in the participation of the Mountain and East Coastal States. Despite the multimillion dollar investment contemplated for Guayana, urban employment in that region will rise from only 3 to 5 per cent of the national total over the next generation (Appendix Table A.8).

The absolute gains projected are nonetheless impressive. The Western Oil States, for instance, comprising Zulia and Falcón, will need to develop 670,000 new job opportunities to meet the requirements of the model. This is nearly three times the total amount of manufacturing employment in the country at the present time (1963). Anzoátegui and Monagas, together comprising the Eastern Oil States, will need 340,000 job additions; Guayana, an additional 240,000; and the East Central States will top all other areas with a projected increase of nearly 2 million urban jobs.

The employment model is premised on an explicit policy of regional decentralization and strengthening of a series of potential core regions throughout the country. The relative stability of the interregional structure of employment is therefore surprising. Should the strategy of activation turn out to be unsuccessful in its implementation phase, a slippage of employment toward the east central group of states can be expected. In other words, the natural tendency of development would be for the periphery to "collapse" upon the center.

The regional structure of manufacturing employment departs significantly from the pattern for all nonfarm jobs (Appendix Table A.9). The East Central States stand out, with better than half of the total employment, followed by Zulia (Western Oil), Guayana, and the Eastern Oil States (chiefly Anzoátegui). Industrial development in other regions will be negligible from a national standpoint.

The relative concentration of manufacturing employment can be seen from the index in Table 10.1, which relates the percent-

231

Table 10.1. Index of Manufacturing Concentration,
1990±5

Group of States	Index	Group of States	Index
Western Oil	0.8	Llanos	0.4
Mountain	0.5	Eastern Oil	1.0
West Central	0.6	East Coastal	0.5
East Central	1.1	Guayana	2.2
		Venezuela	1.0

Source: Appendix Table A.9.

age of total employment in manufacturing to the percentage of the total labor force of the country in each region.

The exceptionally high degree of industrial development in Guayana—more than double of what might be expected purely on the basis of the region's urbanization—is immediately apparent. Substantially "underindustrialized" areas are, according to these projections, the Mountain, West Central, Llanos, and East Coastal States, with a combined estimated population of nearly 7 million.

The same story can be told from a different perspective by an index relating the number of nonmanufacturing jobs to those in manufacturing. For every worker in manufacturing between 1985 and 1995, Table 10.2 lists the number of persons who will be employed in the trades, services, or construction.

Again, Guayana stands out, with only 1.3 jobs in tertiary and quaternary activities for every worker in industry. This contrasts

Table 10.2. Number of Nonmanufacturing Jobs for Every
Job in Manufacturing, 1990±5

Group of States	Index	Group of States	Index
Western Oil	4.7	Llanos	12.0
Mountain	9.0	Eastern Oil	3.4
West Central	5.5	East Coastal	11.0
East Central	3.1	Guayana	1.3
		Venezuela	3.6

Source: Appendix Table A.9.

232

sharply with the Llanos, where the average ratio is 1:12; this underscores the predominantly trade-center function of cities in that region. The low ratio for Guayana, on the other hand, is explained by the absence of an extensive trading area for Santo Tomé de Guayana. Guayana trade will continue to be channeled to a large extent, through Barcelona–Puerto la Cruz.

b. Nonurban employment. The shifting pattern in agricultural employment is clearly apparent from Table A.10. The total projected increase of 760,000 in farm workers will be "absorbed" in primarily three regions—the Llanos, the Western Oil States (chiefly Zulia), and the Eastern Oil States (especially Monagas). However, despite sharp relative declines in rural employment, the overpopulated, downward-transitional areas of the Mountain and East Coastal States will continue to gain. This suggests that farming in these areas is likely to continue in a depressed condition for at least another generation, despite extensive outmigration.

Guayana, which includes the Orinoco Delta, is shown with the rather sizable increase of 70,000 farm jobs over those existing in 1961, a greater increment than that projected for the Mountain States. Whether this gain will, in fact, be realized will to a large extent depend on the outcome of current investigations into the feasibility of large-scale agricultural development in the Delta.

Final Comments: Summary. The principal projections are summarized in Table 10.3. They suggest a pattern of population and employment that, organized around a small number of metropolitan centers, seems reasonable for an economy that has achieved a high degree of industrial development, and most of whose 20 million inhabitants will be living in relative comfort as members of a thoroughly urban society. The proportional measures indicate rather minor shifts in the demographic and employment structure of Venezuela, in particular in the relative importance of the central region.

One becomes aware of the real significance of the projections only by studying the absolute numbers involved: the emergence of multimillion metropolitan regions, the gradual shift to predominance in urban service occupations, the great drift of popu-

Table 10.3. Some Regional Economic Projections to 1990±5

Group of States	Total Population 1990±5 (*millions*)	Principal Core Region	Total Population 1990±5 (*millions*)	Rank Order	Employment 1990±5		
					Mfg.	Other Urban (*thousands*)	Non-urban
Western Oil	3.4	Maracaibo	*ca.*1.8	2	160	750	250
		Specialization: food products, textiles, machinery, transport equipment, chemicals and chemical products					
Mountain	1.6	San Cristóbal	*ca.*0.5	3	20	180	250
		Specialization: food products, forest products, furniture, ceramics, textiles (especially woolens)					
West Central	1.6	Barquisimeto	*ca.*1.0	3	60	330	140
		Specialization: food products, farm-related industries, construction materials, apparel, shoes, furniture					
East Central	6.8	Caracas / Valencia- / Maracay	*ca.*4.4 / *ca.*2.4	1 / 1	610	1,890	110
		Specialization: consumer goods of all types, chemicals and chemical products, transport equipment (especially automobiles and shipbuilding)					
Llanos	2.6	San Juan de los Morros°	*ca.*0.2	4	20	240	420
		Specialization: food products and farm-related industries, lumber and wood products, paper pulp					
Eastern Oil	2.0	Barcelona-Puerto la Cruz	*ca.*0.9	2	100	340	230
		Specialization: food products, textiles, shoes, apparel, machinery, chemicals and products, metal fabrications, transport equipment					
East Coastal	0.8	Cumaná°	*ca.*0.2	4	10	110	110
		Specialization: marine products, textiles, other labor-intensive industries					
Guayana	1.2	Santo Tomé de Guayana	*ca.*0.6	1	120	160	90
		Specialization: heavy metals, machinery, industrial chemicals, ferroalloys, paper pulp, electric energy					
Venezuela	20.0				1,100	4,000	1,600

° Taken as a representative center.

234

lation from the mountains into the plain states, and the revitalization of the economy in the eastern third of the country. The emerging new pattern gives its proper due to history, in that the existing spatial structure, as it has evolved over the centuries, will continue to be expressed in the relative distribution of population and employment over the major regions of the country, in the hierarchy of core regions and in the broad east-west orientation of the morphology of the settlement pattern. Yet, although the old may be recognized in the new features, the projected pattern represents a major expansion of Venezuela's space economy in heretofore unexplored directions. New regions, such as Guayana, will be drawn into its orbit as permanent integral elements; urban areas confronted with the dangers of incipient economic decline will be given an important new role as major foci in the nation's life; and the rural economy will be more closely related to the basic urban structure of the country. Older regions, such as the Mountain and East Coastal States, will continue to pose problems of equity and internal adjustment; but their relative importance will have substantially declined (in demographic terms, from 29 per cent in 1936 to 12 per cent by about 1990). In short, the regional problem, seemingly so urgent in the 1960's, will have shrunk to vestigial proportions, while policy will come increasingly to focus on internal problems of metropolitan organization.

Sources and Derivations of Appendix Tables A.1 to A.5

All historical data were calculated from the 8th and 9th National Censuses, for 1950 and 1961, respectively. The projections of total, urban, and nonurban populations for the country as a whole were used as parameters and were taken from Tables 9.2.

The allocation of total population in 1990 ±5 by major groups of states was guided, in the main, by the proposed system of core regions as diagramed in Map 11.

The distribution of urban and nonurban populations for 1990 ±5 was accomplished by first distributing total nonurban population—which is the smaller increment—according to estimated absorption capacities of different areas, being guided in this by Map 12. Urban population was treated as a residual. In the second round of estimation, urban population was estimated independently for each group of states, based on proposals for the hierarchy of core regions. Finally, a number of iterative adjustments were made in both sectors to arrive at the distribution shown.

Appendix to Chapter 10

Table A.1.   Percentage Distribution of Total Population, 1936–1990±5

Group of States	1936	1950	1961	1990±5
Western Oil	15	16	17	17
Mountain	19	16	13	8
West Central	12	10	9	8
East Central	24	28	32	34
Llanos	10	10	10	13
Eastern Oil	7	8	8	10
East Coastal	10	8	6	4
Guayana	3	3	3	6
Venezuela	100	100	100	100

Because of rounding, total may not add to 100.

Table A.2.   Total Population, 1936–1990±5
            (*in thousands*)

Group of States	1936	1950	1961	1990±5	Increase 1961–1990±5
Western Oil	500	800	1,200	3,400	2,200
Mountain	600	800	1,000	1,600	600
West Central	400	500	700	1,600	900
East Central	800	1,400	2,400	6,800	4,400
Llanos	400	500	800	2,600	1,800
Eastern Oil	200	400	600	2,000	1,400
East Coastal	300	400	500	800	300
Guayana	100	200	300	1,200	900
Venezuela	3,400	5,000	7,500	20,000	12,500

Because of rounding, regional totals may not add precisely to the total for Venezuela.

Table A.3. Urban-Nonurban Distribution of the Population, 1936–1990±5
(in thousands)

Group of States	1936			1961			1990±5			1961–1990±5		
	total	urban	nonurban	total	urban	nonurban	total	urban	nonurban	total	urban	nonurban
Western Oil	490	140	350	1,260	800	460	3,400	2,500	900	2,140	1,700	440
Mountain	640	50	590	1,000	300	700	1,600	700	900	600	400	200
West Central	420	60	360	660	320	340	1,600	1,100	500	940	780	160
East Central	800	380	420	2,440	2,050	390	6,800	6,400	400	4,360	4,350	10
Llanos	350	10	340	780	260	520	2,600	1,000	1,600	1,820	740	1,080
Eastern Oil	220	20	200	630	320	310	2,000	1,200	800	1,370	880	490
East Coastal	340	60	280	490	160	330	800	400	400	310	240	70
Guayana	100	20	80	260	130	130	1,200	900	300	940	770	170
Venezuela	3,360	740	2,620	7,520	4,340	3,180	20,000	14,200	5,800	12,480	9,860	2,620

237

Table A.4. Percentage Distribution of Urban and
Nonurban Population, 1936–1990 ± 5

Group of States	1936		1961		1990 ± 5	
	urban	nonurban	urban	nonurban	urban	nonurban
Western Oil	19	13	18	14	18	15
Mountain	7	23	7	22	5	15
West Central	8	14	7	11	8	9
East Central	51	16	47	12	45	7
Llanos	1	13	6	16	7	28
Eastern Oil	3	8	7	10	8	14
East Coastal	8	11	4	10	3	7
Guayana	3	3	3	4	6	5
Venezuela	100	100	100	100	100	100

Because of rounding, totals may not add to 100.

Table A.5. Urban-Nonurban Composition of the Population
by Groups of States, 1936–1990±5
(*percentages*)

Group of States	1936		1961		1990 ± 5	
	urban	nonurban	urban	nonurban	urban	nonurban
Western Oil	30	70	64	36	74	26
Mountain	8	92	30	70	43	57
West Central	15	85	48	52	29	71
East Central	50	50	84	16	94	6
Llanos	2	98	33	67	38	62
Eastern Oil	8	92	51	49	62	38
East Coastal	17	83	33	67	50	50
Guayana	20	80	51	49	73	27
Venezuela	22	78	58	42	71	29

238

Table A.6. Urban and Nonurban Distribution of Population
and Estimated Rate of Labor Force
Participation, 1990 ± 5
(*in thousands*)

Group of States	Total Population	Percentage of Total Population		Labor Force Participation Ratios		Number in Labor Force		
		urban	*nonurban*	*urban*	*nonurban*	*urban*	*nonurban*	*total*
Western Oil	3,400	74	26	38	28	950	254	1,204
Mountain	1,600	43	57	30	28	210	254	464
West Central	1,600	69	31	37	28	407	142	549
East Central	6,800	94	6	42	28	2,660	114	2,674
Llanos	2,600	38	62	28	28	280	420	700
Eastern Oil	2,000	62	38	35	28	455	226	681
East Coastal	800	50	50	32	28	128	114	242
Guayana	1,200	73	27	38	28	300	86	390
Venezuela	20,000	71	29	38	28	5,390	1,610	7,000

Sources and derivation: Column 1, Table A.2; columns 2 and 3, Table A.5; columns 4 and 5, estimated on basis of an assumed 35 per cent labor force participation rate nationally. In general, the more urbanized a group of states, the higher was its labor force participation rate assumed to be. Nonurban employment data for past years is grossly understated because of the exclusion of many women workers. In the absence of a precise concept of rural labor force, it was assumed that rural labor force participation would not vary significantly among regions. Throughout this study, a minimum population of 5,000 defines the urban status of a settlement. Consequently, the estimate of nonurban labor force made here includes some local service employment, in addition to employment in farming, forestry, and fishing.

239

Table A.7. Estimated Urban Labor Force,
1953, 1960, and 1990 ± 5
(*in thousands*)

Group of States	1953 number	1953 per cent	1960 number	1960 per cent	1990±5 number	1990±5 per cent
Western Oil	190	16	330	18	950	18
Mountain	120	10	130	7	210	4
West Central	90	8	130	7	410	8
East Central	510	44	850	48	2,660	49
Llanos	80	7	110	6	280	5
Eastern Oil	80	7	130	7	460	8
East Coastal	70	6	70	4	130	2
Guayana	30	2	50	3	300	6
Venezuela	1,170	100	1,800	100	5,400	100
Unemployment	130		420		280	

Sources and derivation: For 1953, Joint Center estimate, based on 1950 Census of Population and 1953 Central Bank estimates of total employment by sector; for 1960, distribution based on Central Bank estimate for December 1960 of total employment in the nonagricultural sector. Urban population by states as given in the 1961 Census of Population was used as an allocator; for 1990±5, cf. Table A.6.

Table A.8. Estimated Urban Employment,
1953, 1960, and 1990±5
(*in thousands*)

Group of States	1953 number	1953 per cent	1960 number	1960 per cent	1990±5 number	1990±5 per cent	Increase 1960 to 1990±5 number	Increase 1960 to 1990±5 per cent
Western Oil	170	16	240	17	910	18	670	18
Mountain	110	11	110	8	200	4	90	2
West Central	80	8	100	7	390	8	290	8
East Central	450	43	640	46	2,500	49	1,860	50
Llanos	70	7	90	6	260	5	170	4
Eastern Oil	70	7	100	7	440	9	340	9
East Coastal	60	6	60	4	120	2	60	2
Guayana	30	3	40	3	280	5	240	6
Venezuela	1,040	100	1,380	100	5,100	100	3,720	100

Because of rounding, totals may not add to 100 per cent.
Sources and derivation: Cf. Table A.7. Difference between labor force and employment estimates accrues to unemployment. Total estimated unemployment for the nation was allocated among regions in rough proportion to the urban labor force in each. The resulting totals were subtracted from urban labor force estimates in each region to yield the net figure for unemployment above.

Table A.9. Estimated Employment in Manufacturing
and Other Urban Employment, 1990±5
(*in thousands*)

Group of States	Manufacturing Employment	Per Cent	Other Urban Employment	Per Cent	Unemployment	Index of Concentration	$\frac{c}{a}$
	a	b	c	d	e	f	g
Western Oil	160	15	750	19	40	0.8	4.7
Mountain	20	2	180	4	10	0.5	9.0
West Central	60	5	330	8	20	0.6	5.5
East Central	610	55	1,890	47	160	1.1	3.1
Llanos	20	2	240	6	20	0.4	12.0
Eastern Oil	100	9	340	8	20	1.0	3.4
East Coastal	10	1	110	3	10	0.5	11.0
Guayana	120	11	160	4	20	2.2	1.3
Venezuela	1,100	100	4,000	100	300	1.0	3.6

Because of rounding, totals may not add to 100 per cent.

Sources and derivation: National total from Table 10.1. Distribution was guided by location of potential core regions (Map 11) and estimated competitive advantages for manufacturing at each. Ratios in columns (*f*) and (*g*) were subsequently used for iterative adjustments of the basic data. The index of concentration was calculated by dividing the percentage of manufacturing employment in each region by the corresponding percentage of urban labor force (cf. Table A.7).

Table A.10. Estimated Nonurban Employment,
1953, 1960, and 1990±5
(*in thousands*)

Group of States	1953 number	1953 per cent	1960 number	1960 per cent	1990±5 number	1990±5 per cent	Increase 1960 to 1990±5 number	Increase 1960 to 1990±5 per cent
Western Oil	90	12	120	14	250	16	130	17
Mountain	170	23	190	22	250	16	60	9
West Central	90	12	100	12	140	9	40	5
East Central	120	16	110	13	110	7		
Llanos	120	15	140	17	420	26	280	36
Eastern Oil	60	8	80	10	230	14	150	20
East Coastal	70	10	80	10	110	7	30	4
Guayana	30	4	20	2	90	5	70	9
Venezuela	750	100	340	100	1,600	100	760	100

Sources and derivation: For 1953, Joint Center estimate, based on 1950 Census of Population and 1953 Central Bank estimate of total employment by sector. For 1960, distribution was based on Central Bank estimate of employment in agriculture, forestry, and fishing and allocated in accordance with the distribution of nonurban population (cf. Table A.4). For 1990, cf. Table A.6.

CHAPTER ELEVEN

PROBLEMS OF INPLEMENTATION

Policy as Process

Regional policy involves more than the formulation of a set of abstract principles emblazoned on a document. It involves much more than a statement of objectives to inspire a popular response. To identify some regions and describe their problems constitutes barely a start.

Policy is a living thing. It is best viewed as a system of related processes occurring at different levels of decision and authority. It includes *informing, planning, programming, commitment,* and *action,* each of which, in turn, consists of comparable component processes. The parallel is to one of those Japanese toys that delight children who never seem to tire of playing with boxes within boxes, each one smaller than the preceding one. Now, these processes occur not only at different levels of decision; they are also present in every major phase of regional policy: project location, urbanization, resettlement, resource development, agricultural adjustment, and transportation-communication. In the aggregate, therefore, regional policy appears as a ramified and complexly woven network of organizational relationships that is incapable of being frozen into a masterplan or blueprint.

If regional policy consists of related processes, implementation requires that they be separately initiated. The real issues have to do with organizational arrangements rather than "guidelines," with human motivations rather than "decision rules." Although the intended outcome, as the objective content of decisions, is important, it cannot be guaranteed in advance. It is more significant to design a system of informing, planning, programming, commitment, and action that is self-adjusting to new

242

information and, over the long pull, will lead to an increase in the average number of "correct" decisions as viewed in an historical perspective.

The design of such a system must be adapted to certain conditions present in Venezuela. The following constraints will have to be respected:

1. Intense regional competition for development exists within a democratic system that is sensitive to political pressures. There is consequently a tendency to politicize the process of regional investment allocation and to search for mechanically egalitarian formulas.

2. Little experience with regional policy and planning has yet accumulated. Few government officials are trained to think in regionally relevant terms nor do they understand the relationship of spatial organization to economic development.

3. Competent professionals are normally unwilling to work for extended periods of time in the provinces. They express a strong preference for residence in cosmopolitan Caracas, where they are less isolated intellectually and closer to the centers of effective power.

4. Information useful to regional policymakers is scarce, and no regional economic information is currently collected on a continuing basis.

5. Information available to individual government offices is frequently handled in a secretive manner. Partly this reflects the resistance of line agencies to having their work coordinated on a regional or local basis.

These constraints to regional policy implementation are not the whole of reality, however. Venezuela also offers conditions that greatly facilitate the carrying out of a national policy for regional development. The country can boast of an experienced and effective national planning agency (CORDIPLAN). Recognition of the need for a regional policy is widespread. The general level of professional competence is high. And the current government of Venezuela may be regarded as progressive in its political stance and firmly established in power for the period it was elected to serve.

Problems of Activating New Core Regions

As a strategy, the activation of new core regions is so central to regional policy that clarification is needed on how it may be carried out. No other policy aspect poses problems of nearly the same magnitude. By the same reasoning, if satisfactory arrangements can be made for dealing with activation, other policy aspects may be fitted into the framework for policy decision with relative ease.

A common misconception is to think of the process of activation as involving an effort on the scale of Guayana. One is impressed with the proportions and the drama of a powerful government corporation planning and building facilities worth billions of dollars: a new metropolis, iron ore mines, a steel plant, electric power dams. This image fits the notion of activating new core regions. But the fact is that Guayana, as a resource frontier and as Venezuela's only current example of this genus, represents a rather special case. In the foreseeable future, it will not have a serious rival. In distinction to Guayana, other core regions in Venezuela have an already established urban-metropolitan center with fields of influence that extend over densely settled agricultural areas. But if Guayana is not the appropriate model, how should resources become selectively concentrated on major centers? To answer this question, the Guayana experience will need to be more carefully examined. After all, it may not be the substance of the program, but its method that will provide a clue.

Regional Programming Staffs. The success of Guayana may in significant measure be ascribed to the effectiveness of its *regional programming*. This is a device for

a. The systematic collection and interpretation of regional and other relevant data.

b. The statement of medium and long-term development objectives and derived requirements for investment.

c. The formulation and evaluation of investment projects.

d. The arrangement of investment projects into a sequence, so that a coherent and internally consistent program of development evolves within the framework of the long-term regional strategy and national planning.

e. The continuing assessment of what has been accomplished and of the changing environment for decision.

The emphasis in programming is on the short- and medium-term; its focus is on projects. It is by knowing precisely in what projects to invest and in what temporal order they should be undertaken that a strategy for the activation of core regions acquires meaning. In Chapter 10, core regions were identified on the basis of rather crude criteria. The evidence of projects will be needed to demonstrate the wisdom of this choice.

A certain concentration of investments in core regions is inescapable. But, instead of applying a sterile formula for allo-cating a fixed proportion of national revenues among regions, programming will draw the attention of national planners to realistic possibilities at each location. The presumption is that by putting programming staffs into selected metropolitan centers, proportionately more possibilities for effective action will be discovered there than in areas for which no comparable staff work has been done.

Each Regional Programming Staff would be composed of from five to ten economists, geographers, and engineers. Staff duties would include

a. Carrying out an initial survey of the metropolitan region, covering historical, economic, demographic, social, and cultural aspects; the relation of the region to other parts of the country; and a careful assessment of the area's economic potentialities.

b. Initiating a process for the systematic and continuing collection of planning data for the region, including an appraisal of the area's resources.

c. Undertaking a comprehensive projection of the regional economy, in the light of regional objectives and in keeping with national planning guidelines. These projections would be revised to coincide with periodic revisions of the national plan itself.

d. Preparing a development map of the region, reflecting the statistical projections undertaken in (*c*) above. This map (or series of maps) would ultimately be incorporated into a regional planning atlas.

e. Identifying the principal problems of regional development, and formulating appropriate strategies for action in accordance with national guidelines and program indications.

f. Identifying existing investment opportunities within the region and suggesting the approximate order of priority in which they should be undertaken.

g. Preparing specific project proposals for investment in collaboration with functional government agencies.

h. Reviewing for central clearance all functional agency projects to be located in the region.

i. Studying the implications of regional investment proposals for urban physical development.

j. Counseling private groups concerning investment possibilities in the region.

Personnel policies. A frequently raised objection to proposals such as the foregoing is that it will be impossible to discover professionals of a sufficiently high caliber to undertake programming work. Indeed, there is a great shortage of regional programmers and difficulty in attracting qualified professionals of whatever kind to work for extended periods in the provinces. But pessimists tend to overlook the existence of simple administrative devices that can be used to overcome these obstacles.

All programming staff should be employed directly by CORDI-PLAN. They would thus belong to a prestigious *national* organization with which they would also be identified in the public mind. A regular rotation schedule could be worked out so that all staff would eventually gain experience in the provinces as well as at headquarters in Caracas. Special incentive payments could be offered for residence in the field. In addition, an intensive flow of communications between field offices and Caracas should be maintained to reduce any possible sense of isolation. Regular staff meetings in Caracas for all staff may be considered as a part of such an effort. Close review by the central office in CORDIPLAN would ensure the continued high quality of work performance in the field.

Problems of coordination. Programming entails a measure of coordination. But this is true only with respect to research, project formulation, and sequencing. For implementation, the

246

formal coordination of activities—though desirable—may not always be essential. This point is worth underscoring, as it runs counter to much established opinion. Coordination is fiercely resisted whenever it is sensed as a restriction on organizational autonomy for decision and action. Limited coordination, restricted in advance to a specific task, can usually be obtained as an ad hoc arrangement. In this event, however, the agencies do not commit themselves to a pattern of collaborative action beyond the task itself.

A special case arises in connection with the spatial coordination of activities that are not limited to a given task but rather are of a general nature. This would require the coincidence of all administrative regional boundaries, one for each agency. However, this is not now the case in Venezuela and would be difficult to bring about. Administrative efficiency, operational convenience, and tradition are usually cited to explain the divergence of the boundaries of administrative regions. The advantages of having common geographic limits for both programming and administration are in most cases obscure, and provide insufficient justification for riding roughshod over the opposition of line agencies to such a move.

Central clearance. In the absence of formal coordination procedures for the implementation of programs, however, another device must be used to ensure at least a minimum of consistency in the programs of line agencies. The device is that of central clearance for project proposals prior to their inclusion in the national budget. Accordingly, line agencies would be unable to undertake any investment that had not previously been reviewed and approved by a Regional Programming Staff. Any conflicts arising from this procedure and not capable of being resolved on the local scene, would have to be argued at the national level through an established procedure for review.

Programming regions. The concept of programming regions is bound to cause practical problems of definition and geographic delimitation. Until now it was assumed that programming regions would somehow be centered on core regions, starting with those of national importance, and moving downward in sequence to successively lower orders. But what of the physical extent of

247

the region thus centralized for programming purposes? Three options may be considered.

First, the programming region can be made to coincide with the whole field of influence of the central city (or cities). This has merit on theoretical grounds; but the boundaries of such a region would undergo frequent changes, and administrative problems would arise where the urban field spreads over more than a single state or province.

Second, the programming region could comprise one or more whole states, significant portions of which may be covered by the existing or potential fields extending from each core region. An ordering such as the following may be suggested:

Core Region	Order	States
Caracas	1	Federal District, Miranda
Valencia-Maracay	1	Carabobo, Aragua, Cojedes, Guárico, Apure
Guayana	1	Bolívar, Delta Amacuro
Maracaibo	2	Zulia, Falcón
Barcelona–Puerto la Cruz	2	Anzoátegui, Monagas, Sucre, Nueva Esparta
Barquisimeto	3	Lara, Yaracuy, Portuguesa, Barinas
San Cristobal	3	Táchira, Mérida, Trujillo

The difficulty with this alternative is that it would blanket the whole country with programming regions, a result that is opposed to the basic principle of selective concentration. Programmers will need to be aware of activities in the remoter areas of their urban realm. But awareness of *what is* happening and programming for *what should* happen are quite different things. The multistate approach to programming for the activation of new core regions may be administratively more convenient than the first alternative, but it would also result in too great a dispersion of investment funds.

The third option would follow the example of the Guayana program where a novel concept of the programming region is being used. The area of primary program impact is drawn narrowly to coincide with the physical boundaries of Santo Tomé de Guayana and a strip of land running for some distance along both banks of the Caroní River. Essentially, the focal region overlaps with the metropolitan economy of Santo Tomé de Guayana. But the authority to act on the part of the Guayana Corporation extends beyond it to any area capable of making a direct contribution to the development objectives for the focal region. This wider area is left unspecified. All that needs to be demonstrated is that projects undertaken by the Corporation outside its focal region will be of benefit within it.

This is the most flexible of the arrangements. The metropolitan economy would for each core region be the focal or primary impact region for detailed programming and would have to be administratively defined for this purpose. On the other hand, a multistate region might be used for statistical purposes. Programming staffs would further be authorized to consider projects outside the focal region if their immediate relevance to the growth pole program can be demonstrated. In this way, the principle of selective concentration is adhered to without confinement to the artificial boundaries of a priori regional concepts. Possible jurisdictional conflicts will have to be resolved on a case basis. Since over-all control over Regional Programming Staffs would rest with CORDIPLAN, no major difficulties are expected from working with sets of unspecified regions so long as their respective centers are known.

Physical urban planning. Regional programming should be tied to urban spatial planning and design. The functioning of the metropolitan regional economy will in part depend on the efficient arrangement of its parts in space, but the physical environment must also be livable. All urban investment—housing, infrastructure, productive facilities—will together determine the form of the city. Urban designers will receive projects from the regional programming staff as elements to be incorporated into the physical plan; but project possibilities may also be derived from the plan itself, a system of public transportation, for instance.

In Venezuela, responsibility for urban planning is lodged with the Ministry of Public Works. It would be desirable for this

Ministry to establish urban planning staffs in the principal core regions similar to CORDIPLAN's economic programming units. (At present, urban planning consists largely of drawing up masterplans, which, however, have no legal force. Regardless of the city, these plans are always prepared in Caracas.) Whenever possible, joint offices should be occupied to encourage the close cooperation between economic programming and physical planning staffs. Every project should be judged in a specific environmental context, while urban design should be oriented to projected investments. Because of this relationship, a person acceptable to both CORDIPLAN and the Ministry of Public Works should be appointed as the technical director for every regional programming and planning operation.

Regional Development Advisory Councils. The programming process has been discussed so far exclusively in administrative terms. But a way must be found for responsible local opinion to influence the choices of public officials and hold them within the bounds of popular acceptability. In every core region, therefore, a Regional Development Advisory Council, broadly representative of the local population, should be appointed by the President of the Republic on the basis of nominations submitted by local interest groups. Councils would have the power to review and evaluate (but not to veto) projects, programs, and physical plans submitted by the Regional Programming and Urban Planning Staffs. This review function would be obligatory. Members might also participate, individually or as a group, in various phases of project development and urban planning. Councils would provide for a regular channel of communication between the population at large and the planners. Without a measure of active local participation, regional programming would be in danger of losing its sense of reality and proportion.

CORDIPLAN Regional Policy Staff. A permanent linkage to national planning must be established for the purpose of reconciling competing regional claims, integrating regional programs into a national plan, and providing adequate technical support to Regional Programming Staffs. A parent body of planners—or Regional Policy Staff—should therefore be established within CORDIPLAN and charged with the following responsibilities:

a. Prepare a document setting forth a philosophy to guide regional development planning in Venezuela.

b. Establish Regional Programming Staffs in major core regions.

c. Provide administrative "backstopping" to regional programming staffs: supplies, contacts with ministries at the national level, responsibility for consultant contracts, and so on.

d. Provide continuing technical advice and assistance to Regional Programming Staffs. Prepare an Operating Manual.

e. Analyze and review regional programs and projections, including the program budget.

f. Coordinate regional plan proposals in the preparation of the regional chapters of the national plan. These chapters should provide a synthesis of regional programming. All project locations should be identified.

g. Review regional program budgets and incorporate them into the national program budget.

h. Maintain a continuing flow of information to Regional Programming Staffs. Experiment with rotation of personnel among regional offices and Caracas headquarters. Establish a news bulletin as house organ.

i. Review all projects submitted by line agencies for their consistency with regional policy criteria. Verify that they have been cleared by Regional Programming Staffs.

j. Prepare and maintain a set of regional economic planning data, uniform for the country as a whole. Supply Regional Programming Staffs and line agencies with common interregional projections of basic economic and demographic variables.

k. Contract for a series of basic interregional flow studies.

l. Provide continuing advice at the national level on the spatial implications of national policies.

m. Sponsor short-term, intensive training courses in methods of regional programming.

The Regional Policy Staff represents the key to establishing a *system* of regional policy within the context of national planning. It must be established as the initial measure; remaining suggestions may be subsequently carried out.

Summary. The main elements of organization for the activation of core regions may now be summarized. They include

a. The identification of a limited number of key metropolitan regional economies as primary programming regions.

b. Establishment of Regional Programming and Urban Design Staffs by CORDIPLAN and Public Works, respectively, under a common technical director in each of the several programming regions.

c. Appointment of a broadly representative Regional Development Advisory Council in each programming region. The council would have powers of project and program review, and its members would actively participate in aspects of regional programming and planning.

d. Establishment of a system of central regional clearance for all project expenditures to be included in the national program budget.

e. Establishment of a Regional Policy Staff in CORDIPLAN.

As an initial step, Regional Programming Staffs should be organized in the Caracas and Valencia-Maracay areas. In the third core region of national importance, Santo Tomé de Guayana, development is now being coordinated by a single agency. The Guayana Corporation (CVG) is not only responsible for economic programming and urban design but also for program implementation. It is not suggested that control over the programming of Guayana's development should pass to CORDI-PLAN. In all other cases, however, regional programming can be effectively separated from implementation, and programming staffs should represent the national planning agency directly. When programming offices have been installed and are working satisfactorily at all first-order poles, the programming system may be extended to the next lower order in the hierarchy.

None of the proposed measures would interfere with other forms of regional planning organization. The system of regional programming for the activation of core regions is fully consistent with state-wide planning under the direction of state governors, with planning for the development of Guayana by the CVG, or with the work of the Andean Development Corporation. It is not only consistent with these efforts but a multiplicity of approaches to regional development is desirable to the extent that it gives local populations alternate access to the national centers of decision making and enriches the information on which decisions can be based. So that multiplicity in regional planning organization can be constructive, certain conditions have to be met.

First, there must be a mechanism for resolving interest conflicts on a reasonably objective basis. In Venezuela, the final arbiter is the President of the Republic; but his staff includes CORDIPLAN, and all interest conflicts would first have to pass through a screening process at the level of national planning. Second, one organizational pattern must be given official priority over the others. In the present case, this is the proposed system of regional programming and planning for selected core regions. Because of the attention it will receive, this system can be expected to perform in a fashion superior to alternative planning efforts. This will contribute to implementing the general policy of selective resource concentration.

It remains to be seen whether the activation of core regions will require "large and discontinuous" investments, as one critic has put it. At the present time, the possible directions of regional development in the context of national planning are inadequately known for key growth poles or, indeed, for most parts of Venezuela. Again, Guayana is the great exception and demonstrates the method of attack that must be used. National planners lack a basis for assigning a percentage of total investment to a particular core region until they know the purposes for which the money will be used. It is only on the basis of projects and programs whose costs and benefits can be compared that rational allocative decisions can be made. Regional programming treats the selection and location of investments as part of the same process. It serves as the vehicle by which a national plan is broken down regionally and passes into achievement. The efficiency of a planning-programming system will at first be rather low. Some loss of information between planning and its implementation phases is inevitable: outside interference or "noise" will always filter in. Indeed, the results of planning are often so remote from the original intention—the apparent efficiency of planning is so low—that cynics are led to question whether the inputs into the process are justified. In reply to them one may express the hope that, with the proper institutional arrangements, and given time, the efficiency of a planning-programming system can be raised to a point where its desirability will pass unquestioned.

Additional Measures

To complete the steps necessary for implementing regional policy in Venezuela, two more proposals should be entertained. First, CORDIPLAN should take the lead in establishing an Inter-Agency Commission for Rural Resettlement. This would be composed of members from the Ministry of Agriculture, Ministry of Public Works, the Andean Development Commission, Community Development, the Ministry of War, and the Ministry of Transportation, in addition to the usual CORDIPLAN representatives. Intensive work should be initiated simultaneously in the Andean region and in the East Coastal States.

Second, CORDIPLAN should help each ministry concerned with economic questions to establish small project planning and location staffs. They would submit projects generated within the ministry to a careful review, testing them against technical and economic criteria, and incorporating them into a functional spatial plan for national development. The Ministry of Agriculture, for instance, would prepare a national program for irrigation, with its component parts carefully laid out in actual geographic space. Similar programs, spatially integrated along functional lines, would be developed for transportation, housing, industrialization, electrification, communications, water supply and sewers, education, and health. The availability of functional spatial plans should help CORDIPLAN in the review of activation programs for growth poles, just as it would assist Regional Programming Staffs in their own work. Projects and programs are the essential linkage between objectives for national product and employment, on the one hand, and their achievement, on the other. The sooner project planning is undertaken at the min-

isterial level, the sooner will national planning be in position decisively to influence the course of economic development itself.

A Practical Planner's Wisdom

Implementing a policy means to become engaged in action. But the logic of action differs from that of thought. It is a pity that many intellectuals regard the former as a falling from grace, a shameful compromise with the Platonic purity of thought. Very likely, this is one reason for the frequently cited failure of academically schooled experts to influence the decisions of politicians and administrators.

It would be wrong, of course, to claim priority for either thought or action. So that either may be powerful, it must be joined to the other; and in so doing, it adapts itself to the conditions of the other. The rules under which one may pursue philosophical or scientific truth are well established; but what are the requirements for action? Viewed as rules for successful problem-solving, the following should be regarded not as a counsel of despair, but as a practical planner's wisdom.

1. Learn to live with an imperfect world that is perfectible in the part only, never in the whole.
2. Learn to appreciate that some improvement is better than none at all.
3. Do not try for symmetry in the design of solutions: tailor solutions to local circumstances and needs.
4. Do not attempt to solve all problems at once; do not even try to understand them all; you will find yourself plumbing a bottomless pit. Concentrate on the truly important things first. Some problems may vanish if you leave them alone.
5. Proceed stepwise, incrementally, along the path of least resistance: among the important things to do, turn first to those that are easy to solve.
6. Do not be overly concerned with overlapping functions, fuzzy boundaries, conflicting jurisdictions. Some redundancy may be worthwhile, uncertainty makes one proceed with caution, competition is also a problem-solving device.

7. Step back occasionally to regard your handiwork: assess the total situation with a keen, objective eye, divine the changes in values that have occurred, if necessary redefine your problem, clarify your objectives, critically review your strategy and tactics.

These rules are not meant as an invitation to license. They are not easy to obey and yet obtain the best results achievable. Their purpose is to bring the planner to an awareness of some features of the real world—a world in movement, apparently capricious, elusive, and understood only in fragments. Mind seeks to act on such a world. To gain a measure of success, it must do so in awareness not only of its own severe shortcomings but also of the characteristics of the situation it wishes to transform and of which it is a part itself.

NOTES

CHAPTER ONE

1   Europäische Wirtschaftsgemeinschaft, *Ziele und Methoden der Regionalpolitik in der Europäischen Wirtschaftsgemeinschaft* (Brussels, March 23, 1964); *Massnahmen der Regionalpolitik in den Mitgliedstaaten der EWG* (Brussels, March 24, 1964); and *Strukturverbesserung in alten Industrieregionen* (Brussels, March 25, 1964).

2   Henri Bourginat, *Espace économique et intégration européenne* (Paris: SEDES, 1962).

3   Stefan H. Robock, *North-East Brazil: A Developing Economy* (Washington D. C.: The Brookings Institution, 1963); Benjamin Ward, *Problems of Greek Regional Development*, Research Monograph Series No. 4 (Athens: Center of Economic Research, n.d.); and Malcolm D. Rivkin, *Area Development for National Growth: The Turkish Precedent* (New York: F. A. Praeger, 1965).

4   This model is based on empirical materials developed in Chapter 6.

5   Gerald M. Meier and Robert E. Baldwin, *Economic Development: Theory, History, Policy* (New York: John Wiley & Sons, 1957), Part II.

6   N. S. B. Gras, "The Development of Metropolitan Economy in Europe and America." *The American Historical Review*, Vol. XVII, No. 4 (July 1922), pp. 695–708.

7   Raúl Prebisch, *The Economic Development of Latin America* (New York: United Nations, 1950); Theodore Morgan, "The Long-Run Terms of Trade between Agriculture and Manufacturing," *Economic Development and Cultural Change*, Vol. VIII, No. 1 (October 1959), pp. 1–23; Werner Baer, "The Economics of Prebisch and ECLA," *Economic Development and Cultural Change*, Vol. X, No. 2 (January 1962) pp. 169–182; and Charles P. Kindleberger, "Terms of Trade for Primary Products," in Marion Clawson, ed., *Natural Resources and International Development* (Published for Resources for the Future, Inc., Baltimore: The Johns Hopkins Press, 1964), pp. 339–366.

8   United Nations, *Economic Survey of Europe for 1954* (Geneva: Economic Commission for Europe, 1955), p. 138.

9   *Ibid.*

10 Harvey S. Perloff and Lowdon Wingo, Jr., "Natural Resource Endowment and Regional Economic Growth," in Joseph J. Spengler, ed., *Natural Resources and Economic Growth* (Washington, D. C.: Resources for the Future, Inc., 1961), pp. 204–205. Two other works should be cited in this connection: Chauncy D. Harris, "The Market Factor in the Localization of Industry in the United States," *Annals of the Association of American Geographers*, Vol. XLIV, No. 4 (December 1954), pp. 315–348; and Edward L. Ullman, "Regional Development and the Geography of Concentration," *Papers and Proceedings*, Regional Science Association, Vol. IV, 1958, pp. 179–198.

11 T. W. Schultz, *The Economic Organization of Agriculture* (New York: McGraw-Hill Book Co., 1953), p. 147.

12   Vernon Ruttan, "The Impact of Urban-Industrial Development on Agriculture in the Tennessee Valley and the Southeast," *Journal of Farm Economics*, Vol. XXXVII, No. 1 (February 1955), pp. 38–56; John Friedmann, *The Spatial Structure of Economic Development in the Tennessee Valley*, Research Paper No. 1, Program for Education and Research in Planning (The University of Chicago, 1955); and William H. Nicholls, "Industrialization, Factor Markets, and Agricultural Development," *Journal of Political Economy*, Vol. LXIX, No. 4 (August 1961), pp. 319–340.

13   Douglass C. North, "Agriculture in Regional Economic Growth," *Journal of Farm Economics*, Vol. XLI (1959), pp. 143–951.

14   Vernon Ruttan, *Comments* on preceding article by D. C. North, *op. cit.*

15   Gunnar Myrdal, *Economic Theory and Underdeveloped Areas* (London: Duckworth, 1957); Albert O. Hirschman, *The Strategy of Economic Development* (New Haven: Yale University Press, 1958), Chapter X; and François Perroux, *L'économie du XXe siècle* (Paris: Presses Universitaires de France, 1961), Part II. Perroux's thesis was first stated in his essay "Les Mésures des Progrès Economique et l'Idée d'Economie Progressive," *Cahiers de l'Institute de Science Economique Appliquée*, Serie I, No. 1 (December 1956). The influence of his writings both in Europe and in Latin America has been considerable.

16   Albert O. Hirschman, *op. cit.*, p. 194.

17   John Friedmann, "Regional Planning: A Problem in Spatial Integration," *Papers and Proceedings*, Regional Science Association, Vol. V (1959), pp. 167–180.

18   L. Lefeber, *Allocation in Space: Production, Transport, and Industrial Location* (Amsterdam: North Holland Publishing Co., 1958).

19   Continued metropolitan growth must be regarded as one of the prime facts of modern civilization. The case of the New York Metropolitan Region may be cited as a typical example. In 1960, the region had already reached a total population of 16 million; projections suggest 26 million by the year 2000. To be sure, the region's share of national population has been gradually declining since 1940, when it accounted for 9.5 per cent of the United States population. Sixty years later, however, the New York region is still expected, conservatively, to have between 7 and 8 per cent of the U.S. total, and in absolute numbers, metropolitan population will have more than doubled. (Regional Plan Association, *Spread City: Projections of Development Trends and the Issues They Pose, The Tri-State New York Metropolitan Region, 1960–1985*). It may be true that, as Balassa suggests, "diseconomies arise as the further influx of capital leads to the congestion of urban areas, overcrowding transportation facilities, increased cost of social utilities, and rising factor prices." [Bela Balassa, *The Theory of Economic Integration* (Homewood, Ill.: Richard D. Irwin, Inc., 1961), p. 196]. Probably it is also true that such diseconomies "lead to a divergence between social and private productivity. Entrepreneurs base their investment and production decisions on private profitability and take into account the agglomeration economies appropriated by the firm, whereas the external economies and diseconomies created through the activity of the enterprise are not subject to cost calculations." (*Ibid.*). Nevertheless, such supermetropolises as Paris, London, Moscow, or Tokyo continue to grow, blandly unmindful of any government efforts to control their expansion. It may well be that a total calculus of social costs and benefits stemming from further agglomeration would show a *net gain* to society in terms of productivity, future growth, and cultural attainment. Vaguely aware of this possibility, governments have perhaps been unwilling to exercise their powers to the full in preventing further migration to metropolitan areas. In any event, efforts to define the optimum scale of cities have been notoriously unsuccessful. (Otis Dudley Duncan, "Optimum Size of Cities," in Paul K. Hatt and Albert J. Reiss, Jr., eds., *Cities and Society* (Glencoe, Ill.: The Free Press, 1957), pp. 759–772.

20   This slant in perception is brought out clearly in Albert O. Hirschman, *op cit.* Hirschman writes: "The external economies due to the poles, though real, are

consistently over-estimated by the economic operators." (p. 185). On some of the considerations which enter location decisions in developing countries, see Albert Lauterbach, "Managerial Attitudes and Economic Development," *Kyklos*, Vol. XV, No. 2 (1962), pp. 374–400.

21   George H. Borts, "The Equalization of Returns and Regional Economic Growth," *American Economics Review*, Vol. L. No. 3 (June 1960), p. 326.

22   See especially Rufus B. Hughes, "Inter-regional Income Differences: Self-Perpetuation," *Southern Economic Journal*, Vol. XXVIII (1961), pp. 41–45; F. T. Bachmura, "Man-Land Equalization through Migration" *American Economic Review*, Vol. XLIX (1959), pp. 1004–1017; B. H. Lubke and John F. Hart, "Migration from a Southern Appalachian Community," *Land Economics*, Vol. 34 (1958), pp. 44–53; and Bernard Okun and R. W. Richardson, "Regional Income Inequality and Internal Migration," *Economic Development and Cultural Change*, Vol. IX (1961), pp. 128–143.

23   Richard A. Easterlin, "Long-Term Regional Income Changes: Some Suggested Factors," *Papers and Proceedings*, Regional Science Association, Vol. IV (1958), pp. 313–325.

24   *Ibid.*, p. 325.

25   *Ibid.*

26   Bela Balassa, *op cit.*, p. 204.

CHAPTER TWO

1   George H. Borts and Jerome L. Stein, *Economic Growth in a Free Market* (New York and London: Columbia University Press, 1964); Harvey S. Perloff (with Vera W. Dodds), *How a Region Grows: Area Development in the U.S. Economy* (Committee for Economic Development, Supplementary Paper No. 17, New York, 1963); and the essays in Part III, "Theory of Regional Development," in John Friedmann and William Alonso, eds., *Regional Development and Planning: A Reader* (Cambridge, Mass.: The M.I.T. Press, 1964).

2   Charles M. Tiebout, *The Community Economic Base Study* (Committee for Economic Development, Supplementary Paper No. 16, New York, 1962).

3   Charles Morse, "Potentials and Hazard of Direct International Investment in Raw Materials," in Marion Clawson, ed., *Natural Resources and International Development* (Published for Resources for the Future, Inc., Baltimore, Md.: The Johns Hopkins Press, 1964), pp. 367–414.

4   Robert E. Baldwin, "Development Patterns in Newly Settled Areas," *Manchester School of Economics and Social Studies*, Vol. 24, No. 2 (May 1956), pp. 161–179. Reprinted in Friedmann and Alonso, eds., *op. cit.*

5   For the concept of economic maturity, see Borts and Stein, *op. cit.* pp. 13–17.

6   V. W. Ruttan and L. T. Wallace, "The Effectiveness of Location Incentives on Local Economic Development," *Journal of Farm Economics*, Vol. XLIV, No. 4 (November 1962) p. 972. The author's classification scheme is based on an article by Leon N. Moses.

7   Harvey S. Perloff, Edgar S. Dunn, Jr., Eric E. Lampard, and Richard F. Muth, *Regions, Resources, and Economic Growth* (Published for Resources for the Future, Inc., Baltimore, Md.: The Johns Hopkins Press, 1960), Chapter 3 and pp. 66–67.

8   The role of the city in economic development is discussed in a series of essays contained in Part III, section 2 of Friedmann and Alonso, eds., *op. cit.*

9   On agricultural location, see Michael Chisholm, *Rural Settlement and Land Use* (London: Hutchinson University Library, 1962), especially Chapter 9.

10   Walter Isard, *Methods of Regional Analysis: An Introduction to Regional Science* (New York: John Wiley & Sons, 1960), pp. 404–405.

11   Tibor Scitovsky, "Two Concepts of External Economies," *Journal of Political Economy*, Vol. 62 (April 1954), pp. 143–151.

12 Jean Gottmann, *Megalopolis: The Urbanized Northeastern Seaboard of the United States* (New York: Twentieth Century Fund, 1961; paperback edition by the M.I.T. Press, 1964), p. 261.

13 William B. Nicholls, "Industrialization, Factor Markets, and Agricultural Development," *Journal of Political Economy*, Vol. 69, No. 4 (August 1961), pp. 319–340. Reprinted in Friedmann and Alonso, eds., *op. cit.*

14 John R. Borchert, *The Urbanization of the Upper Midwest: 1930–1960.* Urban Report No. 2, Upper Midwest Economic Study, February 1963, Table 2.

15 Dale E. Hathaway, "Migration from Agriculture: the Historical Record and Its Meaning," *American Economic Review* (May 1960, Part II), pp. 379–391. Reprinted in Friedmann and Alonso, eds., *op. cit.* This article contains references to much of the relevant literature up to that time. See also Simon Kuznets and Dorothy S. Thomas, "Internal Migration and Economic Growth," in *Selected Studies of Migration Since World War II* (New York: Milbank Memorial Fund, 1958), pp. 196–211.

16 Borts and Stein, *op. cit.*, p. 19–20.

17 Robert J. Lampman, "The Low Income Population and Economic Growth," Study Papers No. 12 and 13. Joint Economic Committee, 86th Congress, 1st Session. (Washington, D. C.: Government Printing Office, 1959), pp. 5–7.

18 Borts and Stein, *op. cit.*, Chapter 6.

19 Brian J. L. Berry, "City Size Distributions and Economic Development," *Economic Development and Cultural Change,* Vol. 9, No. 4 (July 1961), pp. 573–587. Reprinted in Friedmann and Alonso, eds., *op. cit.*

20 Bert F. Hoselitz, "Generative and Parasitic Cities," reprinted in *Sociological Aspects of Economic Growth* by the same author (Glencoe, Ill.: The Free Press, 1960), pp. 185–216.

CHAPTER THREE

1 Chauncy D. Harris, "Methods of Research in Economic Regionalization," *Geographia Polonica,* No. 4 (1964), pp. 59–86.

2 John R. Borchert, *The Urbanization of the Upper Midwest: 1930–1960.* Upper Midwest Economic Study, Urban Report No. 2, February 1963; John R. Borchert and Russel B. Adams, *Trade Centers and Trade Areas of the Upper Midwest.* Upper Midwest Economic Study, Urban Report No. 3, September 1963; Russel B. Adams, *Population Mobility in the Upper Midwest.* Upper Midwest Economic Study, Urban Report No. 6, April 1964; and Brian J. L. Berry, "Cities as Systems Within Systems of Cities," in John Friedmann and William Alonso, eds., *Regional Development and Planning: A Reader* (Cambridge, Mass. The M.I.T. Press, 1964).

3 John H. Thompson *et al.,* "Toward a Geography of Economic Health: the Case of New York State," *Annals of the Association of American Geographers,* Vol. 52, No. 1 (March 1962), pp. 1–20, reprinted in Friedmann and Alonso, eds., *op. cit.;* and Richard L. Morrill, "The Development of Spatial Distribution of Towns in Sweden: an Historical-Predictive Approach," *Annals of the Association of American Geographers,* Vol. 53, No. 1 (March 1963), pp. 1–14, reprinted in Friedmann and Alonso, eds., *op. cit.*

4 Derwent Whittlesey, "The Regional Concept and the Regional Method," in Preston E. James and Clarence F. Jones, eds., *American Geography: Inventory and Prospect* (Published for the Association of American Geographers. Syracuse: Syracuse University Press, 1954), pp. 19–69.

5 In the work referred to, Derwent Whittlesey distinguishes between uniform and nodal regions, and this distinction has been widely adopted by geographers. Regions of interdependency is here proposed as a more comprehensive term.

6 For Venezuela, such a system of development regions is shown in Map 12.

CHAPTER FOUR

1   "Criteria for Allocating Investment Resources Among Various Fields of Develop-
    ment in Underdeveloped Countries, A Bibliography and Introductory Notes,"
    United Nations, *Economic Bulletin for Asia and the Far East*, Vol. XII, No. 1
    (June 1961), pp. 30–44.
2   Hollis B. Chenery, "Comparative Advantage and Development Policy," *American
    Economic Review*, Vol. 51 (March 1961), pp. 18–51. On simulation see Edward
    P. Holland, Benjamin Tencer, and Robert W. Gillespie, "A Model for Simulating
    Dynamic Problems of Economic Development," Massachusetts Institute of Techno-
    logy, Center for International Studies, Report No. C/60-10 July 1960. On simu-
    lation of spatial patterns, see Richard L. Morrill, "The Development of Spatial
    Distribution of Towns in Sweden: An Historical-Predictive Approach," *Annals of
    the Association of American Geographers*, Vol. 53, No. 1 (March 1963), pp. 1–14.
3   Thomas A. Reiner, *Regional Allocation Criteria*. Unpublished Ph.D. dissertation in
    Regional Science, University of Pennsylvania, 1963. See also essays by Hirschman,
    Lefeber, Rahman, and Chenery in Part IV (3) of Friedmann and Alonso, *op. cit.*
4   República de Venezuela, Oficina Central de Coordinación y Planificación, *Plan
    de la Nación*, 1963–1966, p. 414.
5   Albert O. Hirschman, *The Strategy of Economic Development* (New Haven, Conn.:
    Yale University Press, 1958), Chapter X: "Interregional and International Trans-
    mission of Economic Growth," pp. 183–201. Reprinted in Friedmann and Alonso,
    op. cit.
6   Albert O. Hirschman and Charles E. Lindblom, "Economic Development, Re-
    search and Development, Policy Making: Some Converging Views," *Behavioral
    Science*. Vol. 7 (April 1962), pp. 211–222.
7   Joseph L. Fisher, "Concepts in Regional Economic Development," *Papers and
    Proceedings*, Regional Science Association, Vol. 1 (1955), pp. W1–W20.
8   Lloyd Rodwin, "Metropolitan Policy for Developing Areas," in Walter' Isard and
    John H. Cumberland, eds., *Regional Economic Planning: Techniques of Analysis
    for Less Developed Areas* (Paris: Organization for European Economic Organi-
    zation, 1961), pp. 221–232. Also "Choosing Regions for Development," in Carl J.
    Friedrich and Seymour Harris, eds., *Public Policy*, A Yearbook of the Graduate
    School of Administration, Harvard University, Vol. XII (1963), pp. 141–162. Re-
    printed in Friedmann and Alonso, eds., *op. cit.*
9   The existence of social diseconomies from concentration is frequently asserted but
    rarely demonstrated. See, for instance, P. N. Rosenstein-Rodan, "Reflections on
    Regional Development," Massachusetts Institute of Technology, Center for Inter-
    national Studies Report No. C/63-25, July 1963. Also Catherine Bauer Wurster,
    "Urban Living Conditions, Overhead Costs, and the Development Pattern," in
    Roy Turner, ed., *India's Urban Future* (Berkeley and Los Angeles, Cal.: University
    of California Press, 1962),pp. 277–295.
10 Paul N. Rosenstein-Rodan, "Notes on the Theory of the 'Big Push,' " in Howard S.
    Ellis and Henry C. Wallich, eds., *Economic Development for Latin America* (Lon-
    don: Macmillan, 1961), pp. 57–73.
11 For an earlier formulation of this criterion, see John Friedmann, "Integration of
    the Social System: an Approach to the Study of Economic Growth," *Diogenes*, No.
    33 (Spring 1961), pp. 75–97.
12 Walter Isard, *Location and Space Economy* (Published jointly by the Technology
    Press of M.I.T. and John Wiley & Sons, New York, 1956; Cambridge, Mass.: The
    M.I.T. Press, Third Printing, 1962), Chapter IV, for an analysis of the role of dis-
    tance inputs.
13 Problems of cost-benefit analysis are extensively discussed in Otto Eckstein, *Water
    Resources Development* (Cambridge, Mass.: Harvard University Press, 1958).

14 A. Quayyum, *Theory and Policy of Accounting Prices* (Amsterdam: North Holland Publishing Co., 1959).

15 Louis Lefeber, "Regional Allocation of Resources in India," in Paul Rosenstein-Rodan, *Pricing and Fiscal Policies: A Study in Method* (Cambridge, Mass.: The M.I.T. Press, 1964). Reprinted in Friedmann and Alonso, eds., *op. cit.*, p. 644.

16 The assumption here is that the prevailing system of political economy is to be preserved. This assumption is not shared, of course, by revolutionary and other dissident elements among the population who, were they to act rationally, would by every means at their command endeavor to foster excessive imbalances in the hope of pushing the system to the point of internal collapse.

17 Local objectives are discussed in Charles L. Leven, "Establishing Goals for Regional Economic Development," *Journal of the American Institute of Planners*, Vol. 30, No. 2 (May 1964), pp. 100–109. Special issue on Regional Development and Planning edited by John Friedmann. Reprinted in Friedmann and Alonso, eds., *op. cit.*

CHAPTER FIVE

1 Simon Kuznets and Dorothy S. Thomas, "Internal Migration and Economic Growth," in *Selected Studies of Migration Since World War II* (New York: Milbank Memorial Fund, 1958), pp. 198–200.

2 Frederick Harbinson and Charles A. Myers, *Education, Manpower, and Economic Growth* (New York: McGraw-Hill Book Co., 1964), p. 186.

3 The crash program as a planning strategy is discussed with reference to Soviet Russia by Peter Wiles in *The Political Economy of Communism* (Cambridge, Mass.: Harvard University Press, 1962).

4 Myron Weiner, in an unpublished manuscript ("Urbanization and Political Extremism: An Hypothesis Tested," Massachusetts Institute of Technology, Department of Political Science, 1964) argues that long-term residents of cities in developing countries tend to display more extremist political behavior than recently arrived migrants. He submits evidence from voting records in Calcutta. The difference in behavior appears to be caused by a difference in felt deprivations between the two groups.

5 The literature on capital programming is scarce. But see Joel Dean, *Capital Budgeting* (New York: Columbia University Press, 1951); also Frederick C. Mosher, *Program Budgeting* (Chicago, Ill.: Public Administration Service, 1954); and Jesse Burkhead, *Government Budgeting* (New York: John Wiley & Sons, 1956), Chapters 6–8.

6 W. H. Brown, Jr., and C. E. Gilbert, *Planning Municipal Investment: A Case Study of Philadelphia* (Philadelphia, Pa.: University of Pennsylvania Press, 1961). See also Aaron Wildavsky, *The Politics of the Budgetary Process* (Boston, Mass.: Little, Brown and Co., 1964).

7 Kevin Lynch, *The Image of the City* (Cambridge, Mass.: The Technology Press and Harvard University Press, 1960; paperback edition by the M.I.T. Press, 1964) and Donald Appleyard, Kevin Lynch, and John R. Myer, *The View from the Road* (Cambridge, Mass.: the M.I.T. Press, 1964).

8 The literature on optimum size of cities has been reviewed by Otis Dudley Duncan, "Optimum Size of Cities," in Paul K. Hatt and Albert J. Reiss, Jr., eds., *Cities and Society* (Glencoe, Ill.: The Free Press, 1957), pp. 759–772.

9 Kevin Lynch, "Environmental Adaptability," *Journal of the American Institute of Planners*, No. 1 (1958), pp. 16–24.

10 Recent contributions to the geography of frontier settlement and its historical implications include Marvin W. Mikesell, "Comparative Studies in Frontier History," *Annals of the Association of American Geographers*, Vol. 50 (March 1960), pp. 62–73, and Dietrich Gerhard, "The Frontier in Comparative View," *Compara-*

tive Studies in Society and History, Vol. 1 (March 1959), pp. 205–229. For Latin America, the following major statements are pertinent: Silvio Zavala, "The Frontier of Hispanic America," in Walker D. Wyman and Clifton B. Kroeber, eds., *The Frontier in Perspective* (Madison, Wis.: The University of Wisconsin Press, 1957); and Victor Andres Belaúnde, "The Frontier in Hispanic Amerca," *Rice Institute Pamphlets,* No. X (October 1923), pp. 202–213. An interesting account of the frontier in Far Eastern History is given by Owen Lattimore, "The Frontier in History," *Relazioni del X Congresso Internazionale di Scienzi Storiche,* Vol. 1 (Florence: G. C. Sansoni, 1955), pp. 105–138. Two specialized studies of frontier development have been drawn upon rather heavily in the preparation of this chapter: George W. Rogers, *Alaska in Transition: The Southeast Region* (Published for Resources for the Future, Inc., Baltimore, Md.; The Johns Hopkins Press, 1960) and Ira M. Robinson, *New Industrial Towns on Canada's Resource Frontier.* Program for Education and Research in Planning, Research Paper No. 4, and Department of Geography, Research Paper No. 73. (Chicago, Ill.: The University of Chicago, 1962).

11 Douglass C. North, *The Economic Development of the United States, 1790–1860.* (Englewood Cliffs, N.J.: Prentice Hall, 1961), and Robert E. Baldwin, "Patterns of Development in Newly Settled Regions," The Manchester School of Economics and Social Studies, Vol. XXIV (May 1956), pp. 161–179.

12 Richard C. Wade, *The Urban Frontier. The Rise of Western Cities, 1790–1830* (Cambridge, Mass.: Harvard University Press, 1959), p. 1.

13 Otis D. Duncan *et al., Metropolis and Region* (Published for resources for the Future, Inc., Baltimore, Md.: The Johns Hopkins Press, 1960), pp. 200 ff.

14 The fascinating story of the growth and decline of Elliot Lake in Canada, the recent "uranium capital of the world," is recounted in Ira Robinson, *op. cit.,* pp. 95–101. It furnishes excellent testimony of the almost total dependence of resource frontiers on external markets.

15 "Foreign interests" may be defined with respect to both the nation and the region. This dual aspect is emphasized in George W. Rogers' study of Alaska (*op. cit.,* Chapters IV and VIII). A comparable situation exists for Guayana. For the people resident in the region, "foreign interests" include both the bureaucracy in Caracas and the Bethlehem and U.S. Steel Corporations which operate mining concessions in the region.

16 According to Robinson (*loc. cit.*), the largest of Canada's new resource towns— Kittimat—has only 10,000 inhabitants, while the normal size of similar Canadian communities falls within the range of 500 to 2,500. It is interesting to compare these magnitudes with Santo Tomé de Guayana, which has a present population of 60,000 of whom more than 20 per cent, however, are unemployed. (See Banco Central de Venezuela, Departamento de Cuentas Nacionales, *Encuesta Sobre Ocupación y Desempleo en Santo Tomé de Guayana,* August 1962, p. ii). The greater accessibility of Guayana may have something to do with its apparently extraordinary size, as may also the lack of alternative employment opportunities in the rest of the country. However, many of the so-called "employed" among Guayana's population are, in fact, working at absolute minimum wages and may be considered only partially employed by any reasonable standard. Moreover, the labor force participation rate in Guayana has been excessively low, even measured against Venezuelan experience—only 24 per cent—which suggests very much higher average dependency ratios than for Kittimat or any other Canadian resource frontier town. The low ratio for labor force participation is undoubtedly due to the unavailability of permanent jobs in the region, so that relatively fewer people are actively seeking employment. As a result, effective unemployment may be rather higher than the fifth of the labor force officially admitted.

Nevertheless, at the time of the survey mentioned, ten thousand workers were actually employed, a figure that, even if we assume *full* employment, would yield a much higher total population than for Kittimat. The large employment of Guayana must be explained, then, by the efforts of the Guayana Corporation to diversify the economic base of the city and to regard this resource frontier, almost from the beginning, as a part of the national economy to be permanently woven into its fabric. None of the Canadian resource towns has striven to achieve this purpose.

17 High labor costs are viewed as a very serious problem by the management of the Matanzas steel plant. Thus, a public relations pamphlet issued by the Corporación Venezolana de Guayana (*Planta Siderurgica del Orinoco*) informs the reader that "it is evident that the cost of human energy is the factor that will primarily determine whether production of the Steel Plant of the Orinoco can compete with imported products. In short, the success of the steel works as an industrial enterprise depends more on the cost of human energy than it does on any other factor." Therefore, the statement concludes, "it is indispensable to find a level for the cost of human energy that, while appropriate for the work performed and just in view of the social rights of the workers, is also within the limits which make competitive steel production possible, for the benefit of Venezuela and for all Venezuelans." (Author's translation from the original Spanish).

18 A recent survey of income and expenditures has made it possible to arrive at educated guesses about some structural aspects of the Guayana economy during 1962. (Banco Central de Venezuela, "Encuesta sobre Ingresos y Gastos Familiares en Santo Tomé de Guayana, Agosto, 1962," as reported in Corporación Venezolana de Guayana, *Informe Anual*, 1962, pp. 95–96). A rough calculation based on this study suggests that approximately 75 per cent of the population in Santo Tomé de Guayana have family incomes of less than $220 per month. This is equivalent to approximately $80 per capita. Such an income level is close to the actual subsistence minimum as measured by the minimum wage level at which presently unemployed workers in the region would be willing to accept a job (see Banco Central de Venezuela, *Encuesta sobre Ocupación* . . . , *op. cit.*, Table 1–26). It is noteworthy, that only 81 out of the 1291 families included in the income survey had monthly earnings of more than $500. These data give a revealing profile of the current socioeconomic situation in the region.

19 On the rootlessness of the work force in resource frontiers, see Ira Robinson, *op. cit.*, Chapter V, and George W. Rogers, *op. cit.*, Chapter IV.

20 George W. Rogers, *op. cit.*, Chapters IV and VIII.

21 In an insightful memorandum entitled "Immediate Steps Toward Civic Consciousness" (dated June 7, 1962), Roderick Peattie, a member of the Joint Center for Urban Studies Project in Guayana who later succumbed in an automobile accident, writes:
Besides building physical parts of the new city, and controlling such building by others, we must see what we can do to bring about a feeling of belonging on the part of the people who come to live here, and of the people who live here already . . . If they feel that they are citizens of an emerging metropolis, then this feeling will do a lot to help it emerge.
Among the actions that he recommends are encouraging the local radio station to cover events of interest to all parts of the city; referring to the city by its new name instead of using the current names of its several parts; setting up a local newspaper; preparing a street map of the city; publishing local picture postcards to help create an image of place; building a visual symbol of the town, such as a lookout tower, from whose heights the citizens could survey the totality of their urban environment; and installing a local telephone system.

22 Ira M. Robinson, *op. cit.*, Chapter IV.

23 Alvin W. Gouldner, "The Norm of Reciprocity: a Preliminary Statement," *American Sociological Review*, Vol. 25 (April 1960), pp. 161–178.

24 The concept of supply area has been used extensively in an analysis of 50 metro-

politan areas in the United States by Otis Dudley Duncan, W. Richard Scott, Stanley Lieberson, Beverly Dunacan, and Hal H. Winsborough, *Metropolis and Region* (Published for Resources for the Future, Inc., Baltimore: The Johns Hopkins Press, 1960), Part IV.

25 Samuel A. Stouffer, "Intervening Opportunities and Competing Migrants," *Journal of Regional Science*, Vol. 2, No. 1 (Spring 1960), pp. 1–26.

26 Rather substantial portions of land may be unsuited to permanent habitation. In the United States, about 12 per cent of the total land area is administered by the federal and state governments as park or forest land.

27 See, for instance, *Multiple-Purpose River Basin Development*. Part I. Manual of River Basin Planning (New York: United Nations, Economic Commission for Asia and the Far East, 1955).

CHAPTER SIX

1 An earlier version of this chapter was published in a Spanish translation as "El Crecimiento Económico y La Estructura Urbana de Venezuela," *Revista de Economía Latinoamericana* (Caracas), Vol. 11, No. 6 (April–June 1963), pp. 115–204.

2 Richard L. Morrill, "The Development of Spatial Distributions of Towns in Sweden: An Historical-Predictive Approach," *Annals of the Association of American Geographers*, Vol. 53, No. 1 (March 1963), p. 2. (Reprinted in Friedmann and Alonso, eds., *Regional Development and Planning: A Reader* (Cambridge, Mass.: The M.I.T. Press, 1964).

3 W. W. Rostow, *The Stages of Economic Growth* (Cambridge: Cambridge University Press, 1960).

4 *Ibid.*

5 Edwin Lieuwen, *Venezuela* (London: Oxford University Press, 1961), p. 49.

6 W. W. Rostow, *op. cit.*, p. 6.

7 The uneven distribution of wealth is a social phenomenon that can be readily observed by a visitor to Venezuela. The only concrete data, however, are summarized in the excellent study by Carl S. Shoup, *et. al.*, *The Fiscal System of Venezuela* (Baltimore, Md.: The Johns Hopkins Press, 1959), Chapter 1.

8 W. W. Rostow, *op. cit.*, pp. 8–9, Chapter 4.

9 *Ibid.*, p. 8.

10 For projections of economic and social changes during this and subsequent periods, see Chapter 9.

11 See Chapter 9.

12 Philip M. Hauser, ed., *Urbanization in Latin America* (New York: International Documents Service, 1961). Also "The Demographic Situation in Latin America," United Nations Economic Commission for Latin America, *Economic Bulletin for Latin America*, Vol. VI, No. 2 (October 1961).

13 The definition of "urban" adopted here differs from that which is officially in use in Venezuela. To qualify as "urban" in the present study, a place has to have a population of 5,000 or more. The official limit in Venezuela is 1,000. Definition of a "city" by a simple statistical measure must always be, to an extent, arbitrary. The Venezuelan concept of urban is largely a legal one and has little relevance for socioeconomic analysis. The higher critical limit was adopted partly for reasons of convenience in the statistical calculations. In any event, a settlement of 5,000 is likely to display more urban characteristics, particularly a nonfarming occupational structure, than places only one fifth its size.

14 The groups of states which have been adopted as convenient units for statistical analysis are shown on Map 1.

15 Evidence for concentration of government expenditures in the Federal District (which includes Caracas) is hard to come by. One example may perhaps be

allowed to stand for the general trend. According to the nation's public housing agency, the *Banco Obrero*, 78 per cent of all construction financed by the agency between 1929 and 1959 occurred in the Federal District. [International Bank for Reconstruction and Development, *The Economic Development of Venezuela* (Baltimore, Md.: The Johns Hopkins University Press, 1961), p. 364, Table 77].

16   Information on the estimated size of the Caracas market was obtained from numerous interviews with Venezuelan businessmen during the summer of 1962.

17   Ingeneria Municipal del Distrito Valencia, *Información de la Zona Industrial Municipal de Valencia.* Mimeographed, 1962, Unpublished data furnished by CORDIPLAN show the following distribution of manufacturing employment in 1962 for plants with one hundred or more workers: Caracas (15,381), Valencia (5,468), Maracay (4,962), and Maracaibo (3,197); in addition, 13,809 workers were distributed among seventeen other cities. Approximately 3,000 workers were employed at the new steel plant at Matanzas (Santo Tomé de Guayana).

18   This calculation was done on a net basis and was derived by subtracting all out-of-state residents in 1936 from all such residents in 1950.

19   There is both direct and indirect evidence that the rate of migration during the 1950's was even greater than before. Thus, the metropolitan area of Caracas alone had an estimated net gain from migration of 155,000 between 1951 and 1955, compared to a gain of only 105,000 in the preceding five years. See José V. Montesino Samperio, *La Población del Area Metropolitana de Caracas.* Cuadernos de Información Económica, November–December 1955 and January–February 1956 (Caracas), p. 59, Table V.

20   According to Montesino Samperio, the ratio was only 4 per cent in 1920. (*Ibid.*, p. 35).

21   Banco Central de Venezuela, *Cuentas Nacionales*, 1960, pp. 37–40.

22   On the whole, these ratios tend to be accentuated if state populations are normalized to bring out the effect of the distance factor alone.

23   For the concept of "intervening opportunities," see Samuel A. Stouffer, "Intervening Opportunities and Competing Migrants," *Journal of Regional Science*, Vol. 2, No. 1 (Spring 1960), pp. 1–26.

24   The similarity of this patterning of ecological zones to the "ring" of Heinrich von Thünen—reflecting the effects of transportation and a competitive adjustment of land uses—should be noted. Von Thünen's theory is summarized in Michael Chisholm, *Rural Settlements and Land Use: An Essay in Location* (London: Hutchinson University Library, 1962), Chapter 2.

25   Richard M. Morse, "Some Characteristics of Latin-American Urban History," *The American Historical Review*, Vol. LXVII, No. 2 (January 1962), pp. 217–238.

26   For the concept of a "system of cities," see Rutledge Vining, "On Describing the Structure and Development of a Human Population System," *Journal of Farm Economics*, Vol. XLI (1959), pp. 922–942.

27   This information was provided by José Alberto Rivas in an unpublished study of the spatial structure of Zulia (1962).

28   From the National Census of 1890, quoted in Rivas, *ibid.* The state of the Andes included in those days the present states of Táchira, Mérida, and Trujillo.

CHAPTER SEVEN

1   Jorge Ahumada, "Hypothesis for the Diagnosis of a Situation of Social Change: The Case of Venezuela." Center for Development Studies, Universidad Central de Venezuela, 1963 (?), mimeographed, p. 12.

2   Venezuelan social scientists generally distinguish the middle class from what they call the "alta burguesía"—the upper bourgeoisie, composed of the top financial and commercial circles in the country. Only a few dozen families, at the most, would belong to this group.

3   Ministerio de Fomento, *Memoria y Cuenta, 1962* (Caracas, 1963), pp. 1039, 1081.
4   Acción Democrática (El Partido del Pueblo), *Acción Democrática, Doctrina y Programa* (Caracas, 1962), pp. 114–116. Also Manuel Vicente Magallanes, *Partidos Politicos Venezolanos* (Caracas: Tip. Vargas, 1960) for a description of the origin and orientation of the Democratic Action Party.
5   Manuel Vicente Magallanes, *op. cit.,* p. 123.
6   *Mensaje Presidencial,* Caracas: Miraflores, Office of the President, March 12, 1963.
7   Enrique Tejera Paris, *Dos Elementos de Gobierno* (Caracas, 1960), p. 139. See also John Friedmann, *Venezuela: From Doctrine to Dialogue* (Syracuse, N. Y.: Syracuse University Press, 1965).
8   República de Venezuela, Oficina Central de Coordinación y Planificación, *Plan de la Nación,* 1963–1966. Corrected version (Caracas, May 1963), p. xii.
9   A detailed analysis of the Guayana project will be presented in Chapter 8.
10 July 21, 1963, p. D-1.
11 Decreto No. 675, January 8, 1962. In 1964, the commission was replaced by the Andean Development Corporation with headquarters in Mérida.
12 Consejo Municipal de Valencia, *Plan de Crecimiento del Distrito Valencia: Estudio Base* (Caracas: Ed. Arte, 1963).
13 Ministerio de Fomento, *op. cit.,* pp. lxiv ff.
14 *Ibid.*
15 República de Venezuela, Ministerio de Agricultura y Cria, *Estudio Preliminar Para el Desarollo de la Region Centro-Occidental de Venezuela* (Rome, Italconsult, December 1962). The Ministry also has published two atlases, for agriculture and forestry, respectively.
16 *El Nacional,* July 11, 1963, p. C-10.
17 *Plan de la Nación, 1963–1966, op. cit.,* p. 414.
18 John Hackett and Anne-Marie Hackett, *Economic Planning in France* (Cambridge, Mass.: Harvard University Press, 1963). A recent notice (*El Nacional,* December 2, 1964, p. D-1) reports final approval by the National Congress of a Law establishing a development corporation for the Andean Region (CORPOANDES) somewhat along the lines of the Guayana Corporation. This represents a major victory for the forces of regionalism in Venezuela. The ultimate wisdom of this move remains to be proved.

CHAPTER EIGHT

1   For estimates of the value of production, see Alexander Ganz, "Regional Planning as a Key to the Present Stage of Economic Development in Latin America: The Case of the Guayana Region, a Frontier Region," Paper presented at the First Latin American Regional Science Congress, November 12–14, 1962, mimeographed, p. 3; for estimated power potential, see Corporación Venezolana de Guayana, *Informe Anual, 1961,* p. 75; for total investment requirements, see Corporación Venezolana de Guayana, *The Guayana Region: A Portfolio of Investment Opportunities* (Caracas, July 1963), p. 46. This estimate does not include the very considerable sums already invested in the steel plant, Macagua Dam No. 1, and urban facilities, including housing, in the area.
2   Decree No. 430, December 29, 1960.
3   The first official expedition into the Gran Sabana was undertaken only in 1939, and one of the highest mountains in Guayana was discovered as late as 1955. See Pablo Vila, *Geografia de Venezuela,* Vol. 1. (Caracas: Ministerio de Education, 1960), p. 56.
4   Quoted in Eugène André, *A Naturalist in Guayana* (London: Smith, Elder & Co., 1904), pp. 53–54.
5   *Ibid.,* p. 4.

6   *Ibid.*, p. 50.

7   Pablo Vila, *op. cit.* Other major references used for this selection include: Marco-Aurelio Vila, *Aspectos Geográficos del Estado Bolívar* (Caracas: Corporación Venezolana de Fomento, 1950); Ministerio de Agricultura y Cria, *Atlas Agricola de Venezuela*, 1960; and *Atlas Florestal de Venezuela*, 1961.

8   Quoted in Dudley Stamp, *Land for Tomorrow* (Bloomington, Ind.: Indiana University Press, 1952), p. 63. Other outstanding books discussing the development possibilities of the tropical world include Pierre Gourou, *The Tropical World. Its Social and Economic Conditions and Its Future Status* (London: Longmans, Green & Co., 1953) and Douglas H. K. Lee, *Climate and Economic Development in the Tropics* (Published for the Council on Foreign Relations, New York: Harper and Brothers, 1957). In their general evaluation of settlement possibilities in the tropics, these books are in broad agreement.

9   Pablo Vila, *op. cit.*, p. 47.

10   Marco-Aurelio Vila, *op. cit.*, p. 175.

11   The most eloquent and literate among the local patriots of Guayana is undoubtedly Eduardo Oxford-Lopez. See especially his study, *Guayana y sus problemas* (Caracas: Cooperative de Artes Graficas, 1942). For an early statement of intense regionalism, see also the ambitious development project for Guayana submitted by Domingo de Ascanio to the national Finance Ministry in 1820. The author envisioned a geometric growth of the region's population to twenty million. *Boletin Histórico*, Fundación John Boulton (Caracas), No. 1 (December 1962), pp. 35–40.

12   Alberto Adriana, "La Colonización en Venezuela," *Revista de Fomento*, No. 15, p. 249, quoted in Eduardo Oxford-Lopez, *op. cit.*, n.p.

13   The frontier theory of Frederick Jackson Turner is sufficiently well known. It is curious, however, to find essentially the same argument about the shaping influence of the frontier on national character cited by an Australian historian, Russell Ward, in *The Australian Legend* (Melbourne, Australia: F. W. Cheshire, 1957).

14   The El Pao deposits were discovered in the early thirties, but the transport problems in getting the ore from the mine to market were not solved until 1950. The great ore deposits of Cerro Bolívar were discovered in course of an aerial survey in 1946. After eight years of exploration and construction work, a U.S. Steel subsidiary, the Orinoco Mining Company, began to exploit and to export the ore. The facts are recounted in Edwin Lieuwen, *Venezuela* (London: Oxford University Press, 1961), pp. 118–119.

15   Decree No. 430, December 29, 1960, 1960, Chapter 11.

16   Corporación Venezolana de Guayana, *Informe Anual*, 1961, p. 57.

17   *Ibid.*

18   An excellent account of the scheme in all of its diverse aspects is given in Corporación Venezolana de Guayana, *Guayana: Cornerstone of the Development of Venezuela* (Caracas, July 1963).

19   For a short assessment of the region's mineral resources, see the memorandum of Blair Bower, "Some Considerations Regarding Mineral Resources in Guayana, with Particular Reference to the 1963–1966 Proposed Investment Program," Joint Center, Guayana Project, December 29, 1962. For a summary report on the agricultural potential, see Lorand Dabasi-Schweng, *Food and the Industrial Development of the Guayana* Corporación Venezolana de Guayana, Joint Center, Guayana Project, December 5, 1962, mimeographed.

20   Maurice Dobb, *An Essay on Economic Growth and Planning* (London: Rutledge and Kegan Paul, 1960), pp. 6–7.

21   Corporación Venezolana de Guayana, *Guayana: Cornerstone of the Development of Venezuela, op. cit.*, p. 40.

22   *Ibid.*, p. 32.

23   Adapted from Corporación Venezolana de Guayana, *Informe Anual, 1963*, Tables 111-1, 111-3, and 111-4.

24 Corporación Venezolana de Guayana, *Informe Anual, 1962,* p. 94.
25 Corporación Venezolana de Guayana, *The Guayana Region. A Portfolio of Invest-ment Opportunities.* Caracas, 1963, p. 42. Also *Informe Anual, 1962,* p. 92.
26 Corporación Venezolana de Guayana, *Guayana: Cornerstone of the Development of Venezuela, op. cit.* p. 37.
27 George W. Hill, *El Estado Sucre: Sus Recursos Humanos* (Caracas: Universidad Central de Venezuela, 1961), gives a statistical profile that reveals the appalling poverty of that mountainous coastal state.
28 Richard M. Soberman, "The Demand for Freight Transportation in the Guayana Region," Corporación Venezolana de Guayana, Joint Center, Guayana Project, División de Estudios, Planificación e Investigación. File No. B-49, February 13, 1963, Table 5. Soberman's estimate allows for a substantial portion of all com-modities to move by ship.
29 *Ibid.,* pp. 52–56. Ferries moved from their present location at Ciudad Bolívar would provide cross-river service until the new bridge would come into existence.
30 Public Administration Service, *Relation of Nation, States, and Municipalities in the Government of the Republic of Venezuela: A Survey Report* (Chicago, Ill., 1959), p. 73. Since this report was submitted, the *Fundación Para El Desarollo de la Comunidad y Fomento Municipal* has been created (January 1962) to provide technical and financial assistance in support of government programs to commu-nities throughout the whole country.

CHAPTER NINE

1 Recent projections by CORDIPLAN (*Plan de la Nación,* 1963–1966, p. 58), assume a rate of natural increase gradually declining from 3.09 per cent (1961–1962) to 2.81 (1975–1976). However, population projections have usually erred on the con-servative side. The higher rate adopted in this chapter would therefore appear to be the more realistic for policy purposes. Cf. Harold F. Dorn, "Pitfalls in Popula-tion Forecasts and Projections," in J. J. Spengler and O. D. Duncan, eds., *Demo-graphic Analysis* (Glencoe, Ill.: The Free Press, 1956), pp. 69–90.
2 CORDIPLAN projections of GNP (Plan de la Nación, p. 38) are comparable: 1962–1966, 7.9 per cent; 1966–1970; 7.0 per cent; 1970–1975; 6.0 per cent.
3 Alexander Ganz, "Regional Planning as a Key to the Present Stage of Economic Development of Latin America: The Case of the Guayana Region, a Frontier Region," Paper read at the First Latin American Regional Science Congress, Ca-racas, Venezuela, November 12–14, 1962, mimeographed, p. 2.
4 CORDIPLAN (*Plan de la Nación,* p. 38) projects a very much higher rate (8 per cent) for long-term increases in agricultural production. In evaluating this projec-tion, however, it must be borne in mind that increases in agricultural output may be very difficult to achieve under Venezuelan conditions, and that the main short-term need will be the resettlement of large populations in new districts rather than dramatic gains in productivity. Generally speaking, capital-output ratios in the agricultural sector appear to have been underestimated and the simultaneous achievement of agricultural and industrial targets as envisioned by CORDIPLAN may not be feasible under foreseeable conditions.
5 CORDIPLAN, *op. cit.,* p. 171.
6 Compared to 23 per cent in 1960. See CORDIPLAN, *op. cit.,* p. 38.
7 For a summary and careful discussion of the relevant issues, cf. A. K. Sen, *Choice of Techniques* (Oxford: Oxford University Press, 1960).
8 This is not only a problem for Venezuela. A. J. Jaffe, in his fascinating but little-known study, *People, Jobs, and Economic Development* (Glencoe, Ill.: The Free Press, 1959), arrives at similar conclusions, using Puerto Rican and Mexican mate-rials. His main findings are worth repeating (pp. 15–18):

1. . . . Modern enterprises can produce very great quantities of additional products or services without necessarily employing great numbers of additional workers . . . .
2. . . . most of the new job openings which may be created by the introduction of a new factory can be filled by persons from industries and occupations having excess workers (i.e., from the underemployed labor force). The jobs so vacated, in turn, can remain unfilled without in any way affecting the volume of goods and services produced by the nation . . . .
3. . . . the new jobs created as a direct result of the economic development program are better jobs than the persons had previously and provide the holders with more pay. However, there is little secondary effect on levels of employment in other industries; the initial jobs create little, if any, additional employment in supporting industries—retail trade, services, agriculture, etc. . . . .
4. . . . it is entirely possible that the total volume of goods and services produced . . . may have to double or triple before the economy may require additional workers.

9   Central Bank of Venezuela, *Memória* 1961, p. 530.
10   *Ibid.*, Tables 23-1 and 20-1.
11   At the same ratio of employment to production gains, a 15 per cent increase in the output of manufactures would have yielded only 19,000 additional job opportunities, a figure still considerably short of the "target" figure of 30,000.
12   The current labor force participation rate in Caracas is estimated at about 40 per cent. The 35 per cent rate is therefore a conservative estimate for an urban society. Moreover, it is well known that the concept of labor force is an especially elusive one and to a large extent refers to a sociopsychological phenomenon, *viz.*, the desire for wage and salaried employment. A wide margin of error must therefore be accepted as inevitable in any labor force projection, particularly in the agriculture and service sectors.
13   Central Bank of Venezuela, *Memória* 1961, pp. 377–379.
14   Edgar M. Hoover and Raymond Vernon, *Anatomy of a Metropolis* (Garden City, N. J.: Anchor Books, Doubleday and Co., 1959), pp. 25–32. The new industrial estate of Guarenas, for instance, is approximately one hour's driving distance from the heart of Caracas.
15   Except for item (*d*), this summary of location propensities was obtained from a field survey of about thirty modern industrial plants in all parts of Venezuela during the summer of 1962. Amenities, however, can be expected to become more important in location decisions as the industrialization process gathers momentum.
16   Harvey L. Perloff, *et al.*, *Regions, Resources, and Economic Growth* (Baltimore, Md.: The Johns Hopkins University Press, 1960), pp. 87–96.
17   This figure is treacherous. From studies carried on in the New York Metropolitan Region, it appears that practically all commuting into Manhattan takes place from within a 2-hours radius, whereas intrazonal commuting is practically all accounted for by a normal travel time of 60 minutes. (Hoover and Vernon, *op. cit.*, pp. 135–145). Commuting time has tended to increase with the reduction in the average number of hours worked. At the same time, transport improvements have made it possible to extend the physical distance that can be covered by commuters in any given time zone. Automated highways in the future suggest the possibility of normal commuting zones in the United States of up to 150 miles from the central city, while supersonic flight may place all cities within the country only a few minutes apart. Neither of these technological possibilities, however, can be considered relevant for Venezuela over the next generation, and the country's transport technology for internal communication can be expected to reach, on the average, the potentialities inherent in the present United States transport system. This means an effective distance commuting-interaction of only thirty to fifty miles from the central city.

NOTES

18 Unofficial estimates by the economic staff of the M.I.T.—Harvard Joint Center for Urban Studies Group in Venezuela.
19 William H. Nicholls, "Industrialization, Factor Markets, and Agricultural Development," *Journal of Political Economy*, Vol. LXIX, No. 4 (August 1961), pp. 319–340.
20 Michael Chisholm, *Rural Settlements and Land Use* (London: Hutchinson University Library, 1962); also T. W. Schultz, "Land in Economic Growth," in *Modern Land Policy*, Papers of the Land Institute, Urbana, Illinois, 1960.
21 Aníbal Buitrón, *Causas y Efectos del Exodo Rural en Venezuela* (Washington, D. C.: Pan American Union, 1955).
22 CORDIPLAN, *Plan de la Nación, 1963–1966*, Corrected version, May 1963, especially pp. iii–xxi. Also Chapters 1 through 4, *passim*.
23 John P. Lewis, *Quiet Crisis in India* (Washington, D. C.: The Brookings Institution, 1962), Chapter 7.

CHAPTER TEN

1 For the concept of a "nested" hierarchy, see Allen K. Philbrick, "Areal Functional Organization in Regional Geography," *Papers and Proceedings*, Regional Science Association, Vol. 3 (1957), pp. 87–98. For the alternative concept of a "weak" or "partial" ordering, see Otis D. Duncan *et al.*, *Metropolis and Region* (Published for Resources for the Future, Baltimore, Md.: The Johns Hopkins Press, 1960), p. 47.
2 In comparison with other large cities, Caracas still has rather low densities, as suggested in the following data, taken from José V. Montesino Samperio, *La Población del Area Metropolitana de Caracas*. Cadernos de Informacion Económica, November–December 1955 and January–February 1956, Caracas, Venezuela, p. 3 :

Population Densities per Square Kilometer

City	Year	Density
Caracas (City)	1950	6,419
Caracas Metropolitan Area	1950	1,926
Paris	1943	36,316
Greater London	1940	4,849
City of London	1940	12,858
Buenos Aires	1947	15,132
New York	1950	9,818
Chicago	1950	6,576

3 Arthur D. Little, Inc., *Estudio Preliminar Sobre Oportunidades Industriales en Maracaibo y Barquisimeto (Cambridge, Mass., May 18, 1954)*.
4 According to a study done by the Central Bank of Venezuela, the Caracas Metropolitan Area (including the entire Federal District and, as far as industrial location is concerned, practically the entire adjoining state of Miranda) accounted for 68 per cent of total industrial employment in 1958. The East Central group of states, which includes Carabobo as well, represented nearly 80 per cent of the national total (*Memória*, 1961, p. 377).
5 "To sum up, the most intensive farming is highly profitable near cities, but less profitable in other places. The most extensive farming pays best at the rim of commerical agriculture. Farmers tend to specialize according to their location, and this tendency is increased because some crops are relatively intensive users of capital and labor no matter where they are grown. Lettuce, carrots, and even eggs come to mind as examples of more or less intensive products." John T. Schlebecker, "The World Metropolis and the History of American Agriculture," *Journal of Economic History*, Vol. XX (June 1960) p. 190.
6 Regional product, by states and sectors, has been estimated for both 1936 and

1953, in an unpublished study by Dr. Gloria Abilahoud of the Venezuelan Central Bank, Department of National Accounts.

7   Louis Delwart and Sidney Sonenblum, "Regional Account Projections in the Context of National Projections," in Werner Hochwald, ed., *Design of Regional Accounts*. Papers presented at the Conference on Regional Accounts, 1960 (Published for Resources for the Future, Baltimore, Md.: The Johns Hopkins Press, 1961), pp. 199–226.

8   The future tense has been used in preference to the conditional, which would have been logically more satisfying, in order to simplify the exposition.

9   The implied annual rate of resettlement is roughly three times that recommended by the recent World Bank Mission to Venezuela. See International Bank for Reconstruction and Development, *The Economic Development of Venezuela* (Baltimore, Md.: The Johns Hopkins Press, 1961), p. 154.

INDEX

E DUE

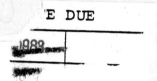

1988